'BELLI DURA DESPICIO'
(I despise the hardships of war)
(*Warspite*'s motto)

Warspite in 1930 (Stan Lawrance)

BATTLESHIP WARSPITE

V. E. TARRANT

Naval Institute Press

Dedicated to my wife, Val,
who guided me through the storm

Published and distributed in the United
States of America and Canada by the
Naval Institute Press, Annapolis,
Maryland 21402.

Library of Congress Catalog Card No.
90-62559
ISBN 1-55750-051-7

This edition is authorized for sale only in
the United States and its territories and
possessions and Canada.

Line illustrations by the author.
Cartography by Sampleskill Ltd, London.

Designed and edited by DAG
Publications Ltd. Designed by David
Gibbons; edited by Michael Boxall; layout
by Anthony A. Evans; typeset by Ronset
Typesetters Ltd, Lancashire; camerawork
by M&E Reproductions, North Fambridge,
Essex; printed and bound in Great Britain by
Courier International Ltd, Tiptree, Essex

Caption abbreviations:
IWM: Imperial War Museum
MPL: Maritime Photo Library

CONTENTS

FOREWORD

BY ADMIRAL SIR CHARLES MADDEN, Bt, GCB, DL

I am proud to have been asked to write a Foreword to this book on *Warspite*. She was by far the most memorable ship in which I served during my forty-six years in the Navy.

I joined her in May 1940 as her Commander, which would now be called her Executive Officer, and was with her throughout Admiral Sir Andrew Cunningham's brilliant series of actions which drove the initially superior Italian Fleet from the Mediterranean. We were his Flagship till we were hit by a bomb in the Battle of Crete. I remained with her through her refit in Bremerton Navy Yard in America, after which she became the Flagship of Admiral Sir James Somerville in the Indian Ocean where I left her in 1942.

Our *Warspite*, the seventh ship of her name, came from a long line of ships dating from the reign of Queen Elizabeth I of which she was the most distinguished. From 1916 to 1944 she was engaged in most of the battleship actions. She was constantly damaged and endlessly repaired. Like the old wooden wall battleships of the Napoleonic wars despite all her wounds she remained unsinkable and always ready for the next encounter.

I had, and retain, a deep affection for her which I know is shared by my shipmates in the 'Warspite Association' and we are delighted that this tribute has been produced to her memory. There is still a *Warspite* in commission, a nuclear submarine – the capital ship of today – to whose company I recommend this book.

Charles Madden.

PREFACE

'There is a saying in the Navy that wherever there is fighting to be done *Warspite* will surely be in it.' So wrote Montague Smith in the *Daily Mail* of 7 June 1944. It was no idle boast, because throughout the Second World War, apart from time spent in dockyard hands while battle damage was made good, *Warspite*'s guns seemed to be almost continuously in action.

She was a ship with a soul of her own, beloved by all who sailed in her but also, as many of her Captains found to their peril, a capricious mistress with a whim for turning complete circles when the fancy took her, which resulted in collisions and hair-raising moments while under the fire of enemy guns.

This is the story of a great ship, the most famous of all British battleships, who covered her name in glory in fighting that spanned from Jutland in 1916 to Walcheren in 1944.

V. E. Tarrant

ACKNOWLEDGEMENTS

I wish to express my sincere thanks to Admiral Sir Charles Madden, Bt, GCB, DL, and Lieutenant R. C. Martin, RN (Rtd), both of whom read my manuscript in its entirety and made constructive criticisms: whatever errors may remain, whether of fact or interpretation, are mine alone. Sincere thanks are also due to the 'Woodpeckers' of the *HMS Warspite Association* who provide photographs and written memoirs on which much of this book relies. I also owe a debt of gratitude to Mr Roderick Suddaby, Keeper of the Department of Documents at the Imperial War Museum; and finally, but not least, to my wife Valerie for typing the manuscript and for putting up with me!

The following individuals and publishers have given me kind permission to quote from the copyright material indicated: Commander Hyde C. Burton, RN from the papers of Commander H. C. Burton, RN; Brigadier G. L. D. Duckworth, CBE from the papers of Captain A. C. Duckworth, RN; Mrs Judith Ellis from the papers of Surgeon-Captain G. E. D. Ellis, RN; Mrs Angela Binney from the log of midshipman D. Binney; Mrs Pamela Walwyn from the papers of Vice-Admiral Sir Humphrey Walwyn; J. J. Bickmore from the papers of Dr. G. H. Bickmore; David Ashton-Bostock from the papers of Commander J. Bostock, DSC, RN; Mrs H. Mckendrick from Viscount Cunningham's *A Sailor's Odyssey*; John Johnson Ltd., from Captain Donald Mcintyre's *Narvik*; Methuen Ltd., from Joy Packer's *Deep As The Sea*; and Collins Ltd., from Captain S. W. Roskill's *HMS Warspite*. Unpublished Crown Copyright material is published by permission of the Controller of Her Majesty's Stationery Office.

1.
THE BEST IN THE WORLD

GENESIS

At the beginning of the twentieth century British naval thinking was dominated by the concept of the big gun – the naval weapon *par excellence*. Big guns, long ranges and accurate shooting – these were the articles of faith of the British naval officer, and to this end tactical systems and the design of warships were subordinated. This was why British dreadnought battleships and battlecruisers of the period always carried guns of greater calibre than contemporary foreign capital ships. For example the three battleships of the British *Bellerophon* class, laid down in 1907, carried ten 12in guns firing a broadside of shell weighing 6,800lb; while the German *Westfalen* class of the same date were armed with twelve 11in guns with a broadside of 5,280lb, or a British superiority of 1,520lb. The *Orion* class and the German *Kaiser* class, both laid down in 1909, had ten 13.5in and ten 12in guns respectively, with broadsides of 12,500lb and 8,600lb, or a British advantage of 3,900lb. Thus when it was rumoured that the new German *König*-class dreadnoughts were to carry 14in guns, and that the United States and the Japanese were arming their new ships with guns of this calibre, Winston Churchill (First Lord of the Admiralty), with the enthusiastic backing of Sir John Fisher (First Sea Lord), decided to go one better and arm the five battleships of the 1912 programme with an even mightier piece of naval ordnance – the 15in gun. However, there was no guarantee that monster weapons of this calibre would prove successful, but as waiting for an experimental gun to be constructed and proof fired (the construction of such guns took between two and three years) would have resulted in a great delay in the laying down of the five battleships, the decision was taken to accept the risk of building ships designed to mount totally untried

weapons. The risk was great but in the event was more than justified as the 15in 42cal Mk I gun proved to be even more accurate than the 13.5in gun, and had 50 per cent greater destructive power after penetration. Each of these gigantic guns was 54 feet long, weighed 100 tons, and was capable of hurling a 1,920lb shell to an extreme range of 23,734 yards or nearly twelve nautical miles: the massive shells were 55 per cent heavier than the largest fired by the German Fleet.

Apart from its superior destructive power, another advantage of the great increase in the weight of the 15in shell over lesser calibres was that it made it possible to dispense with one turret from the standard battleship layout of ten guns in five turrets (i.e., 10 × 13.5in = 14,000lb; 8 × 15in = 15,360lb). The space and weight made available by dropping the midship turret from the design of the new ships, allowed for the provision of additional boilers and a consequent increase in speed of three or four knots over existing classes of dreadnoughts. However, the attainment of the proposed increase in speed was also attendant on another innovation – the use of fuel oil instead of coal. Oil, being a far more efficient fuel, gave a large excess of speed over a coal-burning ship of equal size. In addition, not only did oil allow that speed to be attained with far greater rapidity, but it gave 40 per cent greater radius of action than the same weight of coal. Oil also had the advantage of relieving the ship's company from the exhausting ordeal of coaling ship. With oil it was only necessary to connect a few pipes with the shore or with a tanker, hardly a man having to lift a finger. Indeed less than half the number of stokers was needed to tend oil furnaces.

The final design of the five battleships, named *Queen Elizabeth* (the generic name of the class), *Valiant*, *Barham*, *Malaya* and *Warspite*, was for 25-

knot, heavily armoured battleships of 27,500-ton design displacement carrying eight 15in guns and a secondary armament of sixteen 6in guns. A sixth vessel of the class, to be named *Agincourt*, was ordered under the 1914–15 estimates, but was cancelled on the outbreak of war.

On their completion these five ships were the fastest and most powerful battleships in existence, unrivalled by any existing battleships, building or planned, anywhere in the world as far as guns, armour protection and speed were concerned. Two thousand tons heavier than the German *König*-class battleships (laid down in the same year as the *Queen Elizabeth* class), they were also 4 knots faster in design speed and fired a broadside which was 6,430lb heavier than the German ships (15,360lb v. 8,930lb). 'It can be confidently stated,' wrote Captain Roskill, 'that in the [*Queen Elizabeths*] . . . the art of the big ship and big gun designer reached their peak of success.'[1] Indeed so successful was this class of battleship that they remained in service for more than thirty years.

The high speed of the five *Queen Elizabeths* also gave rise to the possibilities of a new tactical concept, and their perceived role in battle was that of forming a fast division of the battle fleet, which was to act in a detached role, using their superior speed to cross the 'T' of an enemy fleet. Essentially this tactical position was achieved when a line of ships were able to place themselves across the line of advance of an enemy line of battle. This position had the decided tactical advantage of enabling the ships so placed to bring all their broadside guns to bear in concentration upon the van of the enemy line, which in turn was disadvantaged by being able to reply with the forward turrets only.

THE LAUNCH

Laid down in Devonport Dockyard on 31 October 1912, *Warspite* was the second ship of the *Queen Elizabeth* class to be launched. The ceremony took place on 26 November 1913, and was reported in the following day's edition of *The Times*:

'Great interest was taken in the launch of the *Warspite*, the second "all-oil" battleship of the British Navy, which took place yesterday afternoon at Devonport Dockyard. Mrs. Austen Chamberlain named the ship, and the ceremony was witnessed by the First Lord of the Admiralty and Mr. Austen Chamberlain, as well as by an enor-

mous crowd of the general public. For a November day the weather was beautiful, there being little or no wind, while fitful glimpses of sunshine illuminated the scene. The launching weight of the vessel was 12,000 tons, which is said largely to exceed that of any other ship built at a Royal Dockyard. As the *Warspite* stood upon the slip her great beam was noticeable, and this aspect was reflected in the launching platform, which was of unusual width and size . . . According to the programme the launch was fixed for a quarter past three. Half an hour before this time the religious ceremony began, the officiating clergyman being the Rev. E. F. Harrison-Smith, Dockyard Chaplain, the singing of the hymns being led by the choir of the Dockyard Chapel. As soon as the service was over Mrs. Austen Chamberlain named the vessel, breaking over the bows a bottle of wine encased in flowers and accompanying the act with the customary prayer, "God bless her and all who sail in her." In the meantime hundreds of workmen were busily engaged under the keel of the ship cutting away the blocks on which she rested. Then came the bugle signal for everyone to stand clear for the launch. Mr. A. F. Richards, Manager of the Construction Department, held a chisel while Mrs. Chamberlain with a few blows of a mallet severed the cord holding the weights suspended over the dog shores. There was a tremendous thud when these fell, but the ship, though released did not move for some anxious moments. At length, however, with the assistance of powerful hydraulic rams she started and glided majestically down the ways into the water amid the cheers of the ships' hooters and sirens. The launch took place exactly to time.'[2]

After dropping anchors in the Hamoaze to 'bring her up', *Warspite*'s hull was towed to the North Yard of the dockyard for fitting out.

THE NAME

The derivation of the name 'Warspite' dates from the time of Queen Elizabeth I, and was first used as a ship's name during the wars with Spain. The old English word *despight* used as a verb meant 'to treat with contempt'. *Spight*, the contraction of *despight*, with the prefix *war* therefore meant 'to treat war with contempt'. *War-*

The enormous power of the 15in gun. *Resolution* firing a full-charge practice salvo. *Warspite* and her sisters were the first ships in the world to carry this awesome naval ordnance. (IWM)

spight was the most common spelling in use until early in the eighteenth century, when the modern form of *Warspite* came into use. The word *Spight*, however, had a second and quite different meaning in Elizabethan times; it was also the colloquial name of the green woodpecker. This led to the woodpecker being used on the ship's unofficial crest, which she carried on the tampions of her guns and on the bows of her boats.

FITTING OUT

Warspite's fitting out took sixteen months. During this time the ship's first outfit of the awesome 15in guns (eight of the biggest guns in the world), and the four huge 750-ton armoured turrets to house them, were transported by sea from the constructors' yards to be hoisted into position by the dockyard cranes. Four of these great guns, which cost £17,500 each and were built by winding 170 miles of rectangular-section steel wire over a rifled tube, were made by William Beardmore at Parkhead, Glasgow, and the other four by Vickers at the River Don Works, Sheffield. All four turrets were built in the heavy gun-mounting shop of W. G. Armstrong-Whitworth at Elswick, Newcastle-on-Tyne. The life of a 15in gun was about 335 full charges. After firing that number of rounds the worn rifling had to be replaced. This was a costly and complex process, requiring pulling the ship out of line for the guns to be removed and returned to the heavy gun mounting shops. Therefore, to avoid wear on the rifling as far as possible very few full calibre practice shoots were carried out, and a method of sub-calibre firing with reduced cordite charges was adopted. *Warspite* had a new outfit of guns in 1929 and they, in turn, were replaced during the Second World War as she wore them out on war service. To fire a 15in shell a cordite charge of 430lb was required. As *Warspite*'s full outfit of 15in shells was 901, the ammunition weighed more than 1,000 tons.

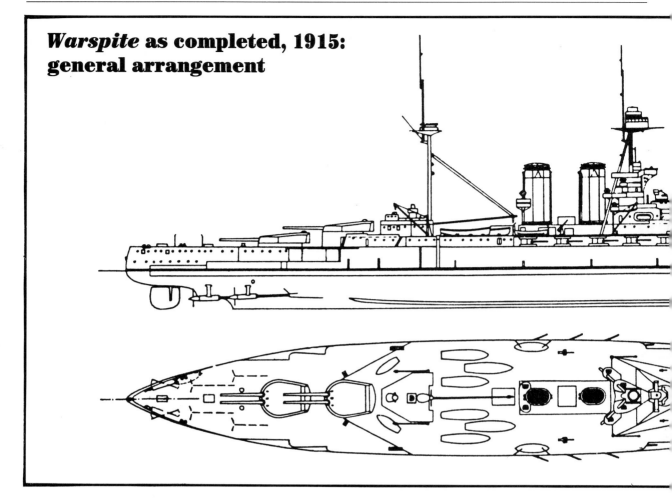

Warspite as completed, 1915: general arrangement

COMMISSIONING

Completed at the beginning of March 1915, six months after the outbreak of the First World War, *Warspite* was commissioned at Devonport into service with the 2nd Battle Squadron of the Grand Fleet, on 8 March 1915, by her first Captain, Edward M. Philpotts. After carrying out her acceptance trials to the west of Ireland (main and secondary armament firing and steaming at full power) in which her officers took her over from the building and machinery contractors on behalf of the Admiralty, *Warspite* joined the Grand Fleet at Scapa, where she arrived in the early hours of 13 April.

During her working up period *Warspite* served with the 2nd Battle Squadron and it wasn't until 2 November 1915 that she formed up with the newly commissioned *Barham* and *Queen Elizabeth* (which had returned to home waters from operations in the Dardanelles) into a separate 'fast division' of the fleet

as originally intended. Designated the 5th Battle Squadron, under the command of Rear-Admiral Hugh Evan-Thomas, who flew his flag in *Barham*, this 'fast division' did not reach full strength until *Malaya* and *Valiant* were commissioned in February and March of 1916 respectively. So formed, the 5th Battle Squadron became, and remained until the end of the war, the fastest and most powerful squadron of battleships in the world. Mounting a total of forty 15in guns, the combined weight of the main armament broadside fire was 76,800lb. In comparison the five 21-knot *Kaiser*-class battleships of the German 6th Division, mounting a total of fifty 12-in guns, could manage a broadside weighing 45,200lb, some 41 per cent lighter. In the might of the *Warspite* and her sisters was epitomized all the grandeur and supremacy of British sea power, which the Kaiser's High Seas Fleet had been created to challenge.

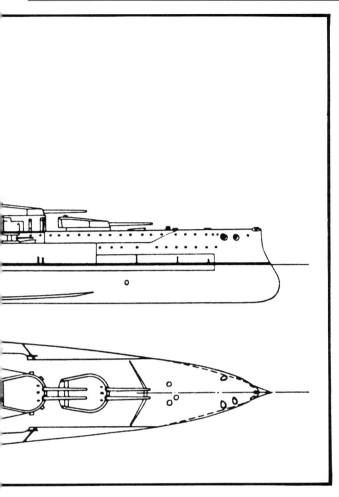

APPEARANCE

The great power embodied in *Warspite* and her sisters was well-reflected in their appearance. These ships were undoubtedly the most ferociously handsome and aggressive-looking ships of the First World War period. The disposition of two of the heavy gun turrets forward of the superstructure and two turrets sited aft on the quarterdeck, gave them a balance and sleekness not possessed by existing battleships with their cumbersome five-turret layout, which were either disposed athwartships of their superstructures or midships, thus dividing the superstructure in two. Apart from carrying the customary heavy tripod foremast, around which the bridge structure was built, the five *Queen Elizabeth*s were the only battleships to date fitted with a tall mainmast fitted aft of the boat deck. This mast added immeasurably to the sense of balance these ships portrayed.

As completed the *Queen Elizabeth* class were fitted with two funnels of equal size, with twin searchlight towers affixed to the after funnel.

Despite the sleekness of her lines, *Warspite*'s appearance was further improved during refits carried out between the two world wars by her twin funnels being replaced by a more modern-looking single funnel, and the entire bridgework being replaced by a solid-looking, watertight square tower. Added to which, the old-fashioned and rather cumbersome tripod mast was replaced by a single, much lighter pole mast erected at the rear of the bridge.

These modifications gave the ship a more graceful and up-to-date appearance, without reducing the impression of power and aggressiveness. Indeed, throughout the various guises which she carried during the thirty years of her career, *Warspite* always retained a sleek menacing appearance which portrayed the very summation of British sea power.

Source Notes
1. Captain S. W. Roskill. *HMS Warspite*, pp 86-7.
2. *The Times*, 27 November 1913.

PARTICULARS OF HMS *WARSPITE* AS COMPLETED, MARCH 1915

Dimensions

Length:	634ft 6in waterline; 639ft 5in overall
Beam:	90ft 6in
Mean draught:	29ft 4½in light; 30ft 2in load; 33ft 5in deep.

Displacement

27,500 tons standard; 33,410 tons deep.

Armour

Main belt:	13in main strake reducing to 6in forward and 4in aft
	6in upper strake
	8in lower strake
	Total width of main belt: 20ft 6in
	(15ft 1½in below waterline; 5ft 4½in above waterline)
Bulkheads:	6in forward; 4in aft
Turrets:	13in face; 11in sides; 4½in roof
Barbettes:	10in to 7in above belt; 6in to 4in below belt

Warspite as completed, 1915: inboard profile, plan and section

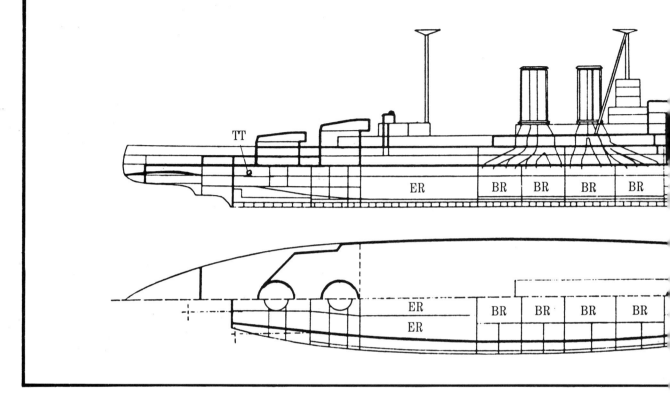

Conning tower:	11in sides; 3in roof; 4in revolving hood
Communications tube:	6in to upper deck; 4in below
Torpedo conning tower:	6in
Torpedo conning tower tube:	4in
Horizontal (deck) armour	
Forecastle deck:	1in over 6in gun battery
Upper deck:	2in to 1¼in from 'A' to 'Y' barbettes
Main deck:	1¼in forward; 3⅛in aft
Middle deck:	1in
Lower deck:	3in in extreme ends; 2½in over steering gears; 1in forward
Vertical armour:	
Torpedo bulkheads:	2in
Magazine ends:	2in

| Funnel uptakes: | 1½in. |

The total weight of the armour was 8,600 tons, 31.27 per cent of the standard displacement.

Machinery
Four Parsons turbines (SHP 75,000 = 25 knots)
Twenty-four large-tube Yarrow boilers.
(On the measured mile *Warspite* achieved 75,510shp =24.65 knots).

Fuel Capacity

Oil:	3,300 tons (2,800 tons was normally carried)
Oil consumption:	41 tons of oil per hour at full speed
Coal:	100 tons (for domestic use)
Radius of action:	8,400 nautical miles at 10 knots.

Complement: 951 peace; 1,048 war.

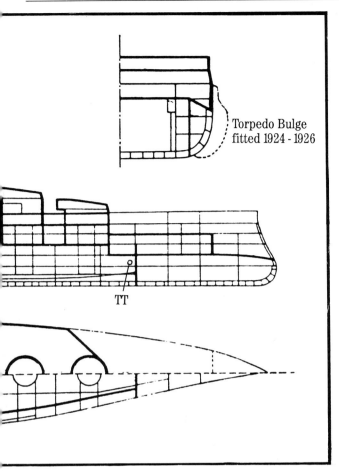

Torpedo Bulge fitted 1924 - 1926

TT

Anchors

Bower:	Wasteney-Smith stockless, 150cwt
Sheet:	Wasteney-Smith stockless, 150cwt
Kedge:	Admiralty Pattern 5cwt.

Main armament

Eight 15in, 42cal Mk I guns

Length of bore:	630in (42 calibres)
Length of gun:	650.4in
Weight of gun:	100 tons
Weight of shell:	1,920lb (4crh = calibre radius head)
Weight of charge:	428lb of cordite
Muzzle energy:	79,890ft-tons (4crh shell)
Muzzle velocity:	2,450fps
Mounting:	Twin Mk I
Revolving weight:	750 tons
Rate of fire:	2 rounds per minute per gun

Maximum elevation:	20°
Maximum range:	23,734 yards
Shell stowage:	773 armour-piercing
	40 high-explosive
	24 shrapnel
	64 practice shells.

Secondary armament

Fourteen 6in, 45cal, Mk XII guns

Length of bore:	270in (45cal)
Length of gun:	280in
Weight of gun:	6 tons, 14 cwt., 56lb
Weight of shell:	100lb
Weight of charge:	28lb 4oz of cordite
Muzzle energy:	5,998ft-tons
Muzzle velocity:	2,940fps
Mounting:	P1X
Rate of fire:	7 rounds per minute per gun
Maximum elevation:	15°
Maxium range:	13,500 yards (4crh shell)
Shell stowage:	150 rounds per gun (1,100 total) + 100 starshells in total.

Twelve of the 6in guns were mounted in casemates around the upper deck. Two were in open mountings on the forecastle deck.

Originally the design called for sixteen 6in guns. This number was actually fitted in *Queen Elizabeth*, four being fitted around the main deck aft. The latter were found to be useless because of their low position, and they were later removed. In *Warspite* these four guns were removed from the main deck position before she was completed; two being re-sited on the forecastle deck. The empty embrasures on the main deck were plated over.

Anti-Aircraft armament

Two 3in High-Angle guns

Weight of shell:	12lb 8oz
Weight of charge:	2lb 8oz
Rate of fire:	29 rounds per minute
Maximum elevation:	90°
Maximum range:	11,200 yards at 45°

Torpedo armament

Four 21in torpedo tubes in two submerged torpedo rooms.

Torpedoes carried:	twenty (280lb charge); range: 18,500 yards at 19 knots.

The total weight of the armament was 4,550 tons, 16.54 per cent of the standard displacement.

2.
A CAPRICIOUS MISTRESS

THE SETTING

The *raison d'être* of the Grand Fleet – the mightiest assemblage of warships in history – was threefold; to protect the British Isles from invasion; to deny egress from the North Sea to German surface warships bent on attacking the Atlantic lanes of Britain's vital seaborne trade; and to bring economic pressure to bear on Germany by cutting off her equally vital maritime trade. The two latter tasks were accomplished by sealing off the North Sea from the outer oceans with two lines of blockade – one stretching 200 miles across the North Sea from the Orkneys to the Norwegian coast, the other across the twenty miles of the Dover Strait. The backbone of the lines of blockade and the means of ensuring the inviolability of Britain from seaborne invasion was the Grand Fleet, strategically based at Scapa Flow.

As the German High Seas Fleet, although it was the second largest in the world, was considered too weak to challenge the Grand Fleet's command of the sea by seeking a battle *à outrance*, it adopted the strategy of a 'Fleet in Being' – a constant threat, tying up the larger numbers of the enemy. Only if the Grand Fleet's numerical strength could be whittled down to a *Kräfteausgleich* – an approximate equalization of forces – would the Germans accept battle. This hoped for *Kräfteausgleich* could be best achieved if the Grand Fleet should steam headlong into the Heligoland Bight with the object of seeking battle. In those shallow restricted coastal waters, mines and torpedo attacks by U-boats and destroyers could inflict a toll on British battleship and battlecruiser strength which could bring about parity or even superiority in capital ships. However, Admiral Jellicoe, C-in-C Grand Fleet, had no intention of playing the German game. Because of the fear of mines and submarine ambush Jellicoe would not accept battle in the southern waters of the North Sea, thus the periodic sweeps of the North Sea by the Grand Fleet were carried out in the waters north of latitude 56°. Conversely, the High Seas Fleet would not subject itself to the disadvantages of fighting in the northern latitudes. During the entire course of 1915 the High Seas Fleet only ventured to sea on five occasions and never did it venture further than 100 miles from its base in the River Jade. Strategically 'the result was like a game of chess in which both players refuse to risk their chessmen by moving over the centre of the board'.[1] As a consequence *Warspite*'s career during the whole of 1915 and for the first half of 1916 consisted of long periods at anchor in the Flow, punctuated by gunnery exercises – sub-calibre shoots inside the Flow and full-calibre firing in the western waters of the Pentland Firth – and sweeps and manoeuvres in the northern latitudes of the North Sea.

LIFE ABOARD *WARSPITE*

During July 1915 Assistant Clerk (Paymaster Cadet) G. H. Bickmore joined *Warspite*, and in his memoirs he gives a description of life aboard *Warspite* during 1915:

'I was extremely lucky in my first ship,' Bickmore recalls. 'Jerry Philpotts was as fine a Captain as a youngster could have for his first ship, and Commander Humphrey Walwyn [later Admiral and Governor of Newfoundland] was an admirable second in command, and *Warspite* was both an efficient and a happy ship. The gunroom [junior officers' mess] where I lived with the snotties [midshipmen] and sub-lieutenants was a very happy mess and H. A. Packer [who was Captain of *Warspite* during the Second World War and later a Vice-Admiral] was a first-class chap. The sub. of a gunroom can make life on board for the junior officers plain hell if he wants to. I know of several gunrooms which were under the control of subs. who were bullies and where the midshipmen and clerks led a very unhappy and harassed life, but there was nothing like that in the *Warspite*'s gunroom, where we were well treated. In most gunrooms it was quite usual for midshipmen to be severely caned for very trivial offences, and even in some cases simply to amuse the sub., but though I served in *Warspite* for nearly a year I do not remember Packer using the cane once.'

Grateful that he did not have to suffer the dirty and exhausting ordeal of 'coaling ship' in *Warspite*, Bickmore found, however, that serving in an all oil-fired ship did have its drawbacks:

'The *Warspite* was one of the first class of battleships to burn oil fuel. This was a great advantage as we did not have to coal ship after a trip to sea, but it had its drawbacks, for the smell of oil fuel is sickly, and the ship, owing to its oil fuel, had a double roll which took some getting used to. In fact I was very much more seasick in *Warspite* of 35,000 tons than I ever was later in 4,000-ton light cruisers. If there was anything like a sea I was always squeamish and the fleet spent a lot of time at sea in the winter of 1915/16. We struck some very heavy weather in the North Atlantic between the Orkneys and Iceland.'

Throughout 1915–16, *Warspite* was based, with the Grand Fleet, in Scapa Flow. During the winter Scapa could be beastly, but in the summer months the heather-clad hills surrounding the Flow could be quite pleasant. For recreation golf courses and football fields were laid out and these were maintained to a high standard. Bickmore has the following recollections of Scapa:

'In spite of being completely land-locked, Scapa Flow was so large an anchorage that when a gale blew up, a very frequent occurrence especially in winter, quite big seas were soon running, and frequently in winter no communication between ships by boat was possible. Ships would let go their second anchor and veer to ten shackles of cable, and even then, would sometimes have to keep up steam on the engines and steam slowly up to their anchors for days on end to avoid dragging. In the summer sailing picnics were held,

when we would go away in one of the cutters and sail to the island of Hoy, land, picnic, and return to the ship in the evening. After dinner on Sunday, all the battleships' bands used to play on deck and the sailors used to dance, while seals attracted by the music, would gather round the ships, floating high in the water and obviously enjoying the music.

'The Flow was full of fish, mostly pollack, and when I would not get ashore, I used to fish with a trout rod from the forecastle. One day the Skipper came up to the forecastle and saw me fishing. He sent for the ship's carpenter and told him to make some circular nets on a frame like a sieve. These were lowered over the side and breadcrumbs sprinkled over them and when a shoal of pollack gathered over the nets they were hauled up and we very quickly caught enough fish to give a fish meal to the whole ship's company of over a thousand officers and men.

'Altogether, apart from active operations, we had a very good time at Scapa. In the early months of 1916 the Fleet spent a great deal of time at sea. Periodical sweeps of the North Sea were made, as well as a great many battle exercises in the North Atlantic, sometimes in very heavy weather. It was quite common to stand on the deck of one's own ship when she was in the trough of a wave and be quite unable to see one's next ahead or one's next astern for the huge rollers which intervened.'[2]

GROUNDED!

Although a happy ship, which *Warspite* undoubtedly was, she was not without her troubles. On Friday 17 September 1915, occurred the first serious mishap in a long chain of misfortunes which punctuated the whole of the ship's long career. On the evening of 16 September *Warspite* sailed from Scapa bound for Rosyth in the Firth of Forth. Suddenly, at about 0530 on the following morning, in foggy weather, land was sighted on an unexpected bearing and despite the helm being swung hard a-port *Warspite* grounded off Dunbar. She was steaming fourteen knots when the incident occurred: in the subsequent inquiry, which was convened aboard *Warspite* on the following Monday, Captain Philpotts explained that he had not reduced speed earlier (despite the fact that the ship was approaching the estuary of the Forth) because he was in submarine-infested waters.

Managing to re-float herself by going astern, *Warspite* moored off Rosyth at 0930. On the following morning her oil fuel had to be pumped off into an oiler, because it was found that her tanks had been damaged by the grounding and were leaking. Such was the extent of the damage to the ship's outer bottom, that she had to be docked in the floating dock of Smith's Docks at South Shields on the Tyne on 22 September, and did not undock until 20 November.

As a result of the Board of Inquiry's findings the Admiralty acquitted the ship's officers of any negligence but considered the 'temporary disablement of this important vessel was due to a grave error of judgement' and Captain Philpotts and the navigator were both reprimanded. Captain Roskill states that 'Captain Philpotts had not reduced speed earlier because he was in submarine-infested waters, and *the destroyer escort which he had expected had not joined*' [author's italics].[3] However, G. H. Bickmore, who was aboard the ship at the time tells a different story:

> 'We arrived off May Island in a fog *and were met by two destroyers* [author's italics] of the Battlecruiser Fleet flotillas, which were to lead us in through the swept channel. By some error, they took us through the small ship channel which had insufficient depth of water for so large a ship, and we went aground, doing considerable damage to the ship's bottom.'[4]

Having rejoined the fleet at Scapa at the end of November, *Warspite* put to sea with the Grand Fleet a few days later for manoeuvres in the North Atlantic, and unfortunately found herself in even greater trouble.

COLLISION!

During the forenoon watch of Friday 3 December, the 5th Battle Squadron was steaming ahead of the battle fleet at a speed of twelve knots, to the NW of Flannan Island. A heavy sea was running. *Barham*, the squadron flagship, which was next ahead of *Warspite*, signalled for a reduction of speed to eight knots. Although the remainder of the squadron read this signal correctly, *Warspite* misread the signal as eighteen knots, and as a result of *Warspite*'s gathering speed while the flagship decreased her rate of knots, the two ships collided. Midshipman A. H. Ashworth, who was serving in *Warspite* at the time, gives his version of events in his diary:

> 'Whilst in the middle of a turn to starboard, *Barham* altered her speed flags and eased to 8 knots, but one of our signal boys, who was the only signal rating on the bridge with the officer of the watch, read it as an increase to 18 knots. The officer of the watch read it the same, and we increased speed, only to find we were closing the *Barham* and pointing our bows at her starboard side, dead amidships.'[5]

Ashworth attributes part of the blame to the signal boy for misreading the flag signal. However, 17-year-old John Chessman, the signal boy in question, puts the blame elsewhere, as he explains in his diary:

> 'I was on watch on the binnacle platform along with the officer of watch, the chief yeoman of signals and a leading signalman [a more likely scenario than Ashworth's contention that a signal

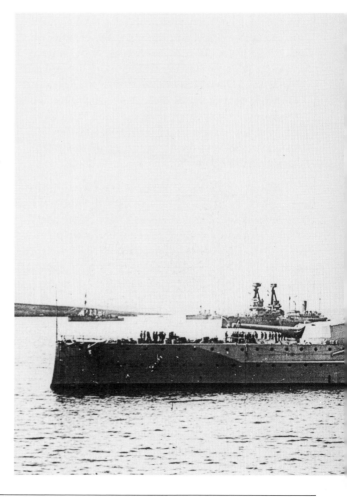

boy was the only signal rating on the bridge]. Any alteration of speed is signalled with flags flying at the yard-arm of the leading ship of the squadron. At that time flag "G" headed the one or two numeral flags indicating the change of speed. Only when that signal was acknowledged by the other ships in company with an answering pennant, the hoisting of which meant the signal had been seen and was understood, was the signal hauled down at the senior officer's discretion. Immediately that did occur the change in engine revolutions were telegraphed to the engine room. If this was carried out correctly the change in speed was smooth and controlled to the extent of there appearing to be no change in bearing or distance. The *Barham* hoisted the signal "G8" which would indicate a reduction of speed equivalent to 8 knots. I was only a small fry, a signal boy and accordingly was expected to make the smallest of noises. I heard

the signalman report to the chief yeoman who in turn reported to the officer of the watch "Eighteen knots sir!" Quickly I jabbed the signalman in the back. "You've made a mistake," I almost shouted. "The signal is 8 knots not 18. Tell him or we'll be in a right bloody mess!" The signal came down, the officer of the watch gave instructions down the engine room tube for the revs. to be raised to the appropriate level for 18 knots. I had been right but was ignored. The result might so easily have cost the lives of men in both ships; and I wasn't even called on to give evidence at the ensuing inquiry. The fault lay with the signalman alone and yet he received not so much as a reprimand."[6]

Warspite at anchor in Scapa Flow among other units of the Grand Fleet. The rangefinder baffles between the funnels date this photograph to the winter of 1916/17. (IWM)

It so happened that Captain Philpotts was making a fleeting visit to the bridge when the danger became apparent. At first he ordered the helm to be put over hard a-starboard and the engines to go full astern to port. However, quickly realizing that this course of action would make *Warspite* cut right into *Barham*'s starboard side dead amidships, he aborted the order and instead completely reversed his decision by ordering the helm to be swung over hard a-port and the engines to go astern to starboard. Finally he ordered full astern both in a last desperate attempt to avoid a collision, but despite *Warspite*'s frantic gyrations and her propellers lashing the sea into a milky foam as they vainly revolved full astern, she collided with *Barham*. According to *Warspite*'s log this happened at 0929.

Because of the heavy sea that was running, *Warspite* was almost upon the flagship when *Barham*'s stern sank into a deep trough, at the same time as *Warspite*'s bows were carried high into the air by a huge wave. When the bows dropped, *Warspite*'s port bow ground against *Barham*'s rising starboard quarter. *Warspite*'s port anchor was torn away along with 17½ shackles of the anchor cable. Down went *Barham*'s stern once more into another trough, while *Warspite*'s bows were lifted clean out of the trough on another wave. When they dropped again they smacked down on the opposite side or port quarter of *Barham*. By this time *Warspite* had at last lost way, but the bows continued to rise and fall, grinding against *Barham*'s port quarter with what John Chessman described as 'a horrible crunching, like a giant robot chewing crowbars'.[7]

Finally the ships drifted apart. *Warspite*'s bows were badly stove in and two of the forward compartments below the waterline were flooded. After heaving-to for the effecting of temporary repairs, *Warspite* got under way again at 1004, speed ten knots, to limp back to Scapa through a driving snow blizzard that had blown up. As there was a danger of the damaged battleship sinking in the heavy sea that was running, she was accompanied by *Barham*, the cruiser *Minotaur* and the light cruisers *Carysfort* and *Castor*. At 1513, when the sea moderated somewhat, *Barham* and *Carysfort* parted company, and at 0820 on the following morning the other two cruisers also parted company when destroyers dispatched from Scapa took up a screen around the battleship. Finally, at 1614 on Saturday 4 December, *Warspite* passed safely through the outer boom of Scapa Flow.

Early on Sunday morning *Warspite*'s damaged bows were raised for inspection by sinking the stern deeper into the water. This was partially achieved by carrying aft 400 15in shells from the magazines of the two forward turrets and stacking them on the quarter deck. After inspection it was decided that nothing short of re-plating the whole of the stricken bows would make good the damage. To effect these repairs *Warspite* was ordered to her home port of Devonport.

A Board of Inquiry was held aboard *Barham* at 0930 on the following Tuesday, and the luckless Captain Philpotts was reprimanded for the second time in two months.

After shoring up the forward bulkheads, and filling the compartments which had been flooded as tightly as possible with canvas and hammocks, *Warspite* sailed from snow-covered Scapa at 0545 on Thursday 9 December, bound for Devonport via the west coast of Ireland. Arriving at 2000 that night, she was taken up harbour by tugs, entering the basin at 2115.

Leave was given to the ship's company while repairs were carried out. But if they entertained any hopes of spending Christmas at home they were disappointed, because *Warspite* arrived back in Scapa at 0932 on Christmas Eve.

The first five months of 1916 passed uneventfully for *Warspite*, other than for a dash with the entire Grand Fleet southward through gales and heavy seas on 24/25th April, when the German battlecruiser squadron, supported to the seaward by the High Seas Fleet, carried out a tip and run raid on Lowestoft, which they shelled. Hopes ran high that the Grand Fleet could cut off the Germans' retreat and bring them to action. Unfortunately the Germans began their homeward journey while the Grand Fleet was still far to the northward, and hopes of bringing them to battle were dashed. However, plans were being prepared by the High Seas Fleet Command for a bolder strategy, which would bring about the greatest sea battle in history: a battle in which *Warspite* was to play a glorious part.

Source Notes

1. V. E. Tarrant. *Battlecruiser Invincible*, p. 86.
2. The papers of Dr. G. H. Bickmore (Imperial War Museum), hereinafter cited as Bickmore Papers.
3. Roskill, *HMS Warspite*, pp. 101–2.
4. Bickmore Papers.
5. The papers of A. H. Ashworth (Imperial War Museum), hereinafter cited as Ashworth Papers.
6. The papers of John Chessman (Imperial War Museum), hereinafter cited as Chessman Papers.
7. ibid.

3.
THE THUNDER OF THE GUNS

JUTLAND, OPENING MOVES

By the spring of 1916, Germany was suffering so badly from the iron grip of the British blockade, that her naval leaders were forced to adopt a bolder strategy in an attempt to break the stranglehold of the Grand Fleet. By May 1916 British numerical superiority had grown to the ratio of 37:21 in dreadnought battleships and battlecruisers, and 105:76 in light forces. Admiral Reinhard Scheer, C-in-C High Seas Fleet, hoped to redress this balance in Germany's favour by luring the Grand Fleet into an ambush of U-boats, which were to lie off the main British naval bases. To entice the British to sea and into the ambush Scheer planned a High Sea Fleet sortie in the form of a raid on Sunderland, where establishments of military importance would be shelled. Seventeen U-boats had taken up their positions by mid May, but in a consequence of the postponement of the sortie, due in the main to repairs to the battlecruiser *Seydlitz* taking longer than expected, the High Seas Fleet did not put to sea until the night of 30/31 May, when an alternative plan for an advance into the Skagerrak was adopted.

The preliminary German movements did not go unnoticed at the Admiralty, and at 1716 on 30 May, both Admiral Jellicoe and Vice-Admiral Beatty (commanding the Battlecruiser Fleet – BCF– based at Rosyth) received an urgent Admiralty signal informing them that intercepted German signals indicated that the Germans intended an operation which was to commence on the following morning, and that the High Seas Fleet would be leaving their base in the Jade, via the eastern route through the minefields in the Heligoland Bight, and out past the Horns Reef lightship. 'Operation appears to extend over May 31st and June 1st,' the signal read. 'You should concentrate to the eastward of the Long Forties ready for eventualities.' (The Long Forties lie about

sixty miles east of the Scottish coast.)

At this time *Warspite* and her sister ships of the 5th Battle Squadron (5th BS) were at anchor off Rosyth in the Firth of Forth with Beatty's Battlecruiser Fleet (BCF). They had arrived in the Forth nine days earlier to take the place of the 3rd Battlecruiser Squadron, which had been ordered to Scapa for gunnery exercises. On arrival at Rosyth *Queen Elizabeth* went straight into dry dock for a refit. She was still there when the forthcoming battle took place.

In response to the Admiralty instructions the BCF and the 5th BS began raising steam for 22 knots at 1800, and they eventually got under way at about 2200. The battlecruisers preceded the 5th BS out of harbour. Signal boy John Chessman remembers that:

> 'The hum of powerful engines filled the air and the smoke-stacks belched smoke. After we had passed under the Forth Bridge the escorting destroyers which had been waiting to join us, took up stations to port and starboard: two to each capital ship. A mighty array steaming into a glorious crimson setting sun. War just a crazy dream in all that loveliness.'[1]

Later that night an observer on May Island at the entrance of the Firth of Forth would have seen the dim, dark shapes of the battlecruisers and battleships speed by without a light showing. First came the long sleek shapes of the six battlecruisers – *Lion* (flying Beatty's flag), *Princess Royal, Queen Mary, Tiger, New Zealand* and *Indefatigable* – followed some distance behind by the great bulks of the 5th BS – *Barham* (flying Rear-Admiral Hugh Evan-Thomas's flag), *Valiant, Warspite* and *Malaya*. With the capital ships went fourteen light cruisers and 27 destroyers as well as a seaplane carrier. After they had melted into the darkness of the warm, summer night, their wash thundered ashore on May Island for a while before the quiet lapping of a calm sea returned.

In the darkness to the north, sailing from Scapa and from Cromarty, Jellicoe, with his flag in the battleship *Iron Duke*, and the battle squadrons of the Grand Fleet, consisting of 24 battleships and three battlecruisers with twelve light cruisers, eight armoured cruisers and 51 destroyers, were heading eastwards for the rendezvous Jellicoe had arranged with Beatty, about 100 miles off the Jutland coast: the rendezvous was timed for 1430, 31 May. In all, 151 warships and 60,000 men of the greatest fleet the world had ever seen were steaming into destiny.

Luckily for the British Fleet the German U-boat ambush lying off the entrance to the various bases was a miserable failure. Only two unsuccessful attacks were made: one on the 1st Light Cruiser Squadron off Rosyth, and one on the 2nd Battle Squadron as it sailed from Cromarty.

THE RUN TO THE SOUTH

At 1415 on 31 May, the BCF and 5th BS, which were five miles NNW off *Lion*'s port quarter, turned from their easterly course to one of N by E with the object of effecting the rendezvous with the Grand Fleet, which was, at the time, some 65 miles distant to the NNW. As the turn to northward was being executed, the light cruiser *Galatea*, scouting to the east of the BCF, sighted a small steamer hull-down to the ESE, stopped and blowing off steam. Closing to investigate, *Galatea* suddenly sighted the mastheads and funnels of enemy light forces in the vicinity. At 1432, on receipt of the exciting signal flying from *Galatea*'s yards, 'Enemy in sight', Beatty, with the battlecruisers, immediately made off at full speed to the SSE with the intention of getting between the enemy and his base. Unfortunately Beatty's general signal by flags to turn SSE (at 1432) was not taken in by Evan-Thomas in *Barham*, and the 5th BS stood on to the northwards for several precious minutes, not turning to follow the battlecruisers until 1439. As a consequence the distance between the 5th BS and the battlecruisers opened from five miles to nearly ten miles; beyond close supporting distance. After the war Evan-Thomas attributed his delay in turning to the fact that the signal was made by flags only, and these could not be distinguished at the distance between the ships and under the prevailing conditions: the battle-

cruisers working up to full speed were '... making a tremendous smoke ... Had signals been made by searchlight, as they had been on other occasions on the same day, they would have been seen immediately.'[2] Further reports from *Galatea* (six were made between 1433 and 1508) made it clear to Beatty that he was up against more than an isolated unit of enemy light forces, and sure enough, at 1530 five German battlecruisers in line ahead were sighted by *Lion*, fourteen miles distant, steering NW. Beatty immediately altered course to ESE (at 1540) and formed line of battle. The German battlecruisers – consisting of *Lützow* (flying the flag of Vice-Admiral Franz von Hipper), *Derfflinger*, *Seydlitz*, *Moltke* and *Von der Tann* – conformed with the turn and a running fight ensued on parallel courses: this phase of the battle became known as the 'Run to the South'.

Because of the distance that had opened between the 5th BS and Beatty, the four battleships were hull down on the horizon when fire was opened by the battlecruisers (1547), and they remained out of range of the German battlecruisers for a further eighteen minutes.

During these preliminary events *Warspite* cleared for action. Commander Humphrey Walwyn, *Warspite*'s Executive Officer, recalls that:

'At 2.40pm., got a message from the Captain by his Messenger "to get the hands up at once". At the same time a signal was brought to me – "Cruiser in sight bearing NE probably hostile." This signal was from the *Galatea* out of sight ahead. I at once sounded off action and passed the word round to everybody to get cleared away as fast as possible. Message from Captain to ask why I had sounded "Action", and that he wanted me.

"Went up to fore bridge and got rather bitten, as apparently the Captain only meant to get the hands shaken up to get some tea early. Anyway I explained that the hands were well on the way clearing away and should like to get everything ready and get tea after if there was time; went on doing this. Intercepted signal reporting 5 columns of smoke bearing NE made from *Galatea* to *Lion*. I remained on fore bridge and it was pretty plain that there was something serious doing; we were now steering SSE. Captain Philpotts decided to go to action stations right away, and we went on clearing everything away for action.

'There was not much time and I was thankful

we had always done everything so thoroughly. Passed the word round to everybody that we were in for the real thing and went all round the mess decks, wetted decks, put all tables and stools on the deck and lit "action candles" (primitive emergency lighting provided by candles in glass cases) etc. Saw all doors and everything closed and went up on deck; they were just finishing washing down the weather decks, and I sent all hands away to their stations and went up and reported everything was ready. There was nothing in sight but our own ships. Hoisted battle ensigns and Union Jack at after struts and masthead.'[3]

From the fore bridge Commander Walwyn made his way to 'B' turret. Orders were received to load and train the 15in guns to port. Looking out through the hood at the rear of the turret Walwyn could not see anything of the enemy ships due to haze and the tremendous amount of funnel smoke being made by the escorting destroyers, which were steaming hard on the port side of the 5th BS.

Signal boy John Chessman had just come off watch (1600) and was going below for his tea, when he was stopped in his tracks at the top of a gangway by the shrilling of the bosun's pipe – "All hands to action stations!" – and the bugler sounding the charge:

'I turned about,' Chessman recalls, 'hunger unsatisfied and made for the Signal Distributory Office situated under the flag deck. It was in there that I kept a small Brownie box camera. To prevent it getting damaged as I thought. I quickly slung it around my neck and went at the double towards my action station. I was the only one not under cover of some description, and I was one out of no more than half-a-dozen of the ship's company of over a thousand who had the opportunity to view the scene which followed wholly and fairly uninterruptedly. My action station was on the small steel platform surrounding the crow's-nest on the foremast. On the platform were a set of miniature numeral flags on shafts. My job was to note the changes of speed as indicated by similar means on the ship ahead. My flags would thus keep the ship astern informed and so on down the line.

'Was this to prove yet another false alarm? I was answered at the same moment by the boom of gunfire, big gunfire. I set my flags and looked in the direction from which the sound came. Although out in the open sea there was maximum visibility and a bright sun shone down warmly on a sea smooth as a pond, the eastern horizon was shrouded in a sea mist, and even with the aid of a telescope no movement was discernible.'[4]

Following some seven miles astern of the five German battlecruisers were the three light cruisers *Frankfurt*, *Pillau* and *Elbing*, speeding south in line ahead with their attendant destroyers. These were sighted in the distance by the 5th BS at about 1550. They appeared as faint outlines owing to mist and the thick funnel smoke of the British destroyers of the 1st Flotilla, steaming hard on the port side of the 5th BS. The destroyers were ordered out of the field of vision (they fell astern) and at 1558 *Barham* opened fire on *Frankfurt* at a range of 18,600 yards. *Valiant* (second in line) opened fire four minutes later (1601) and *Warspite* (third in line) at 1602. Both ships fired at *Pillau*. This was the very first time that *Warspite* fired her guns in anger. The blast was mind-numbing, each of the eight 15in guns having a recoil equivalent to 400 tons. From the muzzles spat flame and huge clouds of dark-brown cordite smoke.

From his position, looking through the hood in 'B' turret, Commander Walwyn could see the fall of shot from *Warspite*'s salvoes – huge columns of water towering 200 feet in the air – but could not make out the enemy cruisers in the mist, other than for their funnel smoke:

'Suddenly saw No. 2 column of smoke [*Pillau*] break out into a bright flame; this dropped astern and at first I thought she was hit, but then it occurred to me that it was a smoke box, as it looked like an enormous calcium life buoy: bright flame and huge white smoke cloud drifted astern.'[5]

In fact neither *Frankfurt* nor *Pillau* were hit, although they were straddled. Both *Frankfurt* and a destroyer dropped smoke boxes, and the enemy turned away to the NE, out of range. The artificial smoke attracted the battleships' salvoes until 1605, when fire ceased. When fire was checked on the disappearing, smoke enshrouded cruisers, the German battlecruisers at last came into view.

'Found we were turning fast to starboard,' Walwyn recalls, 'following our battlecruiser line, and as we came round 8 points I saw 5 enemy battlecruisers on our port bow. They were steaming the same way as we were and going very hard. A mass of black smoke, and I could only see their masts and the tops of their funnels above the horizon and stern waves showing up white and very high.'[6]

Warspite opened fire on *Von der Tann*, the rear ship of the enemy line: range 19,000 yards. The first few salvoes all fell short of the target.

'Time of flight watch boy was splendid,' Walwyn explains, 'and I timed several of our salvoes which fell exactly right by the watch but were short. Blast from "A" turret was awfully bad and blew salt water and dust into my eyes, which watered like blazes. I saw several of their salvoes splash short of us; they fell into an extraordinary small spread and made the devil of a noise. I remember thinking how high their ricochets must be going over us. Saw *Barham* straddled out through the corner of my eye.'[7]

The German battlecruisers repeatedly altered course to throw off the British gun-layers' aim, and the constant deflection in range was very hard to lay on. Hit on the stern by a shell from *Barham*, *Von der Tann* turned away six points to port, and disappeared from view in a cloud of black and white smoke. Walwyn recalls that:

'We turned our attention to No. 4 in the enemy line (*Moltke*), as No. 5 by this time was out of range and the guns were on the stops at 23,000 yards. Guns were constantly bumping the stops, and the gun-layers reported they could not follow the target. It was a wonderful and rather horrible sight to see the constant orange flicker of flame along the enemy line when they fired. I remember timing their salvoes, and when my boy called "stop" they fell about 4 seconds later a bit short. After the flame, when they fired, there was a white cloud, like steam, which was very deceptive and looked like hits.'[8]

All John Chessman, in his exposed position aloft, could see of the enemy line through his telescope was moving blurs, punctuated at regular intervals with flashes of flame from their guns:

'Six huge splashes rose mast high no more than 100 yards away on our starboard side. This was repeated twice; each time the splashes came a little nearer. The third lot soaked me from head to toe. I stared into the mist fascinated . . . like a rabbit looks at a mean snake. This was my baptism of fire. I watched the flames stab the mist, and watched and waited. It seemed a long wait, long enough to conjecture if the last flash had dispatched a shell with your name on it. A whistle overhead, like the introduction to a tornado, and crump! more fountains, rising this time on the other side. I started doing mental sums. Seeing how they had straddled us well and truly, how long before they slide-ruled us out of existence?'[9]

The 'Run to the South', timed from the moment the rival battlecruisers began to exchange fire (1547) until they checked fire (1636), lasted for 51 minutes. During this time Beatty's battlecruisers were quite simply outgunned by superior German gunnery efficiency. The Germans scored 44 hits (42 on the battlecruisers and two on *Barham* – the remainder of the 5th BS were unscathed), while in return they received only seventeen hits (eleven inflicted by Beatty's battlecruisers and six by the 5th BS). However, even when the British gunners scored a hit they were robbed of their rewards, because the armour-piercing shells proved to be defective. The Ordnance Board's professor of statistics calculated that between 30–70 per cent of the British heavy calibre shells were duds! In comparison the German shells wrought havoc on the lightly armoured British battlecruisers. At 1602 *Indefatigable* blew up and sank under a hail of shells from *Von der Tann*.

Twenty-four minutes later (1626) *Queen Mary* also blew up after being struck by two shells from *Derfflinger*. Four minutes after the destruction of *Queen Mary* the strategic situation was suddenly changed when the light cruiser *Southampton*, scouting three miles ahead of *Lion*, sighted the whole of the German battle fleet, under the command of Admiral Reinhard Scheer, steering northwards: sixteen battleships, six pre-dreadnoughts, six light cruisers and 31 destroyers. As a consequence Beatty turned his battlecruisers NW at 1646, with the object of leading the unsuspecting Germans into the arms of the Grand Fleet, sixty miles to the NW.

When the battlecruisers turned north about, the 5th BS was still eight miles distant. Not being in receipt of

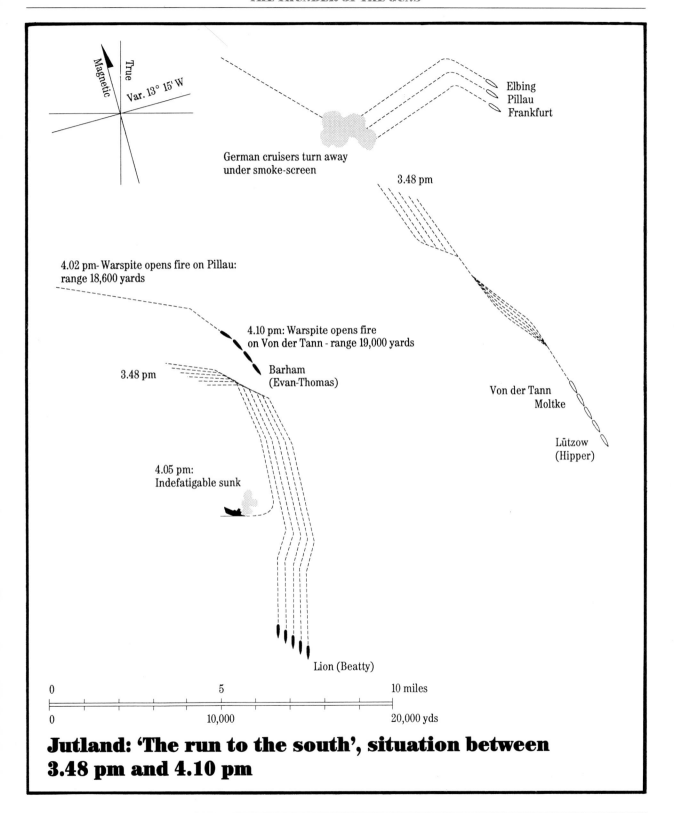

True
Var. 13° 15' W
Magnetic

Elbing
Pillau
Frankfurt

German cruisers turn away
under smoke-screen

3.48 pm

4.02 pm - Warspite opens fire on Pillau:
range 18,600 yards

4.10 pm: Warspite opens fire
on Von der Tann - range 19,000 yards

Barham
(Evan-Thomas)

3.48 pm

Von der Tann
Moltke

Lützow
(Hipper)

4.05 pm:
Indefatigable sunk

Lion (Beatty)

0		5		10 miles

0		10,000		20,000 yds

Jutland: 'The run to the south', situation between 3.48 pm and 4.10 pm

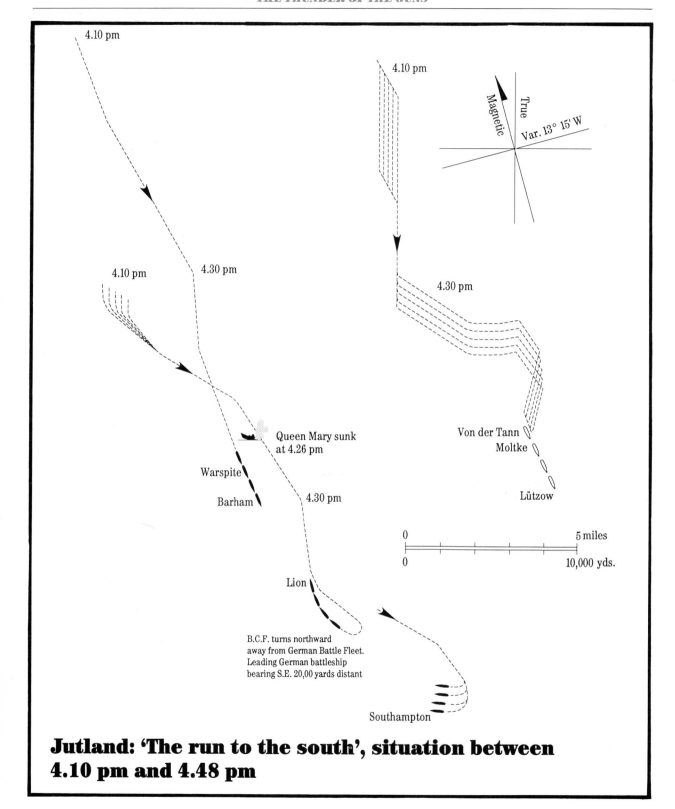

4.10 pm

4.10 pm

Magnetic

True

Var. 13° 15' W

4.10 pm

4.30 pm

4.10 pm

4.30 pm

4.30 pm

Queen Mary sunk
at 4.26 pm

Warspite

Barham

4.30 pm

Von der Tann

Moltke

Lŭtzow

0   5 miles

0   10,000 yds.

Lion

B.C.F. turns northward
away from German Battle Fleet.
Leading German battleship
bearing S.E. 20,00 yards distant

Southampton

Jutland: 'The run to the south', situation between 4.10 pm and 4.48 pm

Southampton's enemy reports and thus being unaware of the close proximity of the German battle fleet, and being unable to read Beatty's flag signal to turn, Evan-Thomas pressed on with the southerly drive. It was only when the 5th BS was almost abreast of the now northward-bound battlecruisers, that Beatty hoisted a flag signal direct to Evan-Thomas ordering him to turn back sixteen points in *succession* to starboard (Compass Pendant). Of course a quicker turn to the northward would have resulted if Beatty had signalled for the 5th BS to turn *together* (Blue Pendant). As it was the Compass Pendant signal offered the Germans a 'turning-point' at which to direct their fire as each of the four battleships turned in succession (beginning at 1658) round the same pivotal point. The turn in succession also led the 5th BS into an unnecessarily close range to the van battleships of the German line of battle. Both *Barham* and *Warspite* received punishment during the turn, and although *Valiant* escaped unscathed, when *Malaya* (last ship of the line) turned, the pivotal point was being deluged with heavy calibre shells from the leading German battle squadron. *Warspite* was hit three times during the turn.

From his position in 'B' turret Commander Walwyn's first indication that the battlecruisers had turned about, was when he saw them passing close by in the opposite direction about four cables distant. He counted only four battlecruisers instead of six, but it didn't cross his mind that the other two had been sunk:

'We then turned 16 points in succession,' he recalls, 'and our turrets trained round full speed to the other beam. Very soon after the turn I suddenly saw, on the starboard quarter, the whole of the High Seas Fleet; at least I saw masts, funnels and an endless ripple of orange flashes all down the line: we were getting well strafed at this time. The noise of their shell falling over and short was deafening. Felt one or two very heavy shakes but didn't think very much of it at the time and it never occurred to me that we were being hit. We were firing pretty fast about Green 120 [30° abaft the starboard beam]. I distinctly saw two of our salvoes hit the leading German battleship. Sheets of yellow flame went right over her mastheads and she looked red fore and aft like a burning haystack; I know we had hit her hard.'[10]

At this time Walwyn received an order from Captain Philpotts to go aft and find out the extent of the damage from a shell which had hit the ship. Walwyn decided to go out over the top of 'B' turret. 'I didn't waste much time on the roof as the noise was awful, and their shells were coming over pretty thick.' As he was climbing down the starboard ladder of 'B' turret, the 15in guns of both 'A' and 'B' turrets fired, making him 'skip a bit quicker'. Making his way below decks and to the stern of the ship, he found nothing wrong and reported as such to the Captain by telephone. Unbeknown to Walwyn the ship had been hit near the stern under the waterline abreast the capstan engine flat. Deciding to make his way forward, he was passing through the forecastle mess deck when:

'A 12in shell came through the side armour on the boys' mess deck. Terrific sheet of golden flame, stink, impenetrable dust, and everything seemed to fall everywhere with an appalling noise. Called for No. 2 Fire Brigade, and they ran up from the flat below and we got hoses on and put out a lot of burning refuse. Several of the fire brigade were sick due to the sweet, sickly stench, but there was no sign of poison gas. The shell hole was clean and about the size of a scuttle; big flakes of the armour belt had been flung right across the mess deck wrecking everything. Many armour bolts came away. Flooding cabinet was completely wrecked and all voice pipes and electric leads overhead were cut to pieces. Everybody busy "souvenir" hunting and had to put a hose on them to make them take cover below again.'[11]

Making his way aft again along the port side of the ship, Walwyn found water pouring in through the scuttles in the Admiral's cabin, and the deck torn up:

'It was obvious the side was blown in below the Admiral's cabin. Stern was very deep due to hard steaming and water was pumping up as we pitched. A 12in shell had also hit right aft going practically fore and aft through 4 bulkheads, flooding the whole of the middle deck aft and ending up in Surgeon Williamson's bunk. Got all No. 6 Fire Brigade out of it as water was gaining fast in the cabin flat and was then about 3 feet deep with men standing on the ladder.'[12]

Surgeon G. E. D. Ellis, who was below decks with the sick bay staff in the Aft Distributing Station, received *Warspite*'s first casualty at this time. Stoker Frederick

Plater was hit in the neck by a piece of shrapnel which perforated the pharynx, causing a considerable frothy haemorrhage. 'He was very collapsed from shock,' Ellis recalls, 'but the bleeding was stopped by packing the wound with thin strips of gauze, and he subsequently recovered.'[13]

THE RUN TO THE NORTH

When the 5th BS turned northward at 1658, *Barham* and *Valiant* engaged Hipper's battlecruisers, scoring hits on *Lützow* and *Derfflinger* and heavily damaging *Seydlitz*, while *Warspite* and *Malaya* fired at the leading German battleships, scoring hits on *Grosser Kurfürst* and *Markgraf*. The running fight to the north continued until 1800 when the junction with the Grand Fleet, which had been racing south-eastward, was at last effected. By this time *Warspite* had been hit a further six times (*Barham* four; *Malaya* seven; *Valiant* 0). Commander Walwyn gives a graphic account of events below decks during the northerly run:

'I was going up the hatch to the casemate lobby when I was called back and told that a shell had just burst in the Captain's lobby. I went aft again and found that my cabin had been completely wrecked. Lobby in an awful state and a hole about 12 feet in diameter in the centre of the deck. Lot of burning débris in my cabin which we put out. My sleeping cabin was not so bad and only spattered with splinters. There were about 4 bursts in the lobby; trunk to steering compartment was wrecked, stanchions cut through, Captain's pantry in heaps and everything in a filthy state of indescribable wreckage. Realized things were pretty warm aft and nothing could be done so went forward again before any more shells arrived. Went past No. 5 Fire Brigade and saw we had been heavily hit port side. Helped with fire brigade in port casemate lobby, plugging fire mains and trying to stop water getting down ventilating trunks. Centre line 2in door was blown off its hinges and whole of the after flat in an awful state, everything blown to pieces and spattered by splinters. I remember columns of water pouring through hole in deck overhead which must have been from shells falling short.

'Ventilating trunks were all holed and blown away near deck and we either unbolted or sledged these away so as to be able to plug the hole in the deck. Three stokers were dead in voice pipe flat, one having his head blown off and another badly smashed to pieces; rather a horrible sight but the burnt ones were far worse.

'A shell had come in further forward and hit 'X' turret barbette armour, killing several of No. 5 Fire Brigade in engineers' work shop and wounding a lot more. Water was pouring through hole in side into Marine Sergeants' mess thus flooding main deck and going down shell hole to centre engine room supply trunk. W/T door had been blown away and killed Sub-Lieutenant Single.

'I realized we could not effectively stop hole inside and decided we must at all costs prevent water getting to engine room down the supply trunk which was exposed. We plugged this by big sheets of rubber shored down with deals, this of course stopped ventilation supply to engine rooms; they got pretty hot down below. Left marines plugging hole in ship's side with hammocks, but a lot of water was coming in and washing all attempts at plugging away.

'Blast of shell put out all lights momentarily but candles were easily relit and did well. Oil lamps as expected went out and were not relit, they are quite useless for action purposes. Electric light bulbs broke in vicinity of shell bursts. Lot of broken glass about the decks made it awkward to get about, also sharp jagged plates were regular death traps. The body of a 12in shell was found above engineers' workshop, unexploded. The filling was sticking out like a chock of wood and a couple of stokers were trying to chip the fuze out. I luckily stopped this little effort.

'Went forward along port side of mess deck and sent Walker to telephone Captain to tell him things were all right. Had a cigarette on the port side of cooks' lobby or rather started one to steady my feelings. Had a yarn with the Paymaster who was wandering about using appalling language as to when the Grand Fleet was going to turn up. Had a laugh together, anyway. Whilst there a 12in came into Warrant Officers' galley and blew down through deck. A stoker alongside me looked up and said, "There goes my — dinner!" Popped up to battery deck port side but found very little damage had been done and everybody was very cheery.'[14]

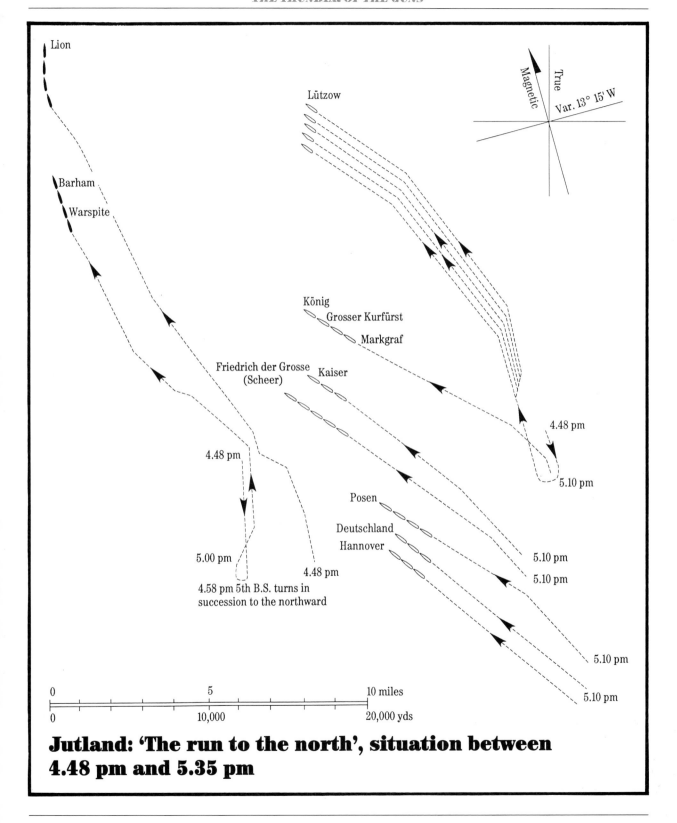

Lion

Lützow

Magnetic
True
Var. 13° 15' W

Barham
Warspite

König
Grosser Kurfürst
Markgraf

Friedrich der Grosse
(Scheer)
Kaiser

4.48 pm

4.48 pm
5.10 pm

4.48 pm

5.00 pm

4.48 pm

Posen

Deutschland
Hannover

5.10 pm
5.10 pm

4.58 pm 5th B.S. turns in
succession to the northward

5.10 pm

5.10 pm

5.10 pm

0		5		10 miles

0		10,000		20,000 yds

Jutland: 'The run to the north', situation between 4.48 pm and 5.35 pm

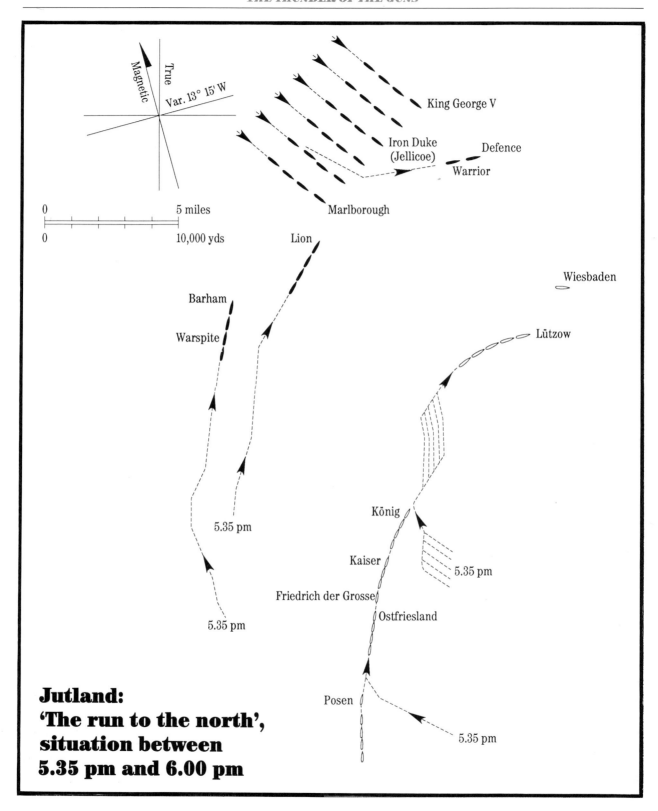

Var. 13° 15' W

0   5 miles

0   10,000 yds

King George V

Iron Duke
(Jellicoe)

Defence

Warrior

Marlborough

Lion

Wiesbaden

Barham

Warspite

Lützow

5.35 pm

König

Kaiser

5.35 pm

Friedrich der Grosse

Ostfriesland

5.35 pm

Posen

5.35 pm

**Jutland:
'The run to the north',
situation between
5.35 pm and 6.00 pm**

JUNCTION WITH THE GRAND FLEET

When the Grand Fleet was sighted by the BCF and 5th BS it was steaming SE with the battle squadrons disposed in six parallel columns. During their approach both Beatty and Evan-Thomas assumed that the Grand Fleet would deploy into single line ahead with the southern-most, or starboard column, leading. As a result both admirals swung their squadrons round on to an easterly course with the intention of taking up their appointed stations in the van of the fleet, in accordance with the Grand Fleet Battle Orders. So disposed, both squadrons would be able to achieve the tactical position of crossing the 'T' of the enemy fleet, which was their tactical prerogative. Jellicoe, however, decided to deploy with the northernmost, or port column, leading. Although the battlecruisers pressed on across the line of fire of the Grand Fleet to obtain the van position, Evan-Thomas, whose squadron lacked the speed to follow Beatty's intention, was forced to swing to port (at 1818) back on to a northerly course to take up his alternative battle station in the rear of the fleet, forming up astern of the starboard battle squadron. During these manoeuvres the 5th BS continued to engage the leading enemy battleships.

WARSPITE'S DEATH RIDE

During the turn to port (1818), while under heavy fire in which she was repeatedly hit, *Warspite's* helm suddenly jammed and she swerved out of line to port, narrowly missing a collision with *Valiant*. Captain Philpotts strove to bring her back into line by use of her engines against the pull of the jammed rudder. All this achieved was to send *Warspite* on a death ride straight towards the enemy battleships at a decreasing speed. A large number of the leading German battleships immediately brought their main and secondary armaments to bear on this fat and inviting target. Unable to bring *Warspite* back to port, Captain Philpotts ordered full speed ahead, letting the ship drive as quickly as possible through a full circle to starboard under the jammed helm. By this means he quickly brought the ship round, heading away from the enemy, but the rudder would not budge, and as it was essential to keep under way rather than become a stationary target for the deadly fire directed at her, Philpotts swung the ship through yet another complete circle. During these impromptu turns *Warspite* was carried to within 10,000 yards of the head of the enemy line and she sustained a total of twenty hits, nine of them definitely heavy calibre, four definitely 5.9in shells from the German secondary batteries, and seven shells of unidentified calibre (i.e., either heavy or light calibre). Throughout her death ride *Warspite* was shrouded in a forest of huge shell splashes from shorts, which deluged the ship in tons of sea water and a hail of shrapnel splinters.

When *Warspite* listed to port during her circular gyrations, Surgeon Ellis, who was below decks, had the impression that she was heeling indefinitely. The list was far greater than that usually produced by an alteration in course, and Ellis braced himself, convinced that *Warspite* was about to capsize. After what seemed like ages, he sighed with relief when the ship eventually regained an even keel.

During the gyrations John Chessman, from his position aloft on the foremast, sighted two British four-funnelled cruisers steaming hard off *Warspite's* starboard beam:

> 'So near were they I could have read their names if I hadn't recognized them as the *Defence* and *Warrior*. I could not resist trying to get a snapshot of the *Defence*, dressed as she was in all her glory with her battle ensigns. I lifted my box camera and wham! it was rocketed from my grasp and high into the air to disappear over the side. Shrapnel of course, it had to be, they weren't throwing eggs. At the same moment, horror of horrors! I watched as over six hundred officers and men shrivelled up in no more than ten seconds flat.'[15]

These two armoured cruisers, which were part of the Grand Fleet's advanced scouting screen, crossed the bows of Beatty's battlecruisers intent on attacking the German light cruiser *Wiesbaden*, which was lying disabled between the rival fleets. As they closed on the crippled *Wiesbaden*, the huge outlines of German capital ships suddenly loomed out of the mist to the southward, less than 8,000 yards away. The result was appalling, as evinced by Midshipman Ashworth at his action station in *Warspite's* 'A' turret. He saw a fire break out on *Defence's* fore part, followed by flames breaking out aft. Another salvo hit her forward and Ashworth saw a huge sheet of flame from her fore turret rise as high as the ship's foretop, then spread aft to the conning tower and thence along the 7.5in turrets, working aft:

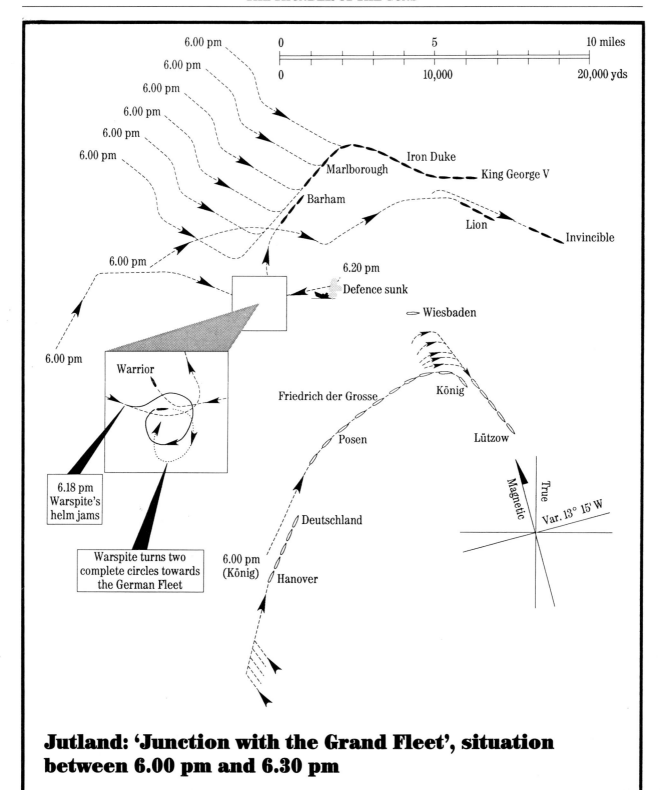

6.00 pm

6.00 pm

6.00 pm

6.00 pm

6.00 pm

6.00 pm

0   5   10 miles

0   10,000   20,000 yds

Iron Duke

Marlborough   King George V

Barham

Lion

Invincible

6.00 pm

6.20 pm

Defence sunk

Wiesbaden

6.00 pm

Warrior

Friedrich der Grosse

König

Posen

Lützow

6.18 pm
Warspite's
helm jams

Warspite turns two
complete circles towards
the German Fleet

Deutschland

Magnetic   True

Var. 13° 15' W

6.00 pm
(König)

Hanover

**Jutland: 'Junction with the Grand Fleet', situation
between 6.00 pm and 6.30 pm**

'I suppose it was working along the ammunition passages, as I could see each 7.5in turret go up in turn, until finally there was a huge burst of flame and smoke which rose at terrific speed till it hid everything, just like a set piece of fireworks going off. This column of flame reached a height of about 300 feet, at the top of which I saw a large black object, presumably a 9.2in gun; it hung there for about 20 to 30 seconds. When it lifted, there was absolutely nothing to be seen, except seething water. No wreckage, survivors or anything. It was an awful sight.'[16]

Warrior, following close astern of *Defence*, was also heavily hit and set on fire. However, as she staggered to the westward to get out of range of the deadly German gun-fire, she was spared the fate of her sister ship by *Warspite*'s circular gyrations, which carried her to the engaged side of *Warrior*, shielding the cruiser from any more punishment.

While this was going on Chessman suddenly found that his hands were covered in blood and his trousers were in tatters. He had been hit by a hail of shrapnel but miraculously suffered no serious injury other than a small gash on the right side of his neck:

'How it missed the jugular I shall never know,' he recalls. 'To stand in the centre of a metal storm and to be cut as I was without a single piece lodging must surely indicate I was born of a miracle.

'Shortly afterwards signalman George Sault from Canada mounted to my platform in order to reclaim a halyard slip out of the yard-arm. "Well cock!" he greeted me, "I thought it was warm down below but jeez! it's bloody hot up here!" "What's with you?" I asked him. "Well," he replied, "they did ask me to come up to give you a bloody medal but I thought you'd sooner have this corned beef sandwich." He was right: I'd had no tea. Was that man cool! After he had recovered the halyard clip he sat on the yard-arm dangling his feet. I tried to raise my voice above the din. "Come in man before you get knocked off your perch," I bawled over the roar of approaching shells. His response was to reach into his pocket and bring out his baccy pouch and papers and coolly roll a smoke.

'There was another comical incident of which I learnt later. Having occasion to visit the upper deck on an errand during the intense bombardment, a friend of mine, signalman Herbert Porter, a cockney and the soul of good humour, had just reached the top of the upper deck gangway just inside the superstructure, part of which formed the bread store. As he turned to reach the door a shell penetrated the store, burst inside, and scattered the loaves of bread in all directions. The force of the explosion lifted the door clean outside the store and of course plenty of bread followed. One or more of these loaves caught Herbert on the head and stunned him to the deck. Just afterwards two casualty checkers arrived on the scene. One said to the other "Hey! there's one here. Looks as if he's had it!" His companion knelt to check pulse and breathing. Just at that moment Herbert's eyelids fluttered, and they were amazed to hear him murmur "Bloody hell! They're firing loaves of bread at us!"[17]

Commander Walwyn records the mayhem below decks during *Warspite*'s death ride:

'Went along starboard side of mess deck and made 6in supply parties spread out more as they would "bunch" together so much. While forward I was told we had been hit port side aft, so ran aft and found we had been hit underneath engineer's office. Looked very bad as a large triangular piece had been blown out of the top corner of the lower strake of main belt, about a foot above water. The fresh water and oil fuel tanks had been blown to pieces and everything in an awful state of dust, oil fuel and filth. Engineer's office completely wrecked and deck all bowed upwards. Men trying to plug the hole but tons of water was coming in and washing them back all the time. As it was all oil fuel they looked like a lot of gold fish swimming about. A marine passed the remark, "This will mean a drop of leave." Tried for a bit to plug and shore up with hammocks but it was hopeless, as the force of the seas was tremendous. I did not realize till later that the bulkhead to stoker petty officers' bathroom had gone and that was flooded too. Decided to fill the whole compartment with hammocks and started a strong party filling the whole show chock full with them. It eventually took nearly 600 hammocks to fill it up which effectually stopped it, but not till late that night. Body of this shell was afterwards found in bathroom.

'The fan supply trunk to WER had been badly holed by this shell and volumes of water was pouring down to the wing engine room. Got down inside trunk and with the chief's assistance we plugged and shoved this hole from inside the trunk with rubber sheets and stopped water getting below. Went up to battery deck port side and looked through 6in control hood. Must have got a direct hit further aft port side with high-explosive shell, as there was a terrific flash and shock and I was knocked endways out of 6in hood, my eyes full of water and dust. Gardner thought I was hit, but it was only shock. Realized it was pretty hot and we were getting heavily hit. Went down to mess deck again to see how the hammock party were getting on and found they had passed a lot in but no sign of bottom yet, many were lost washing out through the hole and it didn't look promising. Crossed to starboard side and a shell burst in battery above. Sheet of flame came down through slits of sliding shutters. Told them to open the shutter with a view to going up the escape to see what had happened, but it was all aglow overhead, so shut it to again. Heard a lot of groaning on battery deck. Went forward to get up fore-end when I was told I was wanted at once as there was a bad fire on superstructure.

'A fragment from the shell bursting by starboard 6in gun had come through the roof of battery deck and actually hit the after 6in cordite case containing 4 full charges. As bad luck would have it they had just given the order to 6in guns to load and the cartridge number had a charge half out of the case in his arms. This box and 4 others went up, cases actually melted and so fired. Whole of No. 6 starboard gun crew were frightfully burned and several more of No. 5 gun. The flash was very sudden and intense heat burnt paintwork and everything near, all leads to No. 6 gun were fused otherwise no damage to gun except the breech screw and carrier were fused up as the breech of the gun was open. Luckily the fire did not spread right along the battery, as the centre-line door was shut and this saved the port battery.'[18]

The fire in the No. 6 gun casemate was fought by three midshipmen – Bostock, Gardner and Batson – Gardner directing the hose while the other two dragged

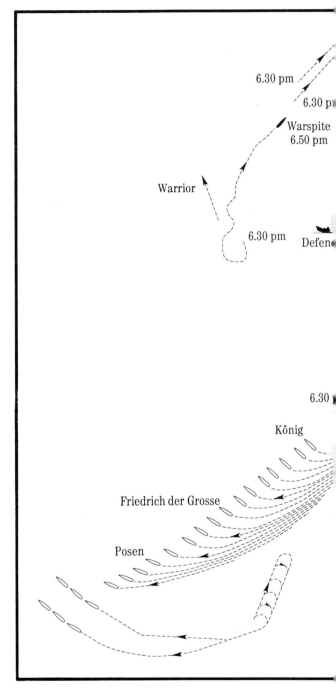

it along behind him. Having to direct a jet of cold, salt water into the casemate filled with screaming, badly burnt gun's crew was horrifying, but it had to be done; if the rest of the cordite had caught fire there was every possibility that it would have spread through the entire starboard 6in gun battery with devastating results.

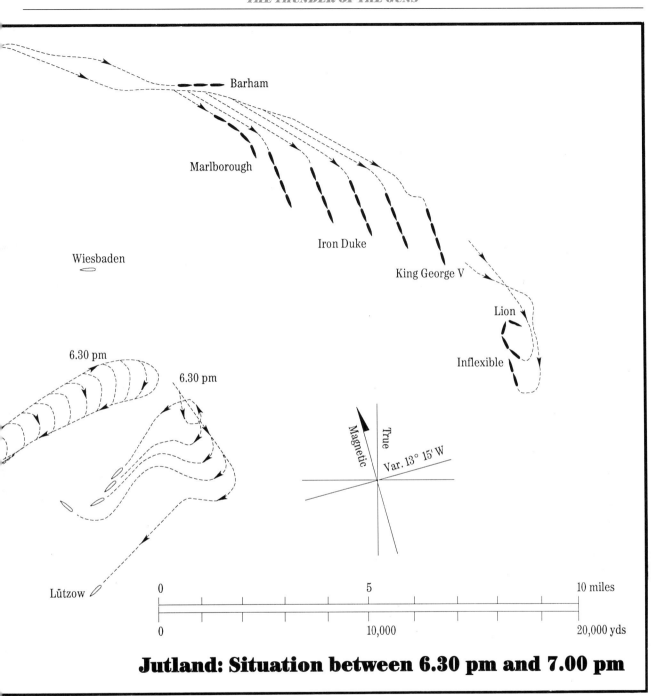

Jutland: Situation between 6.30 pm and 7.00 pm

The wounded from No. 6 gun, all badly burnt by the cordite fire, were taken below to the aft Distributing Station. There were eleven cases in all, including 56-year-old Father Pollen, the RC Chaplain, who had suffered very severe and extensive burns, by rushing into the casemate before the flames were extinguished, in an attempt to rescue the men inside. He was awarded the DSO for his bravery.

To begin with Surgeon Ellis ordered the burns of the wounded to be dressed with pre-prepared picric acid lint. The effect was agonizing (picric acid only aggravated the burns) and the patients tore off the bandages. Dressings of boracic ointment or oil were tried next, and according to Ellis, '. . . this proved more successful, but the restless agony of the patients made it a very difficult matter to keep them protected by dressings . . . injections of morphine seemed to have very little effect on them'.[19] One of the burn cases died before *Warspite* reached base, another two subsequently died in hospital.

Going up on deck Commander Walwyn found that:

'The superstructures were holed everywhere and looked perfectly awful. The noise was deafening, shells bursting short threw tons of water over the ship. The fore superstructure itself was in an awful state of chaos. Port shelter completely gone and starboard side had several big holes in it, everything wrecked and looked like a burnt out factory all blackened and beams twisted everywhere. A 12in shell had come through the after funnel, through beef screen, hit armoured grating over 'B' boiler room and had been deflected upwards, smashing 2nd cutter to matchwood. Apparently it went out through the superstructure sideways without bursting, plating torn to shreds everywhere. On its way through the beef screen the shell had carried with it a whole sheep which was wedged into the gratings; at first I thought it was a casualty. There was a heavy pall of smoke everywhere, terrific rumbling of heavy firing and the whole horizon was lit by orange flashes of gunfire.'

The Grand Fleet battle squadrons had by now deployed into single line ahead: 24 battleships in a line six miles long (not including the 5th BS). The deployment took place while *Warspite* was undergoing her death ride.

Warspite's first complete circle to starboard began at 1820 and was completed at 1830. Her second circle was of only half the circumference, and took only five minutes (1830–1835). Captain Philpotts finally managed to gain some control by steering the ship by the alternative pull of the port and starboard engines. Still under fire from the German battleships *Ostfriesland* and *Friedrich der Grosse*, the ship swerved through an 'S'-shaped course while Captain Philpotts persevered to maintain a course requisite to catching up with the 5th BS, which was some three miles to the NE of *Warspite*'s position by 1900. But with the helm still unmanageable, Philpotts decided to draw off to the NW and stopped engines, with the intention of shifting the steering gear to some other position. At this juncture, Commander Walwyn, black as a sweep and soaking wet, aware that the ship was losing way went to the forward conning tower, from where Captain Philpotts was conning the ship.

'The Captain asked me how things were and I started to tell him. He said, "I don't care a damn about the damage, can we join the line?" I hadn't the faintest idea what the situation was or what had happened and I must have sounded a bit dim, anyway I said, "If she gets another heavy hit on the port side I don't think she will stand it." I was thinking of the wing engine room hit. I did not know anything about the steering gear having been jammed.'[20]

Shrouded in a pall of smoke *Warspite* passed out of sight of the German gunners, and as her guns fell silent, the mind-numbing din of battle receded. She had fired a total of 259 15in shells and a considerable quantity of 6in ammunition.

Learning from Walwyn that the after steering compartment was flooded, Philpotts, realizing that the steering position in the engine room would have to be adopted, and that the extent of the damage made only a moderate speed practical if the danger of serious flooding were to be avoided, set off again at sixteen knots, course NE.

Both the 5th BS and the Grand Fleet were now out of sight from *Warspite*, having disappeared in the smoke and mist to the eastward. The German Fleet, in an attempt to extricate itself from a battle *à outrance* had reversed course to SW and had also disappeared into the mist to the southward. At 1900 the nearest German battleship was nearly seven miles distant from *Warspite*. In the mist, smoke and confusion, Jellicoe was also destined to lose sight of the High Seas Fleet which, apart from fleeting exchanges of fire with the Grand Fleet and having to fight off numerous spirited destroyer attacks during the night, made good its escape back to the Jade.

By 2000, Captain Philpotts, who had still not regained contact with the 5th BS, made a signal by wireless to Evan-Thomas requesting the position of the battlefleet and outlining *Warspite*'s damaged state '. . . two big holes abreast engine room. Wing engine not yet flooded . . . can steam 16 knots'. When this signal was dispatched *Warspite* was some 30 miles northward of the 5th BS. Deciding that *Warspite* was too badly damaged to be risked any further, Evan-Thomas replied (signal dispatched at 2107) that *Warspite* was to retire and make her way back to Rosyth. Accordingly Captain Philpotts shaped course for home.

'It was just getting dusk as the ship turned for home,' Surgeon Ellis recalls, 'and everything was quiet, still and peaceful . . . there was no other ship in sight, or noise of firing anywhere. There was still a dull red glow from the sun left in the sky, low down, but it was very hazy, and impossible to see any distance. The sea was still calm, but there was just enough breeze to make its surface tumbly. As regards the ship . . . only a few hours before she had been one of the cleanest and smartest-looking ships in the fleet; her decks spotlessly white, and her light grey paint, freshly put on only recently, gleaming everywhere in the sunshine. Now her decks were filthy, littered with débris and in places torn up by shells . . . her funnels had ragged holes in them . . . A ragged and dirty White Ensign still flew from her ensign staff.'[21]

After supervising the fighting of a fire which had continued to rage in the sick bay for more than two hours (mainly due to the chemicals stored there), Commander Walwyn made his way to the wardroom (which had been wrecked) where he found, '. . . they had some food of sorts going – sardines and tinned tongue. Had a brandy and soda, biscuits and cheese: everybody was very cheery.' The ship's company also stood down for a meal, although all guns continued to be fully manned. It was also essential to 'darken ship' with the fall of night, but although attempts were made to cover the numerous shell holes with canvas, the ship was so badly riddled by splinter damage that it proved to be a hopeless task. Despite a heavy swell blowing up, the hours of darkness passed uneventfully, and after the bulkheads of the flooded compartments had been shored up, Philpotts was able to increase speed to eighteen knots, zigzagging all the while as a precaution against attack by U-boats.

Daylight on the morning of 1 June found *Warspite* 140 nautical miles ENE of the entrance to the Firth of Forth. The hands were employed getting *Warspite* as ship-shape as possible. As all the ship's boats had been smashed to bits during the action, the carpenters were busied constructing rafts out of mess tables and benches. Finding the Captain's cabin a foot deep in water, Walwyn got a hand-operated 5-ton pump underway to dry it out. The hands at the pump worked all through the forenoon watch without making any impression. Walwyn was still ignorant of the fact that the capstan engine flat had been holed below the waterline, and as fast as the sea water was pumped out it re-entered through the hole in the side below. 'My fault entirely,' Walwyn admitted later, 'felt very foolish afterwards.'

By 0930 *Warspite*, some 100 miles ENE of the Forth, had entered the operational area of the U-boats, which had been positioned off the Firth of Forth as the original ambush to attack outgoing warships, and were now lying in wait for the returning warships of the Grand Fleet. Five minutes later *Warspite* was sighted by one of these boats – *U51* (Walther Rumpel) – which, despite the heavy sea, managed to keep at periscope depth and approach to within 650 yards of the battleship. Luckily for *Warspite* the bows of the U-boat dipped violently in the steep swell just as the torpedoes were fired from the bow torpedo tubes. According to Rumpel's report only one torpedo left the tubes and by breaking surface it betrayed the presence of *U51*. As the torpedo sped across *Warspite*'s bows, Captain Philpotts swung the ship round hard a-starboard, and increasing speed to 21 knots made off north-westward away from the U-boat's suspected position. It was a close shave and as a precaution the number of lookouts was doubled, and a wireless signal was made to the C-in-C Rosyth requesting a destroyer escort.

According to Walwyn, at 1050 fire was opened by the port 6in battery, range 800 yards, on another U-boat. Eight rounds were fired, and a gun-layer swore he saw a conning tower briefly break surface. The first attack must have caused the jitters, because German records are adamant that no U-boat was in the close vicinity of *Warspite* at this time.

At 1142, however, lookouts in *Warspite* definitely did sight the periscope of a U-boat just ahead of the ship. Captain Philpotts immediately increased to full speed in order to ram the U-boat, but the transmission of orders to the helmsman at the steering position in the engine room, took so long that the manoeuvre failed. The U-boat was *U63* (Otto Schultze) which was on her way home from her position off the Forth with a disabled starboard engine. Through the periscope Schultze suddenly sighted *Warspite* not more than 100 yards away, bearing down on him and firing her forward port

6in gun. *U63* immediately crashed-dived to 160 feet and *Warspite* was too slow in changing course to catch her.

Danger from further U-boat attack was reduced at 1330, when two destroyers and four torpedo-boats from Rosyth appeared and took up a screening position around the battleship. Finally, at 1530, with her funnels belching smoke from their many perforations, *Warspite* passed under the Forth Bridge. 'I am bound to say I heaved a sigh of relief', Walwyn recalls, 'as we passed under the Bridge, and the cheers from the troops made one feel quite gulpy.'[22]

Warspite was immediately dry docked for repairs in No. 1 dock.

'We were the first ship to return from the battle,' Surgeon Ellis recorded in his diary. 'The battlecruisers came in the following day, with the crew of the *Warrior* [which had subsequently sunk while being towed home by the seaplane carrier *Engadine*]. The officers of both the *Queen Elizabeth* and the *Dreadnought* [both undergoing refits at Rosyth] were exceedingly kind in offering sleeping accommodation to those of us whose cabins were unusable.

'After spending the night on the *Queen Elizabeth*, I went, next morning, and had a look all round the *Warspite* as she lay in dock. It may seem emotional, but I felt I just loved her. And I think now that there is no other ship in the world like her. *Warspite* – may her name always be honoured.'[23]

When the 5th BS returned to port (*Barham* and *Malaya* went to Scapa, *Valiant* to Rosyth for docking) Evan-Thomas signalled to Captain Philpotts:

'I am much grieved at the sad losses *Warspite* has sustained. I warmly congratulate you on the way she was handled both during the action and afterwards, under most difficult circumstances – with the result that she arrived safely in port. It is hoped that it will not be long before she is able again to take her part in the same gallant manner she did on Wednesday.'[24]

By the time she reached Rosyth, *Warspite* was drawing 35½ feet aft instead of her normal 31 feet. Considering the large amount of damage she had sustained at Jutland, her casualties were remarkably light. Only one officer and thirteen men had been killed; while four officers and 13 men had suffered wounds, out of the ship's company of 1,048 officers and men. More importantly, despite being hit 29 times, *Warspite*'s fighting efficiency had not been vitally impaired. There can be no finer tribute to the sturdiness and the effective scale of armour protection of this class of ship.

Source Notes
1. Chessman Papers.
2. Evan-Thomas's letter to *The Times*, 16 February 1927.
3. Memoir by Commander H. Walwyn, among the papers of Captain E. M. Philpotts (Imperial War Museum), hereinafter cited as Walwyn Memoir.
4. Chessman Papers.
5. Walwyn Memoir.
6. ibid.
7. ibid.
8. ibid.
9. Chessman Papers.
10. Walwyn Memoir.
11. ibid.
12. ibid.
13. The papers of Captain G. E. D. Ellis (Imperial War Museum), hereinafter cited as Ellis Papers.
14. Walwyn Memoir.
15. Chessman Papers.
16. Ashworth Papers.
17. Chessman Papers.
18. Walwyn Memoir.
19. Ellis Papers.
20. Walwyn Memoir.
21. Ellis Papers.
22. Walwyn Memoir.
23. Ellis Papers.
24. Philpotts Papers.

CHRONOLOGICAL LIST OF HITS FROM ENEMY GUNFIRE SUFFERED BY HMS *WARSPITE* DURING THE BATTLE OF JUTLAND

Information compiled from the papers of Captain E. M. Philpotts (Imperial War Museum): Naval Staff Monograph 'Grand Fleet Gunnery and Torpedo Memoranda on Naval Actions 1914–1918'; and 'Final Reports Of The Projectile Committee Reporting On The Battle Of Jutland' (Naval Historical Library).

(Heavy calibre shells were either 11in or 12in, light calibre were 5.9in)

1st HIT

Shell's angle of descent: ?
Thickness of plates penetrated: 6 inches
Distance of burst from point of impact: 12 feet
Damage caused:
Heavy calibre shell penetrated upper strake of armoured belt about 3 inches below the waterline, and burst in after capstan flat. Explosion blew down 237 bulkhead and flooded both flats on middle deck.

2nd HIT

Shell's angle of descent: ?
Thickness of plates penetrated: ¾in
Distance of burst from point of impact: 1–2 feet
Damage caused:

Heavy calibre shell struck hull plating on the waterline, near the stern, between main and middle decks, below Admiral's day cabin. A 4-foot × 3-foot hole was blown in the hull and a split was caused along the edge of the plates for a length of 20 feet to the sternpost and compartments above. Considerable damage was caused to the after compartments and the Admiral's cabin was partly flooded. The main deck plates ($\frac{5}{16}$in) were distorted above the burst. The nose cap of the shell was found in an adjacent cabin, having pierced four $\frac{3}{16}$in bulkheads. It appears that the shoulder of the shell struck the hull, hence the undamaged nose cap.

3rd HIT

Shell's angle of descent: 5–10°
Thickness of plates penetrated: 6 inches
Distance of burst from point of impact: 6 feet
Damage caused:

Heavy calibre shell hit the upper strake of the armoured belt on the starboard side, just forward of the foremost 6in gun, and burst on the boys' mess deck six feet from impact. A hole 2 feet × 18 inches was punched in the 6in armour, and considerable damage was caused to voice pipes, fire control leads and all structure in the vicinity. The 1¼in upper deck was holed in two places, and the ⅜in main deck was riddled with holes below the burst. One large fragment of the shell came to rest in the magazine flooding cabinet 30 feet from the explosion, while smaller pieces were driven across the athwartship gangway to the port side of the ship.

4th HIT

Shell's angle of descent: 15–20°
Thickness of plates penetrated: 1¼ inches
Distance of burst from point of impact: 10 feet
Damage caused:

Heavy calibre shell struck the upper deck port side, midway between 'X' and 'Y' barbettes, about 20 feet from the edge of the upper deck. A hole, 7 feet 6 inches by 1 foot 8 inches, was torn in the deck at the point of impact. The shell burst in the after casemate lobby between the upper deck and main deck. Apart from wrecking the light steel work up to 16 feet distant, the blast also wrecked the main deck magazine flooding cabinet; a 2in-thick door was blown off its hinges in the bulkhead of the flooding cabinet. The 5in main deck plates were riddled and the base plug of the shell tore through the main and middle decks lodging in the 'X' magazine cooler casing, 20 feet from the point of burst. Apart from holing a large number of ventilation trunks on the main deck, the fire-main was also broken. Water from this poured into 'Y' and 'X' magazine cooler spaces and burnt-out the pumps.

5th HIT

Shell's angle of descent: 5–10°
Thickness of plates penetrated: 6 inches
Distance of burst from point of impact: failed to explode.
Damage caused:

Heavy calibre shell struck the port side 6in upper strake of the armoured belt, 4 feet below the upper deck and 5 feet forward of 'X' barbette. Shell pierced the armour, leaving a 12in diameter hole, without exploding and broke into two pieces. The largest piece tore through two ¼in bulkheads and the exhaust vent trunk leading from the centre engine room. Striking the 4in armour of 'X' barbette, it tore off 2¼in of the armour surface, before being deflected downwards through the ⅜in main deck plates, finally coming to rest on the starboard side of the ship in the Engineers' Workshop, killing three of the No. 5 fire brigade and wounding several more.

6th HIT

Shell's angle of descent: 5–10°
Thickness of plates penetrated: ½ inch
Distance of burst from point of impact: 40 feet
Damage caused:

Heavy calibre shell struck 1½in side plating just below the upper deck in line with the after part of 'Y' barbette. Entering the Commander's sleeping cabin, it tore through three ¼in bulkheads and a 7in midships pillar, bursting 40 feet from the point of impact on the main deck, blowing a hole, 4 feet 6 inches × 3 feet, in the 1¼in deck plating. The blast caused severe damage to structures 30 feet from the point of burst; a ¼in bulkhead was blown away and a hole, 7 feet × 3 feet, was blown in the ½in side plating of the Commander's cabin, the frames being twisted and smashed. Escape trunk to the steering compartment was also badly damaged, which admitted water into the trunk, flooding the steering compartment to a depth of 4 feet.

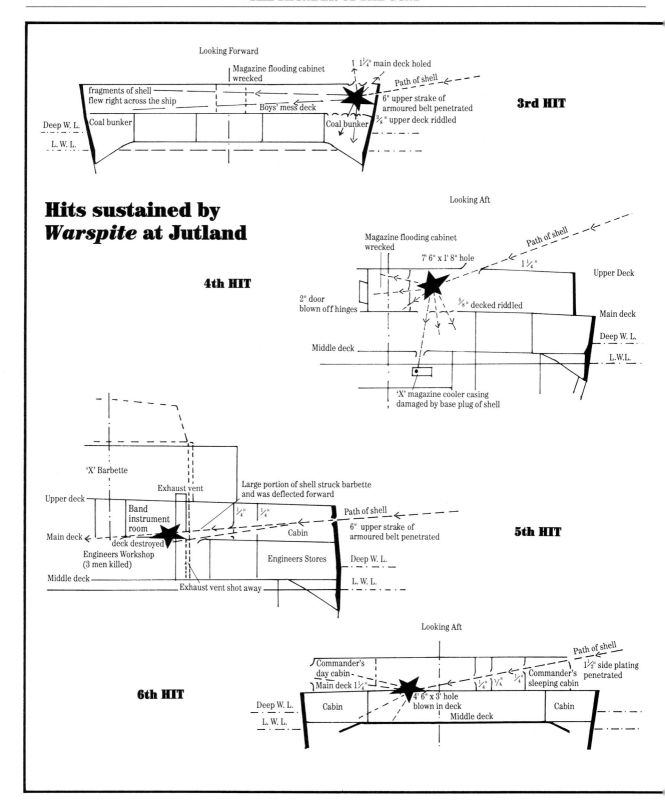

Looking Forward

$1\frac{1}{4}$" main deck holed

Magazine flooding cabinet wrecked

Path of shell

fragments of shell flew right across the ship

3rd HIT

Boys' mess deck

6" upper strake of armoured belt penetrated

$\frac{3}{8}$" upper deck riddled

Deep W. L.

Coal bunker

Coal bunker

L. W. L.

Hits sustained by *Warspite* at Jutland

Looking Aft

Magazine flooding cabinet wrecked

Path of shell

4th HIT

7' 6" x 1' 8" hole

$1\frac{1}{4}$"

Upper Deck

2" door blown off hinges

$\frac{5}{8}$" decked riddled

Main deck

Deep W. L.

Middle deck

L.W.L.

'X' magazine cooler casing damaged by base plug of shell

'X' Barbette

Large portion of shell struck barbette and was deflected forward

Exhaust vent

Upper deck

$\frac{1}{4}$" $\frac{1}{4}$"

Path of shell

Band instrument room

Cabin

6" upper strake of armoured belt penetrated

5th HIT

Main deck

deck destroyed

Engineers Workshop (3 men killed)

Engineers Stores

Deep W. L.

Middle deck

L. W. L.

Exhaust vent shot away

Looking Aft

Path of shell

Commander's day cabin

$1\frac{1}{2}$" side plating penetrated

6th HIT

Main deck $1\frac{1}{4}$"

$\frac{1}{4}$" $\frac{1}{4}$" $\frac{1}{4}$"

Commander's sleeping cabin

Deep W. L.

Cabin

4' 6" x 3' hole blown in deck

Middle deck

Cabin

L. W. L.

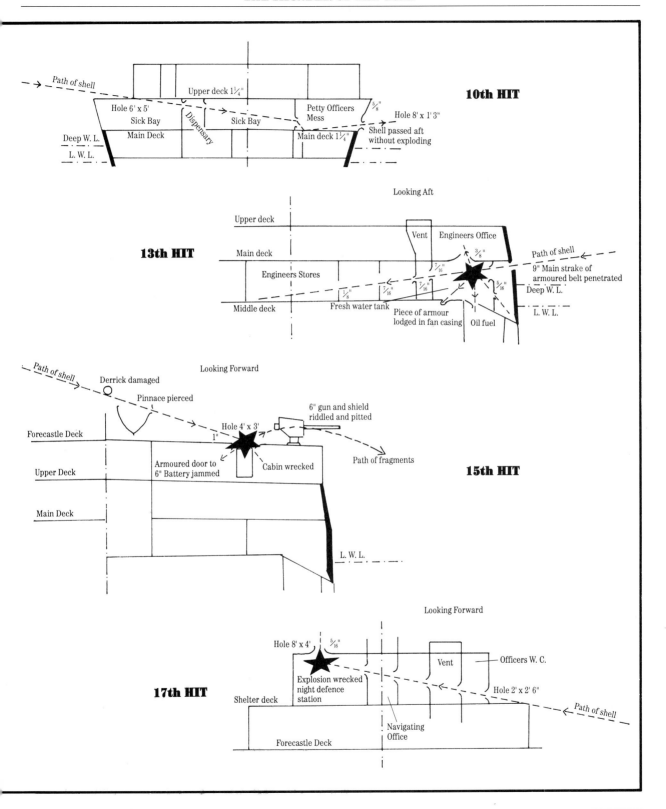

10th HIT

Path of shell

Upper deck 1¼"

Hole 6' x 5'
Sick Bay

Dispensary

Sick Bay

Petty Officers Mess

⅝"

Hole 8' x 1' 3"

Main Deck

Main deck 1¼"

Shell passed aft without exploding

Deep W. L.

L. W. L.

Looking Aft

13th HIT

Upper deck

Vent

Engineers Office

Main deck

⅜"

Path of shell

Engineers Stores

7/16"

9" Main strake of armoured belt penetrated

5/16"

Deep W. L.

Middle deck

⅛"

7/16"

7/16"

Fresh water tank

Piece of armour lodged in fan casing

Oil fuel

L. W. L.

Looking Forward

Path of shell

Derrick damaged

Pinnace pierced

6" gun and shield riddled and pitted

Forecastle Deck

Hole 4' x 3'

1"

15th HIT

Upper Deck

Armoured door to 6" Battery jammed

Cabin wrecked

Path of fragments

Main Deck

L. W. L.

Looking Forward

Hole 8' x 4'

5/16"

Vent

Officers W. C.

17th HIT

Explosion wrecked night defence station

Hole 2' x 2' 6"

Shelter deck

Path of shell

Navigating Office

Forecastle Deck

7th HIT

Damage caused:

Heavy calibre shell burst on centre-line stanchion, wrecking lobby.

8th HIT

Damage caused:

Heavy calibre shell burst in Captain's pantry, causing general damage.

9th HIT

Damage caused:

Heavy calibre shell burst right aft on the waterline, causing local damage.

10th HIT

Shell's angle of descent: 5–10°

Thickness of plates penetrated: 1¼ inches

Distance of burst from point of impact: failed to explode.

Damage caused:

Heavy calibre shell struck 1¼in upper deck in the embrasure near the forward edge of 'A' barbette. It tore a hole 6 feet by 5 feet, in the upper deck, passed across the entire width of the ship causing considerable damage to the sick bay (where spilt chemicals caused a fire). It was deflected down on to the 1¼in main deck, which it dented, and was deflected upwards to pass out of the ship through the starboard ⅝in hull plating.

11th HIT

Damage caused:

Heavy calibre shell struck the upper deck in the starboard embrasure and burst on boys' mess deck, causing local damage.

12th HIT

Shell's angle of descent: 5–10°

Thickness of plates penetrated: ¼ inch

Distance of burst from point of impact: failed to explode.

Damage caused:

Heavy calibre shell struck ¼in plating of a store on the starboard side of the forecastle deck. It tore through a 1½in screen, four thicknesses of the after funnel plating, and a second 1½in screen. It dented the 1in forecastle deck, passed through a boiler-room ventilator on the port side of the ship, before being deflected up by armour gratings through ¼in vertical plating between the forecastle and shelter decks, and out through the ½in shelter deck plates, in which a hole, 8 feet × 3 feet, was torn.

13th HIT

Shell's angle of descent: 10°

Thickness of plates penetrated: 9 inches

Distance of burst from point of impact: 12 feet

Damage caused:

Heavy calibre shell struck the tapered upper part of the main strake and the lower part of the upper strake of the armoured belt, about 23 feet forward of the main-mast. The shell pierced the top corner of an armoured plate tearing a hole, 2 feet × 18 inches in diameter. The actual thickness of the armour pierced was 6 inches at the top of the hole (upper strake) and 9 inches at the bottom (main strake). The shell burst in the port fresh-water tank 12 feet from the point of impact. The explosion blew a large hole in the ⅜in main deck above and, apart from blowing away the bottom of the water tank, badly distorted the 1in middle deck above the port side of the wing engine room and the adjacent oil fuel tank. The ⁵⁄₁₆in bulkhead forming the outer side of the water tank was wrecked, and the forward and inboard bulkheads of the feed tank were holed. Through the latter hole the sea poured into the port wing engine room. The flow of sea water into the water tank was eventually stopped by stuffing 400 hammocks into the tank, and shoring them down until they plugged the hole in the armour belt. One large fragment from this shell tore through the ⁷⁄₁₆in inner bulkhead of the feed tank and on through three thicknesses of plating (one ⅛in and two ⁷⁄₁₆in) before coming to rest 40 feet from the point of burst on the middle deck. A broken piece of the armoured belt was blown into the engine room fan casing.

14th HIT

Damage caused:

Heavy calibre shell burst in after funnel casing. Splinters penetrated the battery deck and completely collapsed boiler room down takes.

15th HIT

Shell's angle of descent: 10°

Thickness of plates penetrated: 1½ inches

Distance of burst from point of impact: 6 feet

Damage caused:

Heavy calibre shell hit the main derrick from the port side, holed the pinnace and burst on the starboard side of the forecastle deck inboard of the forecastle deck 6in gun. Most of the fragments went overboard, riddling and pitting the gun shield and gun. The explosion blew a hole in the 1in forecastle deck and a hole, 4 feet × 3 feet, in the ½in side plating abaft the 6in battery bulkhead, jamming the armoured battery door. Hot fragments from the explosion pierced the after part of the 6in gun battery and ignited four cordite charges. All the crew of the after 6in gun were badly burnt as were some of the crew of the adjacent gun.

16th HIT

Unidentified calibre shell wrecked warrant officers' galley.

17th HIT

Heavy calibre shell – either a richochet or deflected upwards off the edge of the shelter deck – passed through plating totalling $1\frac{5}{16}$ inches in the forward superstructure, and burst 40 feet from the point of impact in the night defence officer's station. A hole, 8 feet × 4 feet, was blown in the $\frac{5}{16}$in deck above the shelter deck. The fire brigade had to wear duffel coats to fight the fire caused by this shell, because of the molten lead dropping on them from the lead-cased electric leads.

18th HIT

Unidentified calibre shell passed through foremost funnel without exploding.

19th and 20th HITS

Two unidentified calibre shells passed through after funnel, showering numerous splinters over the ship.

21st HIT

Unidentified calibre shell. Direct hit on starboard 6in gun shield armour. Wrecked gun mounting and a number of ship's boats.

22nd HIT

Unidentified calibre shell cut through main derrick, which fell across picket boat. Shell wrecked ship's boats and damaged forecastle deck.

23rd HIT

Light calibre shell passed clean through heel of main-mast, wrecking launch and superstructure aft.

24th HIT

Unidentified calibre shell cut communication tube to after director tower, spun the tube through 180°, and wrecked superstructure.

25th HIT

Light calibre shell hit 'X' turret gunhouse side armour. Only superficial damage caused. Nothing was felt inside turret.

26th HIT

Heavy calibre high-explosive shell struck 13in main strake of armoured belt 4 feet above waterline. Shell burst on belt but did not pierce the armour. Splinters showered ship.

27th HIT

Heavy calibre high-explosive shell burst on 13in main strake of armoured belt about 8 feet forward of hit 26. Shell burst on armour without piercing.

28th HIT

Light calibre shell burst on left-hand 15in gun of 'Y' turret, 6 inches from the muzzle. Bulge on gun caused by this hit put the gun out of action.

29th HIT

Light calibre shell tore through deck, through ward-room and out through the side of the ship. Local damage. Splinters from shells bursting short caused minor damage to aft superstructure, main stays, searchlights, 15in director tower, bridges, side plating and compass platform.

In all, *Warspite* suffered a total of 29 hits. As far as can be ascertained from extant records the periods during the battle when these hits were sustained were:

Turn to the northward of the 5th BS = 3 heavy calibre hits.

The run to the northward = 6 heavy calibre hits.

Warspite's 'death ride' (jammed helm) = 9 heavy calibre, 4 light calibre and 7 hits by unidentified calibre shell; total 20 hits.

4.
COLLISIONS, FIRES AND OTHER MISHAPS

A ROYAL VISIT

On 2 June 1916 the majority of *Warspite*'s company were given some well-earned leave, while the ship remained in dry dock having her Jutland wounds repaired. Only 100 men and five officers (one from each branch) remained on board, with Commander Walwyn temporarily in command. A few days after the battle King George V paid a visit to the Battlecruiser Fleet at Rosyth. After he had reviewed the men of the fleet on the parade ground, the King boarded *Warspite* and went all over the ship to inspect the damage she had received. Admiral Beatty accompanied him on the tour. Paymaster Cadet G. H. Bickmore recorded the visit in his diary:

'The King spent about two hours on board, going everywhere, and asking innumerable questions. At one o'clock, Beatty, who like all navy men was used to lunching at noon and who had been getting more and more restive, took the King by the arm and said, "Lunch has been waiting for us aboard the *Lion* since noon sir." The King, who never liked Beatty, turned on him and growled, "I didn't come here to have lunch with you. Let it wait!" and continued to go round the ship for another hour. Beatty was popular enough with the Battlecruiser Fleet, but the Grand Fleet had no use for him, while they just about worshipped Jellicoe whom they called "Hell-Fire Jack".

'Later, when Jellicoe went to the Admiralty as First Sea Lord, and was succeeded by Beatty as C-in-C Grand Fleet [this occurred on 29 November 1916], and the latter came up to Scapa to take over command, there was no spontaneous cheering to greet him, and had not Admiral Sir Cecil Burney, second in command, realized what was happening and signalled an order to cheer ship there would have been no welcome. As it was, the formal cheers were nothing compared with the roar of cheering with which the Grand Fleet said goodbye to Jellicoe.'[1]

Although Beatty initially hoisted his flag as C-in-C Grand Fleet in Jellicoe's old flagship *Iron Duke*, in mid February 1917 he transferred his flag to *Warspite*'s sister *Queen Elizabeth*. From that day until the end of the war the 5th BS was, as a result, composed of only four ships.

HELM TROUBLE AND COLLISION

Warspite remained in dockyard hands at Rosyth for more than seven weeks, and it wasn't until 23 July that she rejoined the 5th BS at Scapa. Considering the amount of serious damage she had received at Jutland, however, seven weeks was not a very substantial time in which to effect the necessary repairs. In fact permanent repairs were not undertaken until nearly twenty years later! In 1935, during the ship's almost complete reconstruction at Portsmouth dockyard, when her hull was stripped of plates down to the frames, it was discovered that much of the damage to her infrastructure had merely been plated over. Even after this reconstruction, distortions and uneven areas of the main deck in her after compartments remained until the end of the ship's long service. More seriously, the complex damage to the steering gear was never properly remedied and sudden jamming of the helm became a curse which dogged nearly every one of *Warspite*'s long line of subsequent captains.

As events were to prove, Jutland was the only occasion on which *Warspite* went into action during the First World War. After Jutland the High Seas Fleet put to sea on only three occasions (19 August 1916; 19 October 1916; and 22 April 1918 – during the latter operation, as far north as the waters off the Norwegian south-west coast). On each of these occasions *Warspite* hurried to sea with the Grand Fleet, but the Germans always retired to base before action could be joined.

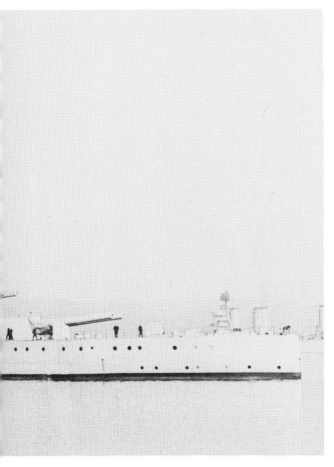

Warspite at anchor off Rosyth, circa 1917–18. Note the hammocks being aired on the forestays. (IWM)

It was during the first of these High Seas Fleet operations (19 August 1916), a mere month after *Warspite* had rejoined the fleet, that the first sign that there were still things amiss with the steering gear first manifested itself. During the early hours of 20 August 1916, when the Grand Fleet was returning to Scapa after chasing south in an unsuccessful attempt to engage the German fleet, *Warspite*'s helm suddenly jammed and she had to haul out of line. She was soon able to regain her position but the experience was extremely disconcerting as no one could tell when it would happen again.

Four months later *Warspite* was once more in serious trouble. On the night of 24 August 1916 *Warspite* was detailed to carry out sub-calibre night firing practice in the waters of Scapa Flow which were reserved for this purpose. The exercise passed without incident, but as *Warspite* was returning to her anchorage the spirit of misrule which dogged *Warspite*'s career struck again. John Chessman, who had been rated to signalman after Jutland, graphically describes what happened:

'No logical reason can be forwarded for what would appear a thoroughly stupid manoeuvre. I was on the upper deck and off watch as we returned to our anchorage, when I saw the unbelievable. In the dark a huge object loomed up directly ahead on our course. Whatever was going on up there on the bridge, they appeared to be in complete ignorance of the threat which then loomed. A few seconds later we hit the obstacle which proved to be our next at anchorage – the *Valiant*. We struck her practically amidships and immediately there was feverish activity on both vessels. The accepted drill on one ship colliding with another is for the colliding vessel to maintain as far as possible her position at the point of contact. The reason for this is to minimize the inrush of water through the breaches of both which may have taken place in both on contact. So there we were in the inglorious situation of resting in the guts of one of our sister ships, and in harbour too! The *Valiant*'s tanks appeared to

have been fractured while *Warspite*'s long-suffering bows were once again stove in.

Poor Captain Philpotts: he appeared to have aged another ten years, but he made no angry protestations, no adverse criticism of anyone else either; just apparent resignation to being in command of the Jonah of all Jonahs. What explanation or excuse could be possibly put forward for this latest débâcle?'[2]

The *Valiant*, which was badly damaged, had been moving out of her anchorage for night firing practice, when the collision occurred, and the subsequent Board of Inquiry blamed both ships equally. The Admiralty ordered the two captains to be tried by court martial, on charges of hazarding their ships. Both Captain Philpotts and Captain Maurice Woollcombe of the *Valiant* were found guilty and sentenced to be reprimanded. Although for technical reasons the sentence on Captain Philpotts was annulled, it is not surprising, taking into account the grounding incident and the collision with *Barham*, that he was relieved of his command of *Warspite* and his career was ruined. He was replaced by Captain Charles Martin de Bartolome on 19 December 1916.

Docked in Rosyth for repairs to her bow on the day following the collision, *Warspite* did not rejoin the fleet until 29 September.

THE LOSS OF *VANGUARD*

Up until the Armistice was signed on 11 November 1918, *Warspite*'s operational career consisted of nothing more than taking part in the numerous sweeps and manoeuvres in the North Sea, and periodic gunnery trials within the Flow and in the Pentland Firth. The long uneventful years of 1917 and 1918 were, however, punctuated by two incidents worthy of recording.

The first of these occurred on the night of Monday, 9 July 1917, when *Warspite* was lying at anchor in Scapa Flow. Midshipman H. C. Burton, who was serving in *Warspite*, recalls what happened:

'After dinner everyone in the gunroom was very merry and noisy and I, feeling very tired, turned in early. I think I dropped off to sleep about

10 o'clock. It seemed scarcely a minute before Midshipman Lingard was at my hammock and I heard him say, "Burton, the *Vanguard* has blown up!" I didn't believe him and said so, and he answered, "Yes she has, everyone is on the quarter deck!" Being only half awake I replied that I couldn't turn out and I lay dozing in my hammock. Then thinking that while I was lying in comfort, men were in the water dead and dying, I jumped out and ran to the quarter deck. A sight never to be forgotten met my eyes. No sign of the stricken ship was to be seen, but on all sides and from every direction, searchlights were being played on the spot where she went down. Boats of every description were already making their way to the empty billet. High in the air was a vast column of smoke, drifting steadily towards the island of Flotta. An eye-witness states that when *Vanguard* blew up there was a huge flash of flame, but the ship could not be seen as she was berthed behind the *Neptune*. The flame was about 200 feet high and a steady rain of burning matchwood was falling everywhere. She sank in less than a minute, so it seems as if she was literally blown to pieces. The water was thick with oil fuel and hammocks and other wreckage was floating everywhere.

'All around were trolling boats and picket boats seeking for survivors and corpses. The *Warspite* was the first ship as far as we could see to have her boats away. Midshipman Ball, who was in the 2nd whaler, picked up the body of some poor wretch, quite naked and black with the oil fuel that was everywhere. Beatty was out in his barge, and Evan-Thomas was seen in the stern sheets of his barge putting on the stern sheetman's sea boots over his bare legs. Everything was carried out quietly and quickly, and the work of rescue went on all the night. The awful part is that being so late, most of the *Vanguard*'s ship's company had turned in so that they must have gone from life to death in a fraction of time. Poor, poor fellows, one is shocked inexpressibly by such terrible loss of life, and yet it is probable that very few felt much pain or even knew anything about it.'[3]

The Board of Inquiry into the loss of *Vanguard* (there were only two survivors out of a complement of more than a thousand) reached the conclusion that: 'The

The 5th Battle Squadron in heavy seas; 1917. View taken from *Warspite*; *Valiant* nearest the camera.

Note the kite ballon being flown from *Barham*, the lead ship. (MPL)

loss of the vessel was caused by a fire starting in a 4in magazine (probably the spontaneous combustion of defective cordite), which quickly spread to either 'P' or 'Q' 12in magazine rooms, setting off the cordite charges therein, and destroying the vessel.'

FIRE!

A far more serious incident which 'but for a very kindly providence might have been the *Warspite*'s last',[4] occurred on the morning of Friday, 1 March 1918, when *Warspite* was at anchor in Scapa Flow. At 0745 Midshipman Burton, who was on the quarterdeck, suddenly noticed thick smoke pouring out of both of *Warspite*'s funnels. This was puzzling as he was aware that the ship was not raising steam for sea. Five minutes later the whole of the forecastle deck was obliterated from view by a cloud of thick oily smoke, which was pouring out through the port wing engine room exhaust. The heat was so intense that the exhaust fumes which came out by the pinnace burnt and blistered the paint on the boat. Fire stations was sounded off, and it was discovered that a fire was raging in the port wing engine room. The fire was caused by an oil feed pipe bursting, the oil gushing from the pipe being ignited when it came into contact with a hot steam pipe. Three engine room artificers, who were on duty in the engine room, had to rush through the flames to make their escape up a ladder and they all suffered minor burns. Fire hoses were played on the fire, but it could not be brought under until one of the artificers, already burnt, rushed back down into the blazing engine room to shut off the oil suction pump, thus stopping the gush of oil from the fractured pipe. The artificer suffered further burns to his face and head, and his boiler suit was on fire when he was dragged out. His action undoubtedly saved the ship. Fortunately the engines were not damaged, but serious damage was caused to the electric leads which had melted in the heat. It took a month of repair work before *Warspite* was seaworthy.

The 5th Battle Squadron at sea, 1917; *Malaya* nearest the camera. *Warspite* and her sisters were very wet forward in even moderate seas. (MPL)

Warspite, 1918. Note the aircraft and flying-off platform positioned on top of 'B' turret. (MPL)

FINALE

Warspite, together with the whole of the Grand Fleet, was berthed in the Firth of Forth when the Armistice was declared on 11 November 1918 (the main fleet base had been moved from Scapa to Rosyth in April 1918). Beatty immediately made the general signal to the fleet from *Queen Elizabeth*, "Splice the main brace." This allowed one tot of rum additional to the daily tot, and unlike the daily tot, was issued to officers as well as ratings. The last occasion on which this had occurred had been on 22 June 1911, when King George V was crowned. At 1900 that evening the 'main brace was spliced' aboard *Warspite* and every other ship in the fleet. On deck the sailors danced, sang, shouted and cheered, while every fog-horn, steam whistle and siren in the fleet was sounded continuously for three hours. Stopping at 2200, the deafening din broke out afresh at midnight.

Warspite's final meeting with her old antagonists at Jutland, took place ten days after the signing of the

Armistice. On 21 November 1918, she put to sea from Rosyth with the Grand Fleet.

Forty miles east of May Island, a rendezvous was made with the nine battleships, five battlecruisers, seven light cruisers and 49 destroyers representing the cream of the German fleet, which, under the naval terms of the Armistice, had come across the North Sea to surrender. When contact was made (0930), the Grand Fleet formed into two columns, six miles apart, and took up position on each side of the German ships, which were in single line ahead. *Warspite* was the 29th ship in line of the 39 capital ships and cruisers which made up the starboard column. *Warspite*'s ship's company, in keeping with every other ship in the Grand Fleet, was at action stations, the guns loaded, ready in case the Germans made a last-minute defiant gesture. Every British ship was bedecked with battle ensigns for the first time since Jutland.

'The German line was led by the battlecruisers, followed by the most modern battleships, which had formed the van divisions of the German fleet at Jutland, and which had inflicted so much damage to *Warspite* during the gyrations of her death ride. But the German ships of November 1918, were no longer the menacing and dangerous enemies of 31 May 1916. Mutiny had spread through the German fleet during 1918, and the ships were now dirty and bedraggled, devoid of the breech-blocks of their guns and all ammunition, which had been left behind in Germany. In funeral-like silence the two fleets proceeded towards the Forth where, at noon, the German ships dropped anchor off Inchkeith, surrounded by the ships detailed to guard them. Seven months later, on 21 June 1919, they scuttled themselves in Scapa Flow.

In the meantime, on 7 April 1919, Beatty's union flag was lowered from *Queen Elizabeth*'s mast-head for the last time, marking the end of the existence of the Grand Fleet, the like of which would never be seen again: the curtain had fallen on the first phase of *Warspite*'s long and glorious career.

Source Notes

1. Bickmore Papers.
2. Chessman Papers.
3. The papers of Commander H.

C. Burton (Imperial War Museum).
4. ibid.

WARTIME ALTERATIONS TO WARSPITE 1915–18

In the light of experience gained at Jutland (in the main the destruction of three battlecruisers by magazine explosions), improvements were made to the scale of armour protection over ships' vitals, and to the anti-flash arrangements of the magazines.

In *Warspite*'s case these improvements consisted of 1in armour plating being added to the middle deck, around the vicinity of the magazines, and the magazine bulkheads: a total weight of 260 tons of extra armour. This increased *Warspite*'s deep load displacement from 33,410 tons to 33,670 tons.

Flash-tight scuttles were fitted in the bulkheads dividing the magazines from the cordite handing rooms. The magazine doors could thus henceforward be kept shut in action. The scuttles operated like revolving doors in a hotel entrance, fitted on the horizontal, so that they were always sealed against a tongue of flame.

The armour-piercing shells which had proved defective, robbing the big guns of much of their punch, were replaced by a new and more efficient shell. These were fitted with a harder cap and improved bursters and fuzes. Despite the urgency of the situation, however, the new shell was not designed until May 1917, a year after Jutland, and they were not delivered to the fleet until April 1918!

1916

1. Main topmast removed.
2. Upper yardarm re-positioned across starfish platform.
3. Ensign gaff removed from foremast and re-positioned below the mainmast tower platform.
4. W/T aerial outriggers fitted to forward arm of starfish platform.
5. Two signal yards (angled aft) attached one each side of the spotting top.
6. Small platform fitted to fore topmast over the 15in gun director.
7. Aerial trunk fitted to starboard of the conning tower on the shelter deck.
8. Carley rafts fitted.

1917

1. Range clock platform fitted on foremast below spotting top.
2. Fog sirens resited on lower platform aft of the rear of mainmast struts.
3. Searchlight platform on aft funnel heightened and range clock added to the starboard side.
4. Deckhouse on port side of after funnel enlarged.
5. Rangefinder baffles temporarily rigged on funnels.

1918

1. Searchlight platform erected on aft superstructure.
2. Searchlight platform erected on rear of mainmast with a hooded control position above.
3. Training scales painted on 'B' and 'X' turrets.
4. Short stump topmast housed on mainmast platform for the rigging of W/T aerials.
5. Plating on aft 6in gun embrasures made flush.
6. More range clocks fitted: two each side of the aft funnel searchlight tower.
7. Range clock platform removed from foremast, two range clocks fitted to a pole arranged ahead of foremast.
8. Flying-off platforms fitted to the roofs of 'B' and 'X' turrets, which were extended over the gun-barrels and supported by angle-bar struts. These were used to facilitate the take-off of a Sopwith 1½ – Strutter and a Sopwith 2F1 Camel. These aircraft were carried for reconnaissance and fall of shot purposes.

An aerial view of *Warspite* with her battle ensign flying at the foremast, on the occasion of the surrender of the German Fleet, 21 November 1918. She is preceded by *Valiant*, *Malaya* and *Barham*. (IWM)

5.
A BRAND-NEW SHIP

THE WASHINGTON TREATY

The scuttling of the Kaiser's Fleet in 1919 left the Royal Navy as the undisputed master of the waves. Britain's 1,300 warships (including 42 battleships and battle-cruisers) with a total displacement of 3,250,000 tons, equalled the naval tonnage of the rest of the world's navies put together. Yet, due to Britain's vigorous commitment to the 'general limitation of the armaments of all nations' envisaged in the Treaty of Versailles, and post-war economic difficulties which invoked a dread of heavy military expenditure, this vast naval prepon-

derance was surrendered with hardly a whimper in the 1921–2 Washington Treaty of Naval Limitations.

The Washington Treaty was designed in essence to defuse Anglo-American–Japanese naval antagonism, which was threatening to escalate into a new naval race as virulent and as prohibitively expensive as the pre-war Anglo-German naval race.

Apart from limiting the size and number of capital ships that the signatory powers (Britain, USA, Japan, France and Italy) were allowed to possess, it was also agreed that no new capital ships were to be built for at

least ten years. The only exception to this was the construction by Britain of *Nelson* and *Rodney*, to offset the retention by the USA and Japan of modern 16in gun battleships. In accord with the terms of the treaty Britain scrapped twenty capital ships (408,500 tons), and four uncompleted battlecruisers (the super *Hood*s) (about 180,000 tons); roughly 48 per cent of the Royal Navy's existing strength in capital ships, which, in those days, was regarded as the very basis of sea power.

A particular clause of the Washington Treaty directly affected *Warspite*. To improve the protection of existing capital ships against both aerial and underwater attack, the addition of a maximum of 3,000 tons on a particular displacement was allowed. Unable, because of the prevailing financial stringency, to improve both deck and underwater protection, the Board

Warspite in 1930, showing the modifications carried out during her November 1924–April 1926 refit. Funnels trunked into one, remodelled bridgework and bulges fitted to the hull.

The top of the upper bulge compartments can be seen just above the waterline (see also overleaf.)

(All Stan Lawrance)

of Admiralty decided that only underwater protection against torpedoes would be improved. This form of protection involved the fitting of 'bulges', external watertight structures fitted to the hull, divided into sections which extended over the vitals of the ship. The bulges were intended to cause a torpedo to explode at some distance from the hull proper, so protecting the boilers, engines and other vital machinery from the full force of the explosion. *Warspite* was the first of the *Queen Elizabeth* class to be so fitted.

WARSPITE'S 1924–6 REFIT

After the Grand Fleet ceased to exist, *Warspite* served in the 2nd Battle Squadron of the newly constituted Atlantic Fleet, commanded by Admiral Sir Charles Madden, until she was paid off (i.e., the ship's company was transferred to other ships and establishments) at

Warspite dressed overall, 1924, before reconstruction, showing the full wartime modifications. The sternwalk was fitted in 1920. (MPL)

Warspite after 1924–6 refit

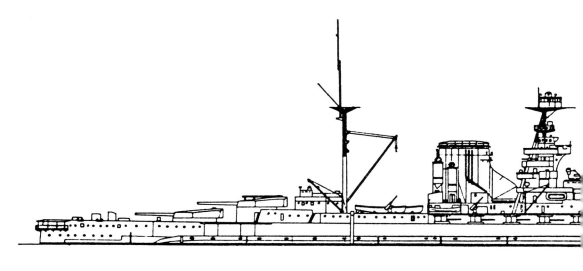

Warspite, September 1932.
(Stan Lawrance)

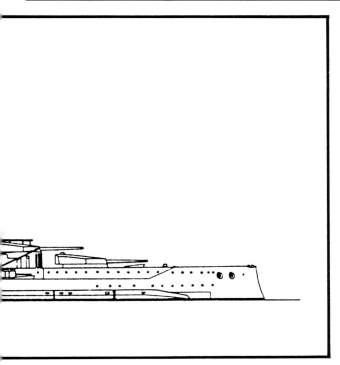

Portsmouth dockyard on 31 October 1924, to undergo her refit. The work took eighteen months, and was completed in April 1926 at a cost of £195,000.

During the refit bulges were fitted to the hull and the bridge platforms were increased in size and re-modelled. To avoid back draught likely to be caused by the new bridge structure drawing the funnel gases back into the bridge, the forward funnel was trunked into the after funnel. And to compensate, in a very small degree, for the financial inability to provide improved deck armour against bombs, the existing 3in High Angle guns were replaced by four 4in Mk V HA guns. The new bridge work and trunked funnel gave *Warspite* a more stream-lined, agressive appearance. The bulges increased the ship's deep load displacement by a further 1,887 tons to 35,557 tons, and increased the beam of the ship from the original 90 feet 6 inches to 104 feet. As a spin-off the increase in the displacement and the greater freeboard afforded by the bulges proved to give *Warspite* greater stability and better seaworthiness, although it must be added that all five ships of the class were regarded as bad sea boats throughout their careers.

Warspite, 1934, before undergoing her second major refit (see also overleaf.) (All MPL)

MEDITERRANEAN FLAGSHIP

Recommissioned at Portsmouth by Captain G. K. Chetwode on 6 April 1926, with a complement of 54 officers and 871 men, *Warspite* spent the remainder of the month carrying out steaming trials and working-up efficiency. Held in home waters due to the General Strike until 12 May (parties of the crew were landed to guard oil tanks, pipelines and a torpedo factory near Greenock), she finally sailed for the Mediterranean, arriving in Malta on 20 May. On the next day she hoisted the flag of the C-in-C Mediterranean, Admiral Sir Roger Keyes.

As Mediterranean flagship she served with her four sisters in the 1st Battle Squadron until July 1928, when she fell victim to yet another of those misfortunes which dogged her career. On 12 July *Warspite* struck an uncharted rock in the Aegean off the Greek island of Skiathos, severely damaging the bottom of her hull. Sent home for repairs, she reduced to two-fifths complement and was dry-docked in Portsmouth harbour.

Recommissioned on 22 January 1929, by Captain A. H. Walker, for further service in the Mediterranean, she sailed for Malta on 14 March 1929, to rejoin her sisters in the 1st Battle Squadron. In July of that year she was with the Mediterranean Fleet at Skiathos to take part in the Fleet annual gunnery competition. Unfortunately she developed turbine trouble and was unable to compete for trophies as she was only capable of steaming at half-speed. Sent to Malta on 19 July for docking, on passage she sighted the small Greek yacht *St. Helene* flying a distress signal. *St. Helene*, which was carrying a cargo of petrol, got into difficulties in high winds and heavy seas off Cape Malea on the 20th. *Warspite* attempted to take the yacht in tow, but, due to the heavy seas and the fact that the vessel was shipping water badly, the tow cable parted twice. The skipper of *St. Helene*, who wrote an article about the incident in the Greek naval periodical *Nautike Hellas*, explains what happened next:

'The warship stood by us. By this time we could do nothing as the ship was full of water and beginning to break up. When the captain [of the *Warspite*] saw the danger he lowered a boat and three officers came alongside and told us to save ourselves . . . we were hoisted on board all wet and miserable. On the *Warspite* we were treated kindly in everyway and taken to Malta. I am unable to find words to express the gratitude of us all to the captain, officers and crew of the English man-of-war. They made a collection of £66 for us in addition to giving us clothes, shoes, etc. The generous spirit of the English is the same wherever England rules the waves.'[1]

Warspite's turbine trouble was not put right until 17 November. On the following day she hoisted the flag of the new C-in-C Med., Admiral Sir Frederick Field. Six months later *Warspite* was transferred to the 2nd Battle Squadron of the Atlantic Fleet based in Home Waters. There she remained until December 1933, when she was reduced to reserve at Portsmouth prior to undergoing a complete reconstruction.

WARSPITE'S 1934–7 RECONSTRUCTION

The reconstruction came about because the economic depression of the early 1930s made it impossible for the government of the day to replace the ageing battle fleet with new construction (by 1937 nine of the fifteen British capital ships in commission would be more than 26 years old). Unable to equip the fleet with modern vessels under a large, new construction programme, the

Opposite page: *Warspite*, 1934, before her second major refit.

Warspite, 1934, midships view, showing the trunked funnel and re-modelled bridge work. (MPL)

expediency of completely modernizing the existing battleships was agreed upon.

Warspite, which was nearly 20 years old, was the first to be taken in hand, and work commenced in March 1934. The nature of the reconstruction had three essential elements: her 20-year-old engines and boilers were worn and in bad order; it was imperative to increase the elevation, and therefore the range, of her 15in guns, because the Americans and Japanese were increasing the elevation of the guns of their existing capital ships; and, in the face of the growing menace to ships from air attack, it was equally imperative to increase the deck armour against bombs, and to improve the anti-aircraft armament.

The task was enormous. To remove the old engines and boilers, and replace them with more powerful modern machinery, practically the whole of the superstructure had to be removed and a huge cavity had to be opened up in the deck amidships. To increase the elevation of the 15in guns by modifying the mountings, the turret roofs were stripped away and the huge guns were lifted out. Having gutted *Warspite* and stripped

much of her hull down to the frames (when the unrepaired damage to the ship's infrastructure incurred at Jutland was discovered), the reconstruction was so extensive as to result in what was, to all intents and purpose, a brand-new ship. The undertaking had been highly problematic because in the stripping down process the dockyard engineers had to avoid structural and internal weight distortions. How this was achieved is not recorded, but their success is testimony to their expertise, at a cost of £2,362,000, which was a mere 31 per cent of the cost of constructing the new battleship *Nelson* (£7,504,000), completed in 1927.

The old, worn-out direct-driven turbines and the 24 Yarrow boilers were removed from the gutted hull and replaced by Parsons geared turbines and six Admiralty three-drum boilers with super-heaters. Although this new machinery, fitted into the existing engine and boiler room compartments, was 1,391 tons lighter than the original fittings, the 'shp' was increased from 75,000 to 80,000, and the overall efficiency and in particular the endurance was greatly increased:

	Before reconstruction	After reconstruction
Shaft horse power:	75,000	80,000
Fuel consumption:	1.22lb/shp/per hour	0.75lb/shp/per hour
Endurance at 10 knots:	8,400 nautical miles	14,300 nautical miles
Fuel capacity:	3,425 tons	3,735 tons
Weight of engines:	1,737 tons	967 tons
Weight of boilers:	1,461 tons	900 tons
Reserve feed water:	497 tons	267 tons

Modifications to the heavy gun turrets improved the elevation of the 15in guns from 20° to 30° which, together with the innovation of shells of a '6 calibre radius head' (crh), increased the range of the heavy guns by 8,800 yards (from 23,400 to 32,200 yards). The 6 crh shells were more sharply pointed than the old 4 crh shells and, encountering less air resistance, were thus able to travel farther.

The better to equip *Warspite* against bombing attacks by aircraft, the horizontal protection was improved. The deck armour on the main deck from 'A' turret barbette to the forward bulkhead was increased from 1¼ inches to 3 inches, and the middle deck armour plate was increased from 2 inches to 5½ inches over the magazines and from 1 inch to 3½ inches over the machinery spaces. To fight off aircraft all the existing High Angle guns were removed and four twin 4in Mk XIX guns were fitted on the forecastle deck, and four multiple Mk VI 2pdr 8-barrelled pom-pom mountings (known throughout the fleet as 'Chicago Pianos') were fitted abreast the funnel. These weapons were supplemented by four 0.5in 4-barrelled machine-guns: two each on the tops of 'A' and 'X' turrets. Wartime experience would prove that both the increased deck protection and the AA guns were inadequate.

Despite the saving in weight afforded by the new machinery and the reduction in the scale of armour

Warspite, July 1937, showing her appearance after her March 1934– March 1937 reconstruction. Note the new bridge work, the smaller, single funnel and the 0.5in machine-gun mountings on top of 'B' and 'X' turret. (Stan Lawrance)

Warspite after 1934–7 reconstruction

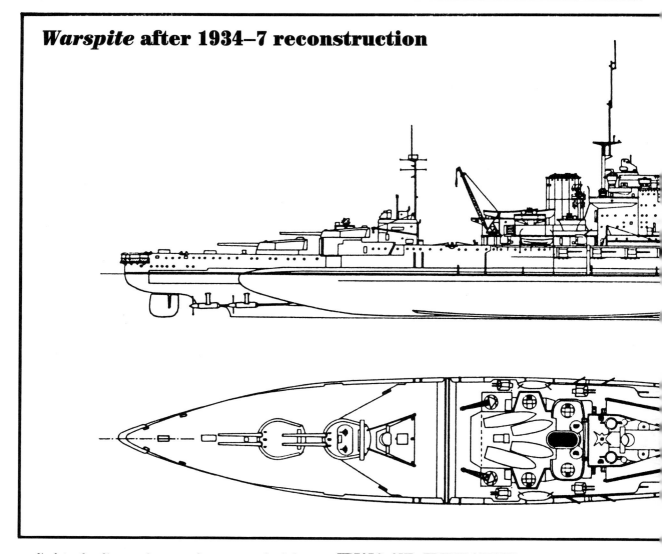

applied to the 6in gun battery, the sum total of these improvements increased the deep displacement of the ship by a further 539 tons to a total of 36,096 tons:

	Weights (tons) before reconstruction	Weights (tons) after reconstruction
Armament:	4,970	5,264
Machinery:	3,691	2,300
Equipment:	1,287	1,420
Hull and protective plating:	16,250	17,130
Armour:	5,431	5,980
Oil fuel:	3,431	3,735
Reserve feed water:	497	267
Deep displacement:	35,557	36,096

TRIALS AND TRIBULATIONS

On completion of her reconstruction *Warspite* sailed from Portsmouth dockyard on 8 March 1937, to carry out her contractors' trials in the English Channel. All was not well. While carrying out a full power steering trial on 12 March the helm jammed hard a-starboard. Despite a new steering engine having been fitted, the capricious curse which had sent *Warspite* careening through her 'death ride' at Jutland had not been eradicated. Three days later, however, the full power steaming trial was carried out without a hitch. *Warspite* managed 80,250shp, attaining 23.84 knots. Notwithstanding the new and more powerful engines and boilers, the adverse effect of the increased weight of the ship and the drag effect of the bulges on the hull made

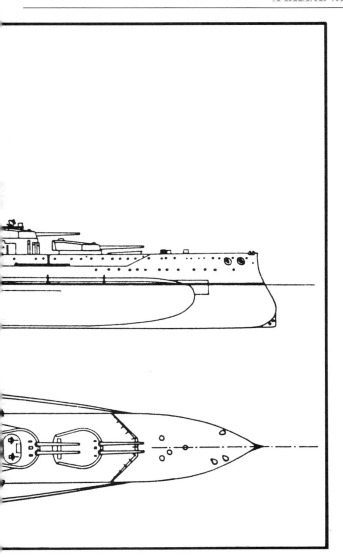

her original speed of 25 knots unattainable.

Her gunnery trials, which took place on 18 March, nearly ended in disaster. Captain Stephen Roskill, who was *Warspite*'s gunnery commander at the time, recalls what happened:

'We took *Warspite* out into the Channel for "gun trials". This included firing all the big guns at extreme elevation, and that meant that the shells would land sixteen or seventeen miles away – almost certainly outside visibility distance from the ship in ordinary Channel weather. So I arranged for a destroyer to be stationed eight miles from the ship. Provided we could see her she should be able to see another eight miles, and so

be able to tell us if the range was clear. This was all carried out as planned, the destroyer reported "all clear," and we opened fire. The programme went without a hitch, and we returned to harbour. I myself feeling well pleased at the way the new turrets had behaved.

'Days had elapsed when my Captain [F. H. W. Goolden] received from the Commander-in-Chief "for report" a letter from the Royal Mail Company. Enclosed in it was one from the Master of one of their large liners written on passage up the Channel from Buenos Aires on the day we had carried out our gun trials. It described how at such and such a time "... a loud explosion had occurred followed by a great column of water about four hundred yards on the port bow of the ship". The Officer of the Watch had promptly altered course, "... thus avoiding a second similar explosion two hundred yards away". (I was amused by the words "thus avoiding", since they plainly implied that the liner was being fired at!). The Master concluded his letter with a remark that, as the passengers were all at breakfast at the time, "... the effect was very disturbing". Doubtless not an overstatement.

'Of course the truth was apparent at once. The destroyer had been unable to see as far as she thought and the liner had passed across our line of fire at exactly the wrong moment. It was, indeed, lucky that we had only near-missed her; for a fifteen-inch shell, even a solid "practice" one, could have done a lot of damage. By such ill chances can a Gunnery Officer's career be jeopardized.'[2]

Further trouble of a different kind was soon to follow. On 29 June *Warspite* commissioned to full complement of 1,218 officers and men for service as flagship of the Mediterranean Fleet, under the command of Captain V. A. C. Crutchley, VC. The prolonged (March until the end of June) trials, and the added burden of making *Warspite* thoroughly shipshape, as befits a flagship, while dockyard and contractors' work on board proceeded continuously, placed heavy demands on the ship's company. This led to a growing atmosphere of disaffection amongst the lower deck, and matters came to a head over the time limit placed on weekend leave. When *Warspite* recommissioned her crew was drawn from Chatham depot, despite the ship being Portsmouth based. Although the Admiralty always tried to avoid commissioning a ship at a different port from her crew's home depot, the neccessity of preserving the drafting balance meant that it was sometimes unavoidable. When it did occur, it made it difficult for the men to see as much as possible of their families, during their last weeks in home waters, before going to a foreign station for several years.

At a subsequent inquiry it was established that half a dozen ratings had stirred disaffection on the lower deck when it was announced that they were required to return for their last weekend at Chatham, before sailing to the Mediterranean, by the usual hour of 0700 on a Monday. For the majority of ratings this meant leaving their homes late on the Sunday night. At 2200 on 30 June it was reported to the Officer of the Watch that a meeting of an 'unlawful character' was in progress on a mess-deck, and the Captain was duely informed. Crutchley immediately assembled the men on the quarterdeck and defused the situation by listening to the

grievance and pointing out the correct manner in which such matters should be represented. Although the Captain reported the incident to the C-in-C Portsmouth the next day, the matter was dropped. Unfortunately a few of the trouble-makers communicated with a newspaper, with the result that the Admiralty had to conduct an inquiry, which was headed by Admiral Sir Max Horton. Their decision was announced in the Press at the end of August. The handling of the situation it was announced, '... could not be regarded as entirely satisfactory', and three officers were relieved of their appointments: the executive officer, Commander D. H. Everett, with Lieutenant-Commander A. F. L. Evans and

Warspite, January 1938. This view clearly shows the 10-ton electric cranes fitted abreast the aircraft hangars amidships. (Stan Lawrance)

Captain, Royal Marines, A. G. C. Langford. Three ratings were discharged from the service and nine were drafted to other ships. Something of the Admiralty's opinion as to the way the situation had been handled can be gleaned from a confidential letter sent to all C-in-Cs in September. It pointed out that discipline '. . . will only be achieved if officers regard their men as human beings with ambitions, hopes and fears, who have private lives and private troubles'.

Warspite was due to sail for Malta during the second week of July, but during the ship's final acceptance trial the helm jammed, yet again, while turning under full rudder, this time with more serious conse-

quences. While *Warspite* was making her way up Portsmouth harbour that evening, it was noticed that the turbine gearing of one of the propeller shafts was making grinding noises. Later inspection revealed serious damage to the coupling between the turbines and the gearing. The damaged couplings were easily repaired, but to discover the cause of the trouble and prevent it recurring was another matter. During the next five months, from August 1937 to January 1938, numerous trials and dockings were undertaken and the trouble was eventually traced to interaction between the inner and outer propellers causing excessive vibration when the helm was put full over at high speed. In the belief that this could be prevented by slowing down the outer propeller shafts, special instructions were given that when the ship was steaming above 200rpm with the use of 5° to full rudder the revolutions of the outer shaft on the outside of the turn must be reduced. To this end special instruments were installed in the bridge and wing engine rooms to give effect to these instructions.

Warspite, January 1938. Amidships view, showing one of the port twin 4in gun mountings above the 6in gun battery deck, and two of the multiple pom-poms abreast the funnel and hangars. (Stan Lawrance)

As events were to prove this did not solve the problem and helm jamming incidents continued to dog *Warspite*'s career until the end of her days.

BACK IN THE MEDITERRANEAN

Warspite finally sailed for Malta from Pitch House Jetty, Portsmouth, at 1145 on 5 January 1938: some five and a half months later than intended. She arrived in Grand Harbour on the morning of 14 January, and almost immediately began her working-up trials and gunnery exercises. 'By the early days of February,' writes Captain Roskill, 'she was fast becoming a ship of which all on board were proud; for it was obvious that she was not only smart but efficient.'[3] None the less, *Warspite* being the Jonah she was, the gunnery exercises did not pass without untoward incident as Captain Roskill explains:

'We had been doing close-range anti-aircraft practice, using all our new rapid-firing multiple weapons at a target towed by a low-flying aircraft. The practices for the day were over. I had rung the "cease fire" bells, and the Captain had turned the ship's head towards the Grand Harbour, when the airman brought the target over the ship once more – probably to let us see if there were any holes in it. Just then the midshipman stationed at one of the multiple pom-poms opened fire again. I stopped him as quickly as I could, but since those weapons fired about eight hundred two-pounder shells a minute there were quite a lot of them already in the air. I said to my captain that they must have fallen in Malta, and remembered, uneasily, how densely populated that island is. I felt distinctly uncomfortable as we picked up our buoys, though I was at least relieved to see that the town of Valetta was not in a state of uproar, and that there were, apparently, no punctures in the roof of the Opera House.

'To my surprise, for several days nothing happened, and I began to think that we had got away with it, when my captain sent for me one morning. He showed me a letter from the C-in-C forwarding one from the Governor, enclosing one

from the General, covering one from the Commanding Officer, 2nd Battalion The Green Howards. The real meat was at the bottom of the pie. It was a description by a platoon commander of the Green Howards who had been exercising his men on a rifle-range not far outside the town: "... when the sound of firing was heard from a warship out at sea, a rain of shells began to fall on the beach and to creep up to the rifle-range". ... The platoon commander had ordered his men to take cover immediately ... Corporal Brown had shown commendable promptitude in getting this order obeyed, and there were no casualties or injuries...

'I wrote the official explanation, and the Captain dealt with the errant midshipman. Meanwhile I suggested to the Fleet Gunnery Officer that, since no damage had been done, we might help to liquidate the affair by calling on the CO of the Green Howards at an appropriate time for liquidations – such as after Church Parade on the following Sunday – and tendering suitable apologies. I also had a brain-wave and got my Ordnance Officer to burnish up a two-pounder shell, mount it on an ebonite base, and inscribe it suitably: "From *HMS Warspite* to the 2nd Battalion, The Green Howards – to commemorate the Bombardment of Pembroke Rifle-range", with the date. We also made a tiny miniature for Corporal Brown – he having been the "best performer". This idea appealed to the Fleet Gunnery Officer, who had a strong sense of humour, and we accordingly proceeded to the Green Howards' barracks on the Sunday, made our apologies, and asked the CO to accept the presentations. It was a huge success with the soldiers, the presentations were joyfully accepted, champagne was opened, and we were invited to their next regimental guest night at which the model occupied the place of honour on their table.'[4]

On 6 February, Admiral Sir Dudley Pound, C-in-C Mediterranean, hoisted his flag in *Warspite* and, after inspecting the ship's company, gave them a thorough dressing down regarding their part in the disaffection aboard the ship the previous June. Both officers and men were indignant, believing his remarks to be unfair as the persons responsible had been removed from the ship. Pound's speech, however, did have the effect of determining the ship's company to prove to the Admiral that he was wrong in his opinion of them, and they accordingly set about their duties with a will. This paid off, when during the following August, on Admiralty orders, *Warspite* carried out battle practice with all her guns to test thoroughly the new equipment fitted during her reconstruction. The exercise took place off Malta on 28 August. Two light cruisers, with complete freedom of manoeuvre, towed battle-practice targets. At a range of 21,000 yards *Warspite* scored almost constant hits with 40 salvoes from her 15in guns. The targets were completely demolished. Admiral Pound was delighted. 'From then on there was no looking back for *Warspite* – only forward to greater deeds and service.'[5]

Combined Home and Mediterranean Fleet manoeuvres carried out in the Mediterranean, March 1938. *Malaya* nearest camera with *Nelson* and *Warspite* in the distance. Note the darker colour of *Nelson* painted in Home Waters grey. (MPL)

Source Notes
1. For this information and the translation from *Nautike Hellas* I am indebted to Lieutenant D. W. Toms, RN (Rtd.): HMS Warspite Association.
2. Article by Captain S. W. Roskill entitled 'Near Misses', in *Blackwood's Magazine*, June, 1949. Hereinafter cited as Near Misses.
3. Roskill, *HMS Warspite*, p. 187.
4. Near Misses.
5. Roskill, *HMS Warspite*, p. 189.

POST-WAR ALTERATIONS TO *WARSPITE*, 1919–20

1919

1. Fore topmast removed.

2. Topmast with an upper W/T yard fitted to mainmast.

3. Two extra searchlight towers, fitted one each side of the after funnel.

4. The two middle engine room vent exhausts on both sides of the mainmast heightened.

5. Thirty-foot rangefinders fitted to rear of 'B' and 'X' turrets: these made it possible for either of these turrets to control the entire main armament.

6. Paravane equipment installed: including two derricks which were positioned port and starboard of the forward shelter deck.

7. Deflection scales on turrets painted out.

1920

1. Fore control top enlarged and High Angle gun control position fitted together with an extra gunnery director tower with a 12ft rangefinder.

2. Main topgallant mast with upper W/T yard fitted.

Warspite, January 1938. In this view the two port 4in gun mountings are visible below the pom-pom platforms. (Stan Lawrance)

Warspite as she appeared at the outbreak of war in 1939. (MPL)

Ensign gaff repositioned on mainmast platform.

3. Searchlights removed from after superstructure and mainmast platform.

4. An Admiral's stern-walk fitted.

5. Aircraft flying-off platform supports removed from the gun barrels of 'B' and 'X' turrets.

6. Two range clocks fitted on 'X' turret.

7. Two 32ft cutters stowed on radial davits abaft the after funnel.

8. Byers anchors adopted as the port and starboard bower anchors.

ALTERATIONS TO *WARSPITE* DURING HER NOVEMBER 1924 – APRIL 1926 REFIT AT PORTSMOUTH DOCKYARD

1. Torpedo bulges fitted to hull.

The bulges were divided into upper and lower bulge compartments. The lower compartment extended some 6 feet from the hull proper, and was divided by watertight transverse bulkheads 20 feet apart. This covered the hull from the lower edge of the armoured belt to the bilge. The upper bulge was narrower, extending only 3 feet from the hull proper. It covered the armoured belt, extending from above the waterline to the top of the armoured belt. It was divided by

watertight bulkheads about 16 feet apart.

2. Aft torpedo tubes removed.

3. Forward funnel trunked into after funnel.

4. Forward superstructure modified:

(a). Compass platform enlarged and fitted with steel screens.

(b). Admiral's platform and searchlight platform enlarged.

(c). Two 36in searchlights replaced by two 24in signal projectors.

(d). Flag deck extended aft to the base of the trunked funnel.

(e). Night gun look-out positions removed.

(f). Torpedo control sight with rangefinder positioned on the charthouse.

(g). Original 15in director refitted on a new platform below spotting top.

(h). Spotting top altered to accommodate a 12ft UB4 rangefinder.

5. Outriggers connected to all arms of the foremast starfish.

6. Short stump mast positioned to the rear of the spotting top, and W/T aerials fitted.

7. Searchlight platform and control positions removed from after superstructure and mainmast.

8. Crossed yardarms and a Type 75 short-range W/T unit fitted on mainmast starfish platform.

9. Admiral's flag pole and larger W/T yard fitted to mainmast.

10. Short-range fire-control aerials installed on aft searchlight tower.

11. All range clocks removed, except for the two on 'X' turret.

12. Fog sirens re-positioned on to funnel.

13. Aerial trunk on starboard side of conning tower moved to port side.

14. Small oil fuel tanks fitted: one on port and two on starboard side of the boat deck.

15. Four single Mk V High Angle guns fitted amidships on forecastle deck. The existing two 3in High Angle guns were removed.

ALTERATIONS TO *WARSPITE* 1926–34

1931

1. High-Angle guns control system (HACS) Mk I fitted on spotting top.

2. Small stump mast removed.

3. Derrick installed between the foremost two 6in guns on the forecastle deck.

4. Type 75 short-range W/T unit fitted at the rear of the spotting top.

ALTERATIONS TO *WARSPITE* DURING HER MARCH 1934 – MARCH 1937 RECONSTRUCTION AT PORTSMOUTH DOCKYARD

1. Existing bridgework and conning tower entirely removed and replaced by gas- and water-tight super-structure.

2. Trunked funnel replaced by a single, much smaller funnel.

3. Tripod foremast replaced by single, lighter pole mast erected at the rear of the bridge.

4. Completely re-engined and re-boilered:

(a). Direct drive turbines replaced by Parsons geared turbines.

(b). 24 Yarrow boilers in four boiler rooms replaced by six Admiralty 3-drum high-pressure boilers in six boiler rooms.

5. New 12ft propellers fitted.

6. Turrets modified to increase elevation on 15in guns from 20° to 30°, which, with the innovation of 6crh shells, increased the range from 23,400 to 32,200 yards.

7. Four of the twelve 6in guns (the two foremost and the two aftermost, port and starboard) removed.

8. Four twin 4in Mk XVI (long-range AA weapons) fitted on the forecastle deck. Existing single 4in mountings removed.

9. Four multiple Mk VI 2pdr 8-barrel pom-pom mountings fitted abreast the funnel and hangars.

10. Four Vickers 0.5in multiple Mk III machine-gun mountings fitted: two each on the tops of 'A' and 'X' turrets.

11. Fifteen-inch gun director control tower fitted on new bridge structure.

12. Original 15in gun director on the control tower repositioned on aft superstructure.

13. Original 6in gun directors repositioned on wings of Admiral's bridge.

14. Two new High Angle gun control systems (Mk III) directors fitted on pedestals immediately abaft 6in gun directors.

15. Two 9ft rangefinders fitted at the forward end of Admiral's bridge platform.

16. Two pom-pom directors fitted on bridge, and two on the after superstructure.

17. Deck armour-protection increased:

(a). Main deck from 'A' turret barbette to forward bulkhead increased to 3 inches.

Warspite at Villefranche during the Mediterranean Fleet's spring cruise of 1938. Off *Warspite*'s stern is the C-in-C's yacht HMS *Surprise*.(Mrs Murrow)

(b). Middle deck increased to 5½ inches over magazines and 3½ inches over machinery spaces.

18. Six-inch gun battery protection reduced in scale.

19. A fixed cross-deck aircraft steam catapult (Type D11H) fitted amidships flush with the forecastle deck.

20. Two aircraft hangars fitted side by side abaft the funnel, each capable of housing one aircraft. Two further aircraft could also be stowed on the catapult.

21. Two 10-ton electrically powered cranes mounted abreast the aircraft hangars to handle the aircraft and ship's boats.

22. Initially Blackburn Shark TSR Seaplanes were carried. These were later replaced by Fairey Swordfish Mk 1 Seaplanes and Supermarine Walrus Amphibians.

23. Two 44in searchlights fitted abreast the fore part of the funnel.

24. Two 36in searchlights fitted on the signalling platform of the bridge.

25. Fore ends of the bulges remodelled: trouble with leakage had been experienced with the original shape.

The King of Greece taking the salute on *Warspite*'s quarterdeck at the march past of the ship's company, July 1938 (off Corfu). (Mrs Murrow)

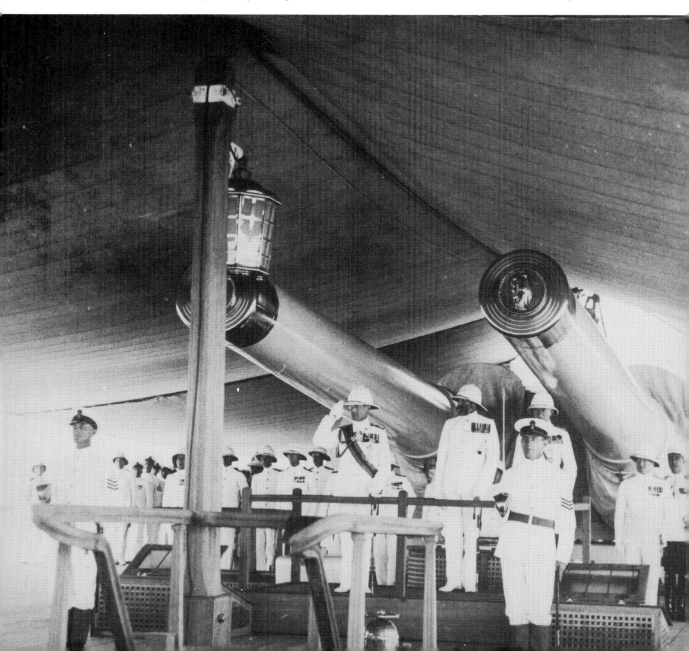

6.
NARVIK

MEDITERRANEAN AND HOME WATERS

The outbreak of the Second World War on 3 September 1939 found *Warspite* in the Mediterranean under the command of Captain Crutchley, serving as flagship to the C-in-C Mediterranean, Admiral Sir Andrew Browne Cunningham (he had hoisted his flag in *Warspite* on 7 June 1939). Admiral Cunningham was known throughout the navy, for obvious reasons, as ABC.

The potential enemy in the Mediterranean was Italy, but she did not declare war on Britain and France until a year after Germany commenced hostilities, with the result that throughout September and October 1939, *Warspite*'s war service consisted of nothing more adventurous than patrolling the eastern basin of the Mediterranean and carrying out battle practice off the Fleet's base at Alexandria. On 27 October, however, *Warspite* was ordered to Home Waters to replace the battleship *Royal Oak* which had been sunk by *U 47* in Scapa Flow on 14 October. ABC struck his flag, and after a brief docking in Malta *Warspite* hastened west.

On arrival at Gibraltar on 6 November, *Warspite* was ordered to proceed immediately to the Canadian port of Halifax to escort the homeward-bound convoy HX.9, of thirty merchant ships, which was in the process of assembling. All the way across the North Atlantic *Warspite*'s progress was impeded by violent gales and heavy seas, and she did not arrive in Halifax until 14 November.

Apart from yet another occasion on which her helm jammed, *Warspite*'s eastward, homeward-bound, progress in company with her convoy, passed uneventfully until she was well out into the Atlantic. Then, on the afternoon of the 24th, Captain Crutchley received orders from the Admiralty to part company with the convoy immediately, steer NNE and make for the Denmark Strait with all speed.

The reason for this sudden and urgent diversion was the appearance in the Iceland–Faeroes gap of the German battlecruisers *Scharnhorst* and *Gneisenau*, which had sank the Armed Merchant Cruiser *Rawalpindi* on the evening of the 23rd. If the German raiders intended to break out into the North Atlantic to attack the convoys, the Denmark Strait route was a strong probability and *Warspite*'s move was designed to block the exit. Punching through a raging gale, she passed through the Denmark Strait between Iceland and Greenland on the 25th. *Warspite* then swung east, passing to the north of Iceland, using her catapult aircraft to widen the area of search. By this time, however, the two German battlecruisers had fallen back on the Norwegian coast and subsequently, due to bad visibility, were able to slip past the British patrols and make good their escape back to Germany unmolested.

Warspite remained with the Home Fleet for the next four months, spending much of the time patrolling with the Fleet in northern waters, protecting Norwegian convoys and Canadian troop convoys. A succession of storms of unusual persistence and severity, and very severe cold of arctic intensity, placed a heavy strain on the ship's company during these operations, and it must have been a great relief when they learnt at the beginning of March that *Warspite* was being transferred back to the sunny clime of the Mediterranean. But it was not to be. Although she had actually sailed from the Clyde, bound for her old station, she was suddenly recalled by the Admiralty on 7 March, and ordered to join the Home Fleet under the command of Admiral Forbes, which had sailed from Scapa for Norwegian waters in response to Admiralty intelligence that unusual enemy naval movements were in progress. On the following day Germany invaded Denmark and Norway with practically their entire fleet in support.

Warspite in Grand Harbour, Malta before the outbreak of war. (Ivor Silcock)

NARVIK – THE SETTING

As part of the operational planning of the invasion of Norway, ten large German destroyers escorting transports carrying 2,000 troops, made their way unopposed up the fiords to Narvik and, overwhelming the defences, disembarked the troops who captured the port on 9 April 1940.

In an attempt to prevent the capture of Narvik, Admiral Forbes ordered Captain B. A. W. Warburton-Lee, commanding the 2nd Destroyer Flotilla which was patrolling off Vestfiord (the approach to Ofotfiord in which Narvik is situated), to proceed up the fiord and sink or capture the German troop transports.

Attacking with five destroyers at dawn on the 10th, Warburton-Lee achieved tactical surprise and sank six German merchant ships and two destroyers in Narvik bay. However, while withdrawing down Ofotfiord, the five British destroyers became embroiled in a running fight with the eight remaining enemy destroyers in which two of Warburton-Lee's ships were sunk and one

was severely damaged (Warburton-Lee was killed and awarded a posthumous Victoria Cross). Thus ended what became known as the First Battle of Narvik.

In a further attempt to destroy the German ships left at Narvik, two squadrons of Swordfish from the aircraft carrier *Furious* launched an attack on the afternoon of 12 April, but, because of low clouds (ceiling 100 feet) and snowstorms (visibility was only 250 yards), only one squadron got through to Narvik and their bombs scored no hits.

As a result of this unsuccessful attack the Admiralty ordered Admiral Forbes to effect the destruction of enemy naval forces in Narvik with a battleship heavily escorted by destroyers. The Admiral decided to employ *Warspite* (which was patrolling in company with the Home Fleet off Vestfiord) and ten destroyers. To command this strike force (designated 'Force B') Forbes chose Vice-Admiral W. J. Whitworth, who, commanding the battlecruiser squadron, was flying his flag in *Renown*.

NARVIK – THE BATTLE

Admiral Whitworth transferred his flag to *Warspite* at 0200 on Saturday 13 April (this was achieved with considerable difficulty as a heavy swell was running) and the whole force assembled inside Vestfiord, about 100 miles from Narvik, at 0730. 'Force B' proceeded up Vestfiord at 22 knots. The weather was overcast, heavy clouds producing intermittent snowstorms; there was a south-westerly wind, Force 3–4, and visibility was ten miles. The snow, lying thickly on the mountains surrounding the fiords, came down to sea level. Conditions on *Warspite*'s decks may be judged from the fact that during the progress up Vestfiord the crews of 'A' and 'B' turrets indulged in a snowball fight on the forecastle. At 0915 Admiral Whitworth made the following general signal to 'Force B':

'We are proceeding to attack the defences of Narvik and any German war or merchant ships met. I am sure that any resistance on the part of the enemy will be dealt with in the most resolute and determined manner. I wish you all every success.'[1]

By 1030, when *Warspite* had reached a position approximately 30 miles from the entrance to Ofotfiord, the destroyers *Icarus*, *Hero* and *Foxhound* took up a position ahead of the rest of 'Force B' and put out paravanes to sweep for mines. At the same time the destroyers *Bedouin*, *Cossack*, *Punjabi*, *Kimberley*, *Forester* and *Foxhound* formed an anti-submarine screen around *Warspite*. The tenth destroyer, *Eskimo*, was at this time patrolling off Tranoy Light farther up the fiord. Her position was fortuitous for at 1045, just as *Warspite* hove into sight, *Eskimo* sighted a U-boat three miles distant, situated between her and the battleship. The U-boat dived and *Eskimo* with some of the destroyers kept it down with liberal depth-charge attacks over the area from which it could threaten *Warspite*, although no ASDIC contact was established.

At 1152, when *Warspite* was five miles west of Baroy Island, at the entrance to Ofotfiord, the battleship's Swordfish seaplane was catapulted off to starboard. Airborne, it proceeded up Ofotfiord to reconnoitre 'with particular reference to the presence of German forces and the position of shore batteries; and to bomb any suitable targets'.[2] The Swordfish was piloted by Petty Officer Frederick Rice; the observer was Lieutenant-Commander W. Brown, RN, and the gunner and telegraphist was Leading Airman Maurice Pacey. They performed sterling service. In his report on the action Admiral Whitworth commented, 'I doubt if

ever a shipborne aircraft has been used to such good purpose.'[3] The Swordfish, which was armed with two 250lb and eight 20lb high-explosive bombs, plus two 100lb anti-submarine bombs, first reported the position of two German destroyers (reports made at 1203 and 1210) about twelve miles ahead of *Warspite*. Both destroyers opened fire on the Swordfish with their AA armament, but scored no hits even though the range was only 3,000 yards. Because of the low cloud ceiling – between 1,000 and 3,000 feet – the Swordfish was forced to fly low. Lieutenant-Commander Brown described the experience of manoeuvring between the steep sides of the fiord and under the low cloud ceiling as 'resembling flying in a tunnel'.[4]

After examining the entrance to Skjomenfiord on the south shore of Ofotfiord, and reporting one destroyer anchored off Narvik, *Warspite*'s Swordfish entered Herjangsfiord (1220) to the north of Narvik. Three minutes later, after flying along the northern shore of the fiord, a U-boat was sighted anchored 50 yards from the jetty at Bjerkvik. This was *U 64*, a large 1,050-ton Type IXB Atlantic boat, under the command of Kapitänleutnant Schulz. Petty Officer Rice put the Swordfish into a dive and released the two 100lb anti-submarine bombs at a height of 300 feet. The first bomb exploded in the U-boat's bows. The second bomb was either a hit or a near miss in the vicinity of the conning tower: the exact point of impact could not be observed owing to the explosion of the first bomb. Pacey, the air gunner, also hit the conning tower with a burst from the rear machine-gun. The U-boat retaliated with her 37mm gun and hit the starboard side of the Swordfish's tailplane; shrapnel from the exploding shell punctured the floats and caused minor damage to the rear of the fuselage. Damage to the tailplane made the Swordfish sluggish to control but she remained airborne. *U 64* sank within half a minute of being hit; 36 of her crew of 48 survived. This was the first U-boat to be sunk by a Fleet Air Arm aircraft in the Second World War. For this and their subsequent excellent reconnaissance work, the pilot was awarded the DSM, the observer the DSC and the air gunner was mentioned in dispatches.[5]

Returning down Ofotfiord towards the advancing *Warspite* and her destroyers, the Swordfish reported all fiords empty with the exception of Narvik itself (1230). This report was qualified six minutes later when she sighted a German destroyer which had manoeuvred into a small bay off Djupvik on the south shore of the fiord. Her bows were pointed to the eastward so that her

Warspite in Ofotfiord
during the Second Battle of
Narvik. View from
Warspite's airborne
Swordfish. (Ron Gilpin)

torpedo tubes bore across the fiord ready to fire at the approaching British squadron at a range of 3,000 to 4,000 yards. Hidden as she was, it was obviously hoped that she could fire her torpedoes before she was sighted. The

destroyer in question, the 2,200-ton *Erich Koellner*, was one of the two destroyers the Swordfish had first reported at 1210. Although undamaged in the First Battle of Narvik, *Koellner* had run aground in Ballangen-fiord and the damage sustained was so severe that the ship was no longer seaworthy. The captain of *Koellner*, realizing that he could not accept action, thus took up a position of ambush in Djupvik Bay. The Swordfish's report nullified the danger by allowing the British ships to train their guns and tubes to starboard, ready to engage *Koellner* the moment she hove into sight.

At 1236, when the report from *Warspite*'s Swordfish regarding *Koellner* was received in the battleship, 'Force B' was 40 minutes' steaming from Djupvik Bay, and other targets presented themselves before *Koellner* was sighted. The first destroyer reported by the Swordfish at 1203 was the 2,400-ton *Hermann Künne*. On sighting the British squadron she immediately retired towards Narvik, exchanging fire with the leading British destroyers at a range of 12,000 yards, which was the limit of visibility. Künne signalled a warning to the six German destroyers at anchor in Narvik harbour the

moment she sighted 'Force B'. On receipt of this signal Captain Bey, the senior officer of the 4th German Destroyer Flotilla, immediately ordered his force to put out to meet the enemy. However, only three, *Hans Lüdemann*, *Wolfgang Zenker* and *Bernd von Arnim*, were able to respond with dispatch. Of the other three, *Georg Thiele* and *Erich Giese* had not got sufficient steam up, and *Diether von Roeder* was too badly damaged (after the First Battle of Narvik) to move from her moorings.

As the three German destroyers cleared the harbour they joined up with *Künne*, and all four began steaming at speed to and fro across the width of the fiord, bringing all their guns and torpedoes to bear on the leading British destroyers, which were three miles ahead of *Warspite*. As the rival destroyers began to engage one another, *Warspite*'s great guns prepared to open fire. Unfortunately the enemy destroyers were obscured by a haze of mist, funnel and cordite smoke, and as there was no breeze the haze hung and progressively thickened. The enemy were also making rapid alterations of course, which meant that only estimated ranges could be passed from the director control tower to the gunlayers. At 1259 the fire gongs sounded on *Warspite* and 'A' and 'B' turrets opened fire at one of the enemy destroyers at a range of 21,500 yards. This was the first time since Jutland that *Warspite* had fired her guns in anger. In four minutes, nineteen rounds in ten salvoes were fired. No hits were scored.[6] As the foremost turrets were firing practically dead ahead, the blast from 'B' turret guns damaged the blast bags of 'A' turret (the bags covered the openings where the guns protruded from the turret) with the result that 'A' turret gunhouse filled with choking cordite smoke, and the gunlayers and sightsetters were temporarily deafened by the blast of the guns. At 1306 aim was shifted to a second destroyer, range 16,300 yards, twelve rounds in six salvoes beng fired from the foremost turrets. All fell short. As sight of this target was lost in the smoke, aim was shifted to a third destroyer observed crossing behind the previous target. An up of 800 yards correction was applied to the range, and eight rounds in four salvoes were fired. Again no hits were scored. Apart from the prevailing conditions, visibility from *Warspite*'s director control tower was further obscured by the great clouds of cordite smoke from the guns of 'A' and 'B' turrets firing on forward bearings.

The destroyers ahead of *Warspite*, engaging the enemy at ranges of between 10,000 and 15,000 yards, did not fare any better than the battleship; scoring no hits with guns or torpedoes. It is indicative of the appalling visibility that the German destroyers also were unable to score any hits during this phase of the battle. However, a target was about to present itself which the British squadron could not miss. At 1300 *Warspite* had ordered her still airborne Swordfish to circle over the German destroyer hiding in Djupvik Bay. This accurately pin-pointed the danger to the approaching squadron, and as two of the leading British destroyers, *Bedouin* and *Eskimo*, passed Djupvik Point at 1312, their guns and torpedo tubes already trained to starboard, they opened a withering fire on *Erich Koellner*. A hail of shells and two torpedoes struck the German ship, and within three minutes she was reduced to a blazing wreck. In return, *Koellner* had managed to fire one salvo from her guns, and two torpedoes, none of which hit. When *Warspite* passed the bay at 1322, the burning *Koellner* was to all appearances out of action, but as men were observed near her torpedo tubes she was given a full broadside from all four 15in turrets and the starboard 6in battery: eighteen rounds of 15in shells and seven salvoes from the 6in guns were fired, all of which hit. At a range of 3,600 yards they could hardly miss. *Koellner* was literally blown apart, and she heeled over and sank.

Meanwhile *Georg Thiele*, having raised sufficient steam, had cleared Narvik and joined the four German destroyers. The haze and smoke of battle had thickened to the extent that spotting the fall of shot was almost impossible. A total of 25 rounds in thirteen salvoes were fired by the two foremost turrets at ranges between 14,000 and 15,200 yards. Again no hits were scored.

During the action torpedoes fired by the German destroyers, having missed the British destroyers, threatened *Warspite*. On the first occasion, course was altered to starboard to avoid five torpedo tracks, all of which passed on the port side, one exploding against a rock on the north shore of the fiord just astern of the ship. In the second instance *Cossack* reported the approach of a torpedo. The track was not observed from *Warspite*, but the battleship manoeuvred to present the smallest target and escaped unscathed. There was no warning on the third occasion, and a violent explosion shook *Warspite* as a torpedo exploded after striking a rock very near or actually under the ship. No damage was incurred.

By this time the German destroyers' room for manoeuvre in the waters at the end of Ofotfiord was

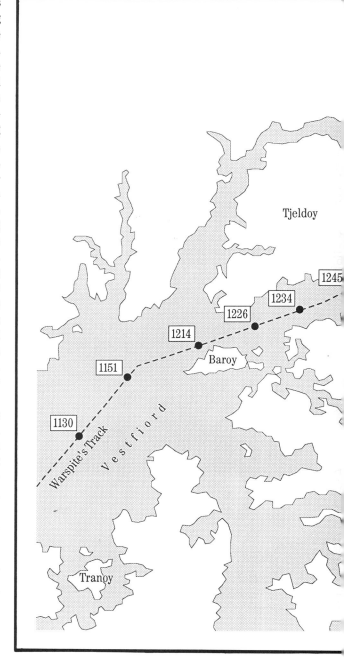

being severely restricted by the relentless progress of 'Force B'. It was obviously apparent to Captain Bey that once the oncoming battleship came into close range her guns would have devastating effect. Moreover, the Germans' position was fast becoming hopeless because they were running out of ammunition, having expended a large quantity during the First Battle. Accordingly, at

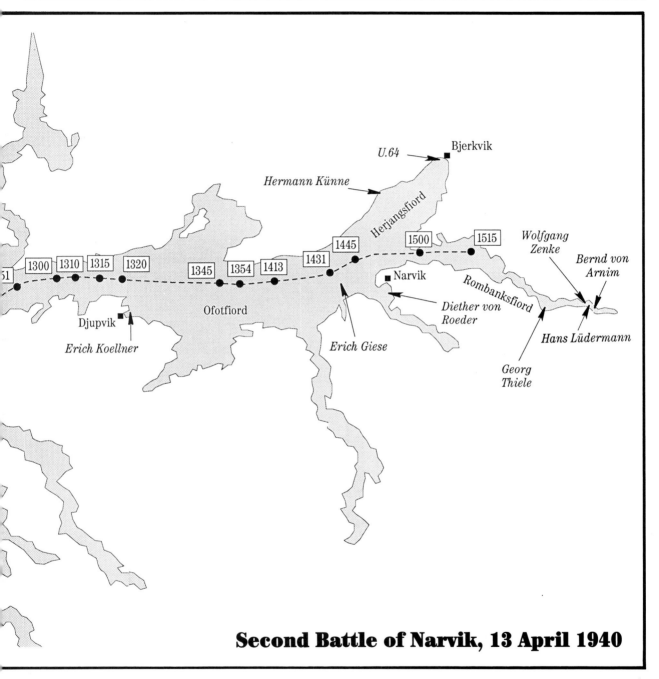

Second Battle of Narvik, 13 April 1940

1350, Captain Bey, with no other alternative open to him, ordered his force to 'Retire up Rombaksfiord'.

It should be mentioned that, up to this point, after 90 minutes of action, not one of the German destroyers except *Koellner* had been hit by either shell or torpedo. This state of affairs was about to change dramatically. *Hermann Künne*, apparently not taking in Bey's signal, tried to escape in the opposite direction to the other four destroyers, making for Herjangsfiord instead. There she beached herself off Troldvik. Her crew scrambled ashore and joined up with the German 139th Mountain Regiment, which was defending the area north of Narvik. Hard on *Künne*'s track, *Eskimo* torpedoed the beached destroyer leaving her a burning wreck.

The burning remains of the German destroyer *Hermann Künne*, after being reduced to a blazing wreck by *Warspite*'s 15in guns. (Ron Gilpin)

Meanwhile, as *Lüdemann*, *Zenker*, *Arnim* and *Thiele* disappeared behind the Narvik headland into Rombaksfiord, *Erich Giese*, which had finally raised enough steam to leave harbour, found herself under fire from almost the entire British squadron the moment she entered Ofotfiord. At 1358 *Warspite* opened fire on what was thought to be a shore battery. Her target was in fact the damaged *Diether von Roeder* which was unable to leave harbour. After *Warspite* had fired five salvoes at *Roeder* (range 16,900 yards), scoring no hits, *Giese* moved across the battleship's line of fire, and the range of *Warspite*'s guns was immediately corrected on to this new target (10,000 yards). *Warspite*'s shells reduced *Giese* to a burning, sinking wreck, and at 1410 her Captain gave the order to abandon ship. With *Giese* destroyed, *Warspite*'s guns turned once more upon the harbour-bound *Diether von Roeder*. Thirty-two rounds were expended at a range of 11,000 yards: only one hit

was scored with the fourth salvo. While the battleship was engaging *Roeder*, *Cossack*, followed by *Foxhound* and *Kimberley*, entered Narvik harbour, where they sank *Roeder* after a short but fierce exchange of fire. During this action *Roeder* scored four hits on *Cossack*, leaving her unable to manoeuvre; *Cossack* went aground 50 yards south of the lighthouse at the entrance to the harbour, where she remained until 0315 the next morning.

Meanwhile the remaining British destroyers (minus *Punjabi* which had been damaged and was temporarily out of action) with *Warspite*'s Swordfish reconnoitring overhead, chased the fleeing German destroyers up the narrow Rombaksfiord, which was only half-a-mile wide in places. During the chase *Georg Thiele* accidentally ran ashore at Sildvika while turning to fire her last torpedoes. One of her torpedoes struck the pursuing *Eskimo*, blowing off her bows and forecastle. *Thiele* scuttled herself, as did the three remaining German destroyers after beaching themselves at the head of the fiord: their crews escaped ashore to join the German garrison at Narvik.

During the chase up Rombaksfiord, *Warspite* had entered the fiord with the intention of carrying out an indirect bombardment of the fleeing German destroyers

The wreck of the German destroyer *Erich Giese* off Narvik. (Ron Gilpin)

at the head of the fiord, should this be necessary. During this time *Warspite*'s aircraft was recalled and hoisted inboard. But as the enemy forces had been successfully dealt with, and the battleship's support was not necessary, Admiral Whitworth decided to return to Narvik Bay. Arriving at 1730 *Warspite* found Narvik to be quiet except for a wild exchange of fire between the grounded *Cossack* and a small gun on shore. In his report Admiral Whitworth stated:

> 'I considered the landing of a party to occupy the town, as the opposition had apparently been silenced. But with the force available only a small party could be landed, and to guard against the inevitable counter-attack, it would be necessary to keep the force concentrated, close to the water front, and to provide strong covering gunfire; in fact, I considered it would be necessary to keep *Warspite* off Narvik.'

But information from a German naval officer taken prisoner by *Foxhound*, led Admiral Whitworth to believe that the fiords were infested by U-boats, and to make matters worse a dozen German aircraft appeared at 1800.

'Apart from the above conditions,' Admiral Whitworth relates, 'I felt that to place, at the end of a long and strenuous day, a party of less than 200 tired seamen and marines in the midst of a force of not less than 2,000 professional German soldiers would be to court disaster, even allowing for the moral effect which the day's engagement must have had on the enemy. The cumulative effect of the roar of *Warspite*'s 15in guns reverberating down and around the high mountains of the fiord, the bursts and splashes of these great shells [134 15in shells were fired in total], the sight of their ships sinking and burning around them must have been terrifying . . . [But the moral effect would not last. To take full advantage of it] . . . would have required a trained, organized military force, ready to land directly the naval engagement had ceased . . . I thereupon decided against keeping *Warspite* stopped in the fiord off Narvik, subject to U-boat and air attack.'[7]

In fact (other than the ill-fated *U 64*) only one other U-boat was present in the fiords during the battle: this was *U 51*, which had submerged in Narvik harbour when the attack began, and had slipped quietly out of Ofotfiord without attempting to attack any of the British ships.

Warspite began to withdraw down Ofotfiord at 1830 protected by a screen of five destroyers, leaving two destroyers behind to assist the disabled *Cossack* and *Eskimo*. But when Admiral Whitworth learned that there were a large number of wounded men in the disabled destroyers, he turned *Warspite* round and returned to Narvik (arriving midnight) with the object of

embarking the wounded in the battleship. This was effected by two destroyers coming alongside at the same time, but even then the last of the wounded were not embarked until 0540. All the while *Warspite's* gun crews remained closed up, expecting attack by U-boats and aircraft. Neither transpired and *Warspite*, unmolested, was able to withdraw down the fiord once more.

Thus ended the Second Battle of Narvik. The risks to *Warspite* in running the enemy to earth in the confined waters of the fiords had been correctly assessed and boldly accepted, and the result was an outstanding success. The Germans lost eight destroyers

resulted in a depth-charge attack by *Warspite*'s screening destroyers.

On 24 April, prior to an assault by an expeditionary force sent to capture Narvik, *Warspite*, in company with the cruisers *Aurora*, *Effingham* and *Enterprise*, went up the fiord again to bombard the enemy defences and the port of Narvik in the hope that heavy shelling would persuade the enemy garrison to surrender. The result of the bombardment is described by Captain Donald Macintyre:

'For three hours the thunder echoed and re-echoed amongst the tumbled mountains, and the houses of the little town shook at the blast and concussion. But little else resulted. Under their mantle of snow, few military targets could be distinguished nor could the result of the shell burst be seen. Recurrent snowstorms frequently reduced visibility to a few hundred yards. Conditions made any reconnaissance impossible, and there was no way of judging what moral effect had been produced on the defenders. A wireless station was destroyed as well as a few sheds and railway rolling stock, and a ferry steamer was sunk. The machine-gun nests could not be located, while the strong-points guarding the harbour water-front were in any case forbidden targets.'[8]

Not surprisingly the Germans in Narvik did not surrender, and it was not actually captured by troops until 28 May. Immediately after the bombardment *Warspite* was recalled to Scapa Flow. There Captain Crutchley was relieved of command of *Warspite* by Captain D. B. Fisher (the ship's twentieth captain) on 27 April. Three days later, after embarking stores at Greenock, *Warspite* sailed for the Mediterranean, where even greater glories awaited her.

and one U-boat, at a cost to the British of two destroyers badly damaged and one slightly damaged. In addition the German garrison occupying Narvik had been virtually isolated.

By the morning of 15 April, *Warspite* was in the open sea cruising off Vestfiord with three screening destroyers, blockading the sea approaches to Narvik. Four days later, on the 19th, while in a position to the south-west of Vestfiord, she had a narrow escape when *U 47* (Prien) launched an attack on her. Prien fired two torpedoes at a range of 1,000 yards. Both torpedoes missed, and the position of *U 47* was betrayed by one of the torpedoes exploding at the end of its run, which

Source Notes
1. PRO ADM 199/473. Admiral Whitworth's Narrative of Proceedings.
2. ibid.
3. ibid.
4. PRO ADM 199/473. Lieutenant-Commander Brown's Narrative of Proceedings.
5. I have based this account on Lieutenant-Commander Brown's official narrative, supplemented with information provided by Lieutenant-Commander F. C. Rice of the HMS Warspite Association.
6. All gunnery information relating to *Warspite* in this chapter is from *Warspite*'s Gunnery Narrative, PRO ADM 199/473.
7. Admiral Whitworth's official narrative.
8. *Narvik*, Captain Donald Macintyre. Evans Brothers, 1959.

PARTICULARS OF THE EIGHT GERMAN DESTROYERS SUNK IN THE SECOND BATTLE OF NARVIK

Leberecht Maass Class

Erich Koellner   Displacement: 2,200 tons
Wolfgang Zenker   Dimensions: 374ft × 37ft × 9½ft
Bernd von Arnim   Armament: Five 5in guns
Georg Thiele   Eight 21in torpedoes
Erich Giese   Complement: 315.

Von Roeder Class

Hermann Künne   Displacement: 2,400 tons
Hans Lüdemann   Dimensions: 384ft × 38½ft × 9½ft
Diether von Roeder   Armament: Five 5in guns.
                     Eight 21in torpedoes
      Complement: 313.

Warspite's Swordfish
seaplane landing
alongside. (F. C. Rice)

7.
'MARE NOSTRUM'

When *Warspite* was transferred to Home Waters from the Mediterranean in October 1939, Admiral Cunningham, in bidding farewell to the Ship's Company of his flagship, prophesied that he was sure he ' . . . should see them back in the spring'.[1] His prophecy was fulfilled with the arrival of *Warspite* at Alexandria on the evening of 10 May 1940. ABC hoisted his flag in the ship on the following day, although *Warspite* had to go immediately into dock for repairs to the extensive blast damage to decks and superstructure, which she had inflicted on herself with her heavy guns at Narvik. She was finally ready for service on 24 May. Seventeen days later Italy declared war on Britain and France (June 10). On the following day ABC took the entire Fleet to sea to sweep the central Mediterranean in search of the Italian Fleet and the Italian convoys which were supplying Mussolini's forces in Libya. The sweep passed uneventfully; most surprisingly, even the *Regia Aeronautica* (Italian Air Force) failed to put in the appearance that ABC had expected. The second foray of the Fleet into the central Mediterranean, which commenced on 7 July, would be far from uneventful, however.

THE BALANCE OF POWER

Mussolini had declared the Mediterranean to be an Italian Lake, or more correctly, '*Mare Nostrum*' (our sea), and to give substance to this claim he had set about creating a fleet which, although numerically inferior to the combined French and British Mediterranean Fleets, was superior to either one individually, especially in light craft. With the capitulation of France on 22 June, therefore, Cunningham found himself contesting control of the Mediterranean with a numerically inferior fleet. In terms of capital ships, ABC, with four battleships (*Warspite*, *Malaya*, *Ramillies* and *Royal Sovereign*) and one aircraft carrier (*Eagle*), believed himself

confronted by five or six Italian battleships. Four of these were of First World War vintage, but, like *Warspite*, all had undergone complete modernization in the inter-war years; while the other two were of the powerful, brand-new, 35,000-ton *Vittorio Veneto* class. To make matters worse for Cunningham, of his four First World War battleships, only *Warspite* had been completely modernized; added to which *Ramillies'* boilers were worn out, which adversely affected her speed. In fact, when Italy instigated hostilities the situation *vis-à-vis* battleships was not as bad as ABC feared. Italy had only the two battleships of the *Cavour* class (*Conte di Cavour* and *Giulio Cesare*) in commission, although another four – the two *Caio Duilio* class (*Andrea Doria* and *Caio Duilio*) under reconstruction and the two new *Littorio* class (*Littorio* and *Vittorio Veneto*) nearing completion – would be commissioned during the remainder of the summer months.

CALABRIA – OPENING MOVES

Late in the evening of 7 July 1940, *Warspite*, flying Admiral Cunningham's flag, led the Fleet to sea from Alexandria. Cunningham's plan was to make an extensive sweep into the central Mediterranean as far as the vicinity of the Italian coast, with the object of covering the passage of two convoys from Malta bound for Alexandria (one carrying evacuees, one stores). The Fleet, which consisted of three battleships, one aircraft carrier, five cruisers and seventeen destroyers, was organized in three groups: five 6in gun cruisers and one destroyer, commanded by Vice-Admiral J. C. Tovey, formed 'Force A'; *Warspite* and five destroyers formed 'Force B', while 'Force C' consisted of *Royal Sovereign*, *Malaya*, *Eagle* and eleven destroyers, under the command of Rear-Admiral H. D. Pridham-Wippell.

Only eight hours after the Fleet had cleared Alexandria, ABC received a signal from the submarine

Phoenix that the Italian Fleet was at sea. *Phoenix* reported that she had made an unsuccessful attack on two battleships and four destroyers at 0515, 200 miles east of Malta, about halfway between Taranto and Benghazi. The enemy fleet was, at that time, heading south towards the North African coast, and their course led ABC to suspect that they might be covering an Italian convoy bound for Libya. After directing the Naval Authority at Malta to send out a flying-boat to shadow the Italian Fleet and to postpone the sailing of the two convoys, ABC altered course and steered north-westwards at 20 knots. His intention was to place himself between the Italians and their base at Taranto.

Throughout the afternoon of 18 July, bombers of Regia Aeronautica (flying from the Italian Dodecanese Islands off the coast of Turkey) unleashed their full fury on Cunningham's Fleet. Between 1205 and 1812 *Warspite* was attacked seven times. The bombers pressed home their attacks in formation in the face of heavy anti-aircraft fire from *Warspite* and her five escorting destroyers. Although 120 bombs were dropped and *Warspite* found herself surrounded by

towering pillars of spray higher than her mast, she came through unscathed. Six attacks were made on 'Force C' also without result, but Tovey's cruisers were not so lucky. During one of the five attacks launched against 'Force A', a bomb hit the compass platform of the cruiser *Gloucester*, killing her Captain, six other officers and eleven ratings.

The second report of the enemy to reach ABC was made during mid-afternoon by a flying-boat from Malta. It reported that the Italian Fleet, which was now 200 miles from Benghazi, consisted of two battleships, six cruisers and seven destroyers, and that they had turned north, obviously heading back to Taranto. Cunningham immediately altered course directly for the Italian base situated in the instep of the Italian boot. The flying-boat continued to shadow until 1715 when, running short of fuel, she was obliged to return to Malta.

The night passed without incident, and daylight on 9 July found the British Fleet 60 miles west of the south-western coast of the Greek mainland. Tovey's cruisers were in the van, eight miles ahead of *Warspite*; 'Force C', comprising the two slower battleships and *Eagle*, were

Warspite in the Mediterranean, 1940. (H. Hawkins)

eight miles astern of the flagship. At 0440 ABC ordered three planes to be flown-off *Eagle* in an attempt to relocate the enemy. Commencing at 0732, these, together with a flying-boat from Malta, began sending back sighting reports of the enemy fleet's position and composition. The Italians were now only 145 miles to the WNW of *Warspite*, and their fleet was found to consist of two *Conte-di-Cavour* class battleships, sixteen cruisers and thirty-two destroyers. With three battleships to the Italian two, Cunningham appeared to have a superiority in this class of ship. But he was well aware that this superiority was purely theoretical. *Warspite* was the only one of the three British battleships to have undergone a complete modernization, with the result that both *Malaya* and *Royal Sovereign* were substantially slower than the 28-knot *Cavour*s (*Royal Sovereign* by 7 knots), and their guns were outranged by 8,500 yards. Although the Italian ships carried guns of a lesser calibre (10 × 12.6in), greater elevation gave them a range of 32,000 yards; equal, that is, to *Warspite*'s guns. Cunningham's numerical superiority, therefore, was cancelled out by the great speed of the Italian battleships and the long reach of their guns. Assuming parity in battleships, there can be no doubting the Italians' preponderance in light forces: 16 to 5 in cruisers, and 32 to 17 in destroyers. As for the presence of the aircraft carrier *Eagle*, her seventeen Swordfish hardly counted at all in comparison with the potentially vast aerial superiority that the Italians could muster from numerous air bases ashore, all within short distance of the scene of the impending action. Cunningham sums up his dilemma:

> 'It was not quite the moment I would have chosen to give battle. They had a large number of cruisers, and we, because the damaged *Gloucester* was not fit to engage in serious fighting, had no more than four, which had little more than fifty per cent of their ammunition remaining (the rest had been expended in fighting off the air attack on the previous day). Moreover, the speed of approach was limited by the maximum speed of the *Royal Sovereign*.'[2]

But to the pugnacious Cunningham any opportunity to engage the enemy was welcome.

By noon the distance between the rival fleets had shortened to 90 miles, and a strike force of nine Swordfish was flown-off *Eagle* with the intention of attacking the enemy battleships with torpedoes in an attempt to slow them down. Unfortunately a temporary alteration of course to the southward by the Italians prevented the aircraft from finding the battleships.

The British Fleet, meanwhile, was still on its northwesterly course and was rapidly closing the enemy. At 1400, having achieved his immediate objective of cutting the Italian Fleet off from Taranto, Cunningham altered course to west to increase the rate of closing, and by 1438 *Warspite* was within 30 miles of the enemy fleet. On *Warspite*'s bridge the general impression prevailed '... that the enemy proposed to vindicate Mussolini's claim of "*Mare Nostrum*" concerning the Mediterranean. The moment for which the Italin Fleet had been built up was at hand, if the Italian C-in-C (Admiral Riccardi) were prepared to accept the gage of battle.'[3]

Smoke from the Italian Fleet was first sighted at 1447 by *Orion*, one of Tovey's cruisers, ten miles ahead of *Warspite*. Visibility was twenty miles, the sky was dappled with thin cloud, the wind was northerly, Force four, and the sea was slight. Five minutes after *Orion*'s sighting, the cruiser *Neptune*, having actually sighted

two enemy ships, signalled to Cunningham 'Enemy battle fleet in sight.' This was the first time such a signal had been made by a British warship in the Mediterranean, since HMS *Zealous* had made her sighting report of the French Fleet to Lord Nelson before the Battle of the Nile, 142 years earlier.

CALABRIA – THE ACTION

The action off Calabria was initiated at 1514 by four of the Italian 8in gun cruisers which opened fire on Tovey's cruisers at a range of 23,600 yards. With the advantage of the sun behind them the Italians' fire was initially good, Tovey's cruisers being straddled several times, but their aim fell off noticeably when the British cruisers came into range and returned their fire at 1522. The western horizon was by now alive with enemy cruisers, and to support Tovey's heavily outnumbered force of four ships (the damaged *Gloucester* had been ordered to retire), *Warspite* increased speed to her maximum 24½ knots. At 1526 her great guns belched forth flame and huge clouds of cordite smoke as the Italian cruisers came into sight, 26,400 yards distant. *Warspite* fired ten salvoes, and as the huge 200-foot-high columns of water thrown up by her shells straddled the Italian cruisers, they turned away out of range under the cover of smoke. *Warspite* scored no hits on the enemy, but the blast from the first salvo of her own guns severely damaged her Swordfish aircraft on the catapult, and it had to be jettisoned into the sea.

To keep his battleships concentrated as far as possible, Cunningham ordered *Warspite* to turn a complete circle, so as to allow *Malaya* and *Royal Sovereign* to catch up. Coming out of the turn at 1533, *Warspite* opened fire again at two Italian 6in gun cruisers which hove into view. Eight salvoes were fired. No hits were scored, but once again the enemy made smoke and turned away. A fifteen-minute lull in the action now ensued, broken by the sudden appearance at 1548 of the two enemy battleships *Giulio Cesare* and *Conte-di-Cavour*. Both battleships opened fire on *Warspite* at extreme range, and with some accuracy. The majority of salvoes fell within 1,000 yards of the flagship, some straddling but nearly all having a wide spread. One closely bunched salvo fell 400 yards off *Warspite*'s port bow, drenching her in cascading water.

It was a full five minutes after the Italian battleships had opened fire, before *Warspite*'s range-takers found the range and her gunners began their deadly reply. At a range of 26,000 yards *Warspite* fired at the leading enemy battleship *Giulio Cesare*, flying the flag of Admiral Riccardi. Fire was opened at 1553, and seven minutes later, at 1600, *Warspite*'s thirteenth salvo straddled her target. From *Warspite*'s bridge Admiral Cunningham saw ' . . . a great orange-coloured flash of a heavy explosion at the base of the enemy flagship's funnels. It was followed by an upheaval of smoke, and I knew she had been heavily hit at the prodigious range of thirteen miles.'[4] Apart from wrecking the light arma-

Italian 12in shells falling near *Warspite* during the action off Calabria. (Ron Gilpin)

ment on *Giulio Cesare*'s upper deck, *Warspite*'s shell put six of the battleship's boilers out of action, reducing her speed to 18 knots; her casualties were 29 killed and 69 wounded. The effect of this hit was immediate: both the enemy battleships made a large turn away and began to lay a smoke-screen. *Warspite* altered course to close the range on the fleeing enemy, but after firing a further four salvoes, ceased fire at 1604 as they had become completely obscured by smoke. *Malaya* finally caught up with *Warspite*, just before the Italian battleships disappeared from view, and managed to fire five salvoes at the extreme range of her guns, all of which fell 3,000 yards short. *Royal Sovereign*, unable to close nearer than three miles from *Warspite*, never got into range and took no part in the action.

From the bridge of *Warspite* the western horizon was now seen to be overlaid with a thick pall of smoke, and all that could be seen of the enemy was a few of their light forces as they dodged in and out of the smoke, engaging in intermittent skirmishes with the British cruisers and destroyers. Between 1609 and 1639 only two targets presented themselves to *Warspite*'s guns. Six salvoes of 15in shells were let loose at a cruiser (range 24,600 yards) and five salvoes of 6in shells were fired at a destroyer. No hits were scored. Cunningham had no intention of plunging into the enemy smoke-screen in hot pursuit. His ability to read signals in the Italian Fleet's code and in plain language enabled him to determine that Admiral Riccardi intended to lure the British ships into a submarine and aircraft ambush, as the Italian ships retired towards the Straits of Messina. While Cunningham was working round to the windward and northward of the smoke-screen, however, one element of Riccardi's ambush was sprung. Commencing at 1640, hundreds of Italian bombers began a series of attacks on Cunningham's Fleet. *Warspite* and the carrier *Eagle* were particularly singled out, each being attacked five times. Despite the scale of the attack no ships were hit. Most of the bombing was extremely wild, being carried out from heights between 10,000 and 15,000 feet. During the attack, frantic signals from Admiral Riccardi were decoded with delight in *Warspite*: the Italian bombers were distributing their cargoes on friend and foe with complete impartiality.

At 1700 Cunningham gained the northernmost edge of the smoke-screen, only to find that the Italian Fleet had vanished. As it was now plainly evident that the enemy had no intention of renewing the action, and that it was impossible to intercept him, ABC, after reaching a position 25 miles off the Calabrian coast, altered course for Malta.

So ended the action off Calabria, in whch the one 15in hit scored by *Warspite* on *Giulio Cesare* had a moral effect out of all proportion to the damage it caused. 'Never again', wrote Cunningham, 'did the Italians face up to the fire of British battleships, though on several subsequent occasions they were in a position to give battle with a great preponderance in force.'[5] In effect *Warspite*'s guns had destroyed the Italians' boast of '*Mare Nostrum*': for the remainder of the war the Mediterranean was to be 'Cunningham's Pond'.

SUBSEQUENT MOVEMENTS

The passage to Malta throughout the night of 9 July passed uneventfully. Reaching a position south of the Island on the morning of the 10th, *Warspite* and the heavy ships of the fleet cruised for twenty-four hours while the destroyers entered harbour to refuel. The two convoys, for whose protection Cunningham had taken the Fleet to sea, before the action with the Italians off Calabria intervened, had in the meantime sailed from Malta for Alexandria with their own escort of destroyers. At 0800 on the 11th, *Warspite* and the Fleet followed.

In an endeavour to avoid the attention of Italian bombers based in the Dodecanese, ABC decided on a southerly route running parallel with the North African coast. But this course only served to attract the unwelcome attention of Italian bombers based in Libya. Between 1248 and 1815 on the 11th, *Warspite* was subjected to five attacks in which 66 bombs were dropped. On the following morning, between 0850 and 1150, seventeen attacks were made and 160 bombs fell around her. Despite these persistent attacks *Warspite* came through unscathed, although on one occasion she completely disappeared from view amidst a forest of huge splashes when two dozen bombs exploded close off her port side simultaneously with another dozen exploding off her starboard bow, all within 200 yards of the ship. Finally at 0600 on the morning of the 13th, *Warspite* entered Alexandria harbour, the two convoys and the remainder of the Fleet also reaching base unscathed from the Italian bombing.

Source Notes
1. Viscount Cunningham of Hyndhope, *A Sailor's Odyssey*, hereinafter cited as Cunningham.
2. Cunningham, p 259.
3. PRO ADM 234/323 The Action Off Calabria.
4. Cunningham, p 262.
5. Cunningham, p 263.

8.
CUNNINGHAM'S POND

FIRST BOMBARDMENT OF BARDIA

A month after the action off Calabria, the appearance of considerable Italian troop concentrations massing on the Libyan/Egyptian frontier, indicated that an Italian advance against the British forces in Egypt was imminent. With the object of causing as much damage as possible to the *matériel* and morale of Italian military concentrations in the forward areas, it was decided that Cunningham's Fleet should bombard the port of Bardia.

Lying half a dozen miles from the Egyptian border and only 250 miles from Alexandria, Bardia was the only sheltered anchorage on the Libyan coast east of Tobruk. The town, which at the time was heavily held by Italian troops and contained various military offices and barracks and a wireless station, stands on cliffs some 300 feet high, north of the harbour. Being the chief supply base for the Italian forces on the frontier, there were numerous storehouses in the vicinity of the town. Also, about ten miles south of Bardia, close to the Egyptian border, was another strong concentration of Italian troops at Fort Capuzzo.

The ships of the bombarding force were organized in two forces: *Warspite* and the cruiser *Kent* which were to fire on the Capuzzo concentration area; and the battleships *Malaya* and *Ramillies* which were to turn their guns on Bardia. All four ships closed the Libyan coast together from the north-east, separating into two groups at 0540 on the morning of 17 August 1940, an hour before sunrise, when they were twenty miles off-shore from Bardia.

With her Swordfish airborne to spot the fall of shot, *Warspite*, accompanied by *Kent*, opened fire a little after 0700. At a range of 24,000 yards *Warspite*'s 15in guns were directed on Fort Capuzzo. Initially ground mist and low cloud prevented the observer in the Swordfish from identifying the proper target, with the

result that the first six salvoes were wide. But after the observer rectified his error, *Warspite* dropped several shells into the Fort. Fire was then shifted, by a previously calculated switch, to a circle of 2,000 yards diameter two miles north of the Fort, where a concentration of troops and guns had been reported. Firing for effect immediately, without ranging, *Warspite*'s gunners dropped every salvo on this target within 300 yards of its centre. As the observer in the Swordfish reported no sign of any troops or guns, however, fire was immediately shifted back to Fort Capuzzo. While *Warspite*'s heavy guns engaged the main targets, her secondary battery of 6in guns fired on Fort Ramla, an old fortification situated on the coast, some six miles NE of Fort Capuzzo, in which stores and mechanical transport had been reported. The range was 10,000 yards and it wasn't until the seventh salvo was fired that a hit was scored. Smoke and dust from this hit prevented accurate spotting and the 6in guns ceased fire after the twelfth salvo. The bombardment by both groups finished at 0720 and they withdrew to the northward, rejoining an hour later. In all, *Warspite* had fired sixty 15in and forty-seven 6in shells, while *Kent*, which had followed astern of *Warspite*, expended ninety-one 8in shells at ammunition and storage dumps north-west of Ramla. Between them *Malaya* and *Ramillies* had also dropped 125 15in and 227 6in shells in and around Bardia.

Although a number of buildings were destroyed and a few storage dumps were set on fire, Cunningham, in his dispatch on the operation, commented that ' . . . the targets offered do not justify a repetition of this type of operation with heavy ships so long as warfare in the Western Desert remains static . . . because the Italians have shown themselves skilful in dispersing mechanical transport and stores over wide areas'.[1] Italian retaliation was minimal. A few 4in shells fell 1,000 yards short of

Malaya and *Ramillies*, while *Warspite* drew no retaliatory fire at all. Italian aircraft did not appear until four hours after the bombardment, when a considerable force of Savoia bombers dropped a large number of bombs on the retiring ships without effect, but at a cost of twelve of their number.

CUNNINGHAM'S POND

From the end of August until the middle of October, *Warspite* put to sea with the Fleet on three occasions, each time with the object of covering convoys to Malta. Although the Italian battleships put to sea on each occasion they hurriedly withdrew before there was any chance of ABC bringing them to action, thus confounding his main aim of crippling the Italian Fleet. The only sign of the enemy during these covering operations was the unwelcome attention of Regia Aeronautica, which carried out frequent bombing attacks. Although she was narrowly missed by one salvo of bombs and four airlaunched torpedoes during these attacks, *Warspite* again came through unscathed. In fact only one cruiser out of the whole Fleet was damaged.

By November 1940, the balance of naval power in the Mediterranean had swung decisively in Cunningham's favour. The Fleet had been reinforced by the aircraft carrier *Illustrious* and *Warspite*'s sisters *Barham* and *Valiant*: the latter being not only fully modernized like *Warspite*, but also equipped with radar (*Warspite* was not so equipped until December 1941). In battleships Cunningham now had parity with the Italian six, and this was suddenly transformed on 11 November, to a British superiority of three, when twenty-one Swordfish, launched from *Illustrious*, attacked the Italian Fleet at anchor in Taranto, sinking three of their battleships in the shallow waters of the harbour. Two were raised six months later and repaired, but *Conte-di-Cavour* was so severely damaged that she took no further part in the war. The effect of this was that Admiral Domenico Cavagnari, the Italian Naval chief of staff, ordered the Italian commanders to avoid confrontation with the British Fleet. The Mediterranean had become indeed 'Cunningham's Pond'.

SECOND BOMBARDMENT OF BARDIA

The 'Fleet in Being' strategy of the Italian Navy mitigated against the prospect of *Warspite* engaging Italian warships. Indeed the only occasion that *Warspite* fired her main armament during the five months subsequent to the Taranto raid, was during the bombardment of enemy shore installations.

The first of these operations took place in the early hours of 19 December 1940 when, as a result of Mussolini's invasion of Greece (28 October), *Warspite* and *Valiant* bombarded the Albanian port of Valona which the Italians were using as a supply base for their campaign. *Warspite* and *Valiant* each fired fourteen salvoes of 15in shells into the port and on to the adjacent airfield. Surprise was complete, and there was no reply to the crushing explosions on shore; about a dozen Italian aircraft were destroyed.

Just over a fortnight later *Warspite* found herself bombarding her old target Bardia once again. Although ABC had stated that a repetition of the previous bombardment of Bardia was not justified, the situation on land had changed to mobile warfare and hence the planned bombardment was of a different nature. The Italians had made their bid to invade Egypt on 3 September, and had driven the British Forces of General Wavell as far as Sidi Barrani, some 50 miles beyond the frontier. Here their advance was halted, and three months later Wavell counter-attacked. By 2 January 1941, British troops were converging on Bardia from the south and south-west. The object of the second bombardment was to neutralize and harass the sector north of the main Bardia–Tobruk road, on which large concentrations of Italian mechanized transport and tanks had been reported, and to prevent the formation of a counter-attacking force.

The bombarding force, which was again directed by Cunningham in person, consisted of the battleships *Warspite*, *Valiant* and *Barham*, the monitor *Terror*, three gunboats and five destroyers. In addition, Cunningham had in company the anti-aircraft cruiser *Calcutta* and four more destroyers acting as a screen to the main force. Farther out to sea was the carrier *Illustrious*, screened by two cruisers and four destroyers, her aircraft providing anti-submarine patrols and fighter protection for the bombarding ships and their spotting aircraft.

The bombarding squadron approached Bardia from the south-east at 15 knots, and fire was opened at 0810 on 3 January 1941. *Warspite*'s first 15in salvoes were aimed on a reported troop concentration in Wadi Raheb, four miles north-west of Bardia. Fire was then shifted on two concentrations of mechanized transport and stores nearby, as they were pointed out in succession by her spotting aircraft (catapulted from *Warspite* at 0718). *Warspite*'s first run past Bardia ended at 0830. Turning 180° she carried out a second run, firing on two groups of mechanized transport, reported by her aircraft, further up the Wadi at a range of 15,000 yards. During the two runs *Warspite*'s 6in guns had fired at an encampment on the clifftop near Hebs el Harram, two miles north-west of Bardia, had twice engaged an Italian battery on Point Bluff, and had fired a 'blind ladder' up the Wadi Raheb. In total *Warspite* fired ninety-six 15in and 116 6in shells, while *Valiant* and *Barham* fired a total of 150 15in, 154 6in and 240 4.5in shells. Apart from some anti-aircraft fire directed against the battleships' spotting aircraft at the opening of the bombardment, the only opposition came from four 4.7in guns on Point Bluff. This battery opened fire at about 0820, some ten minutes after the first run began; but it was temporarily silenced by the 6in and 4.5in secondary batteries of the three battleships. The Italian battery opened fire again when the battleships turned into their second run, only to be silenced once more by counter-battery fire from the destroyers and three salvoes of 15in from *Warspite*.

Warspite's Walrus amphibian being catapulted to port. *Illustrious* in the background. (H. Hawkins)

So far the Italian guns had scored no hits, but as the ships steered away from the coast, two of the four Italian guns began firing again, and at a range of 19,000 yards, splinters hit *Warspite* and *Barham*. In reply *Warspite* and *Valiant* fired a few rounds of 15in from their after turrets at the obdurate gunners.

The bombardment succeeded in its principal object, for the moral effect of the ships' fire sent the Italian troops to ground, and the majority stayed in their shelters until they were taken prisoner when British troops overran their positions on the following day. The *matériel* effect was less positive. Although the weather proved ideal for aircraft spotting, smoke and dust raised by the exploding shells quickly covered the targets. Furthermore, the dispersed mechanized transport, tanks and dumps of stores were not ideal targets for 15in guns. The sum total of material damage was, many

lorries, a few tanks and an anti-aircraft battery destroyed.

ENTER THE LUFTWAFFE

During January 1941 the arrival of the German *Fliegerkorps* X (10th Air Corps) in the Mediterranean theatre added a deadly element to the frequent air attacks on Cunningham's Fleet. Three hundred Ju 87B Stuka dive-bombers, Ju 88s, Heinkel He 111s and Messerschmitt fighters were sited on airfields in Sicily and the southern Italian mainland. The first taste of what these 'complete experts', as ABC described the German airmen, could achieve was experienced on Friday, 10 January 1941. *Warspite, Valiant, Illustrious* and seven destroyers had put to sea from Alexandria to cover the passage of two convoys, and had reached a position to the south of Malta when they were attacked by both Italian and German aircraft. Midshipman Binny, who was serving in *Warspite* at the time, gives a graphic account of what happened:

'Whilst nearing the end of dinner we were surprised by the Pom-Poms and 4in guns opening

fire. "Action!" was not sounded and very soon the firing ceased. I went up on the bridge to relieve midshipman Cunningham. When I reached the shelter deck I heard the fire bells ringing and the order to "stand to!" When I arrived on the bridge midshipman Cunningham told me that the last attack had been made by Italian Savoia torpedo-bombers which had done no damage, although one torpedo had passed under the *Valiant*'s stern. Whilst he was still talking, *Illustrious* opened fire again and looking up at her shell burst I saw several high-flying bombers. A few seconds later we opened fire along with *Valiant* and the enemy bombers were surrounded by puffs of dirty brown smoke. These bombers were Junkers 88. Other planes were then sighted on the starboard beam and we brought the 6in guns to bear on them. Then the dive-bombers came. I saw several bearing down on the *Illustrious*, diving at a terrific angle, then bombs dropped sending up huge water spouts. Yet another swooped over her, this time even steeper and lower, dropping its cargo and straightening up. It was a direct hit. A terrific tongue of flame leapt up aft on the flying-deck, and débris was hurled up in the air amongst which was the wing and half the fuselage of a Fulmar. Thick smoke was pouring from a cavity in the flying-deck, and from the results of another bomb hit just for'ard of the superstructure . . . A Stuka dived at us and I saw a bomb splash on the starboard bow and a huge fountain of grimy smoke floating up.

This bomb struck the shank of the anchor and by throwing it up damaged the hawse-pipe. The dive-bombers departed and in their place came more high-level bombers. We put up a terrific barrage and they were driven away without doing any damage.'[2]

Warspite was fortunate to escape with only a glancing blow on the fluke of the starboard anchor. *Illustrious* was hit by six 1,000lb bombs in ten minutes, but despite sustaining extensive damage and heavy casualties she managed to limp into Malta. After being patched up, she returned to Alexandria at the end of January, prior to sailing to the United States (via Suez) for repairs. Further attacks the next day, resulted in the sinking of the cruiser *Southampton* and damage to the cruiser *Gloucester*.

This inaugural attack by Fliegerkorps X came as a severe shock to ABC who wrote after the action that the 'command of the Mediterranean was threatened by a weapon far more efficient and dangerous than any against which we had fought before. The efforts of the Regia Aeronautica were almost as nothing compared with those of these deadly Stukas of the Luftwaffe.'[3] Just how deadly, *Warspite* was destined to experience first-hand as the war progressed, suffering very severe damage from bombs on two occasions.

German dive-bomber attack
on the carrier *Illustrious*,
January 1941. Views taken
from *Warspite* (Ron Gilpin)

CAPE MATAPAN – OPENING MOVES

During September 1940, British cryptanalysts broke the Italian naval Enigma (cipher machine) settings and were thus able to read Italian high-grade cipher signals. A series of intercepts gleaned from this source in March 1941, alerted Cunningham to the fact that the Italian Fleet appeared to be planning a sortie against the convoys transporting British troops to Piraeus in Greece. Although the Italian Naval High Command was loath to risk its ships, under pressure from the Germans, a fleet under the command of Admiral Angelo Iachino put to sea from Naples late on the evening of 26 March, with the intention of attacking the British troop convoys. Flying his flag in the brand-new, 30-knot battleship *Vittorio Veneto*, Iachino had under his command six heavy cruisers, two light cruisers and thirteen destroyers.

Despite the deciphered signals forewarning the Italian sortie, plus a report from a Malta-based Sunderland during the morning of 27 March, that three Italian cruisers and a destroyer had been sighted 80 miles east of the south-eastern tip of Sicily, steering south-eastward, and notwithstanding increased Italian air reconnaissance over Alexandria throughout the afternoon of the 27th, Cunningham was still not entirely convinced that the Italians were coming out. Nevertheless, after betting his Staff Officer (Operations), Commander Manley Power, ten shillings that they would see nothing of the enemy, ABC put to sea in *Warspite* after dark on the evening of the 27th, in company with *Valiant*, *Barham*, the aircraft carrier *Formidable* (which had been sent into the Mediterranean to replace the damaged *Illustrious*) and nine destroyers. While leaving harbour *Warspite* passed too close to a mud-bank which filled her condensers with mud, reducing her maximum speed from 24 knots to 20 knots. At this speed the Fleet steamed on a north-westerly course throughout the night, to reach a position south of Crete at daylight. Here a rendezvous was to be made with the four cruisers and four destroyers, under the command of Vice-Admiral Pridham-Wippell, which had been operating in the Aegean.

At dawn an air search was flown-off from *Formidable*, and at 0740 one of these aircraft sighted enemy cruisers and destroyers. Forty minutes later Pridham-Wippell sighted the same ships. Cunningham cheerfully paid up his ten shillings to Commander Manley Power and pressed on to support Pridham-Wippell's cruisers, some 90 miles to the north-west, which had come under fire from the Italian heavy cruisers and the 15in guns of *Vittorio Veneto*. Desperate for more speed than *Warspite*'s mud-clogged condensers could deliver, ABC summoned Engineer Captain Wilkinson to the bridge and in colourful language ordered him to do something about it. Temporary repairs were immediately effected, but as the propeller shaft from the affected engine was still only turning at half its usual power, the other three engines were worked to beyond their normal full capacity. Shortly afterwards *Warspite* picked up speed and was quickly foaming along at her full speed of 24 knots.

To help alleviate the pressure on Pridham-Wippell's cruisers, which were in danger of being overwhelmed, ABC ordered *Formidable* to launch an air strike. Although this saved the British cruisers, it had the unfortunate effect of causing the Italian Fleet, which Pridham-Wippell had been leading on to the guns of Cunningham's battleships, to turn about to northwards; Admiral Iachino deciding to cancel the planned attack on the convoys and return to base. As *Vittorio Veneto*, which was capable of 30 knots, was some eighty miles from *Warspite* when she turned about, there seemed little chance of Cunningham bringing her to action during daylight, if at all. However, the odds against bringing Iachino to action increased in Cunningham's favour when, during an air-strike launched from *Formidable* at 1500, a torpedo struck *Vittorio Veneto*'s stern and reduced her speed to 15 knots. More importantly to the course of subsequent events, a small force of Fleet Air Arm Swordfish from the airfield at Maleme in Crete, scored a hit on the heavy cruiser *Pola* which disabled her engines, leaving her dead in the water.

Chafing with frustration, ABC ordered *Warspite*'s

Swordfish to be catapulted at 1745 with one of his staff officers, Lieutenant-Commander A. S. Bolt, aboard to assess the chances of bringing the Italian battleship to bay. At 1830 Bolt reported that *Vittorio Veneto* was 55 miles from *Warspite* making good 15 knots. As she was too far away to catch during what remained of daylight (sunset was at 1930), Cunningham was now faced with a difficult decision: whether or not to engage the enemy at night. As he paced the charthouse deck, his staff officers gave their opinions. The majority of them argued against a night action with all its attendant uncertainties, and the risk of British ships firing on one another in a night-time mêlée. Not since the Battle of the Nile in 1798 had a night battle been decisive, and even then Nelson had actually attacked before dark. Having listened to the objections Cunningham snapped, "You're a pack of yellow-livered skunks! I'll go and have my supper now and see if my morale isn't higher than yours!" To all who knew him there could be no doubt as to what his decision would be. Aggressive and possessed with a bull-terrier's instinct for a fight, at 2040 ABC ordered his destroyers to race ahead at full speed to establish contact with the enemy, while the battleships continued the pursuit. At this stage the Italian Fleet was estimated to be 33 miles ahead of *Warspite*.

CAPE MATAPAN – THE NIGHT ACTION

Only thirty minutes after Cunningham had made his momentous decision, a signal was received from Pridham-Wippell, flying his flag in the light cruiser *Orion*, which was twenty miles ahead of *Warspite*, that he had made radar contact with a ship lying dead in the water five miles to port. Hopes ran high on *Warspite*'s bridge that, crippled by the torpedo hit, *Vittorio Veneto* was no longer able to proceed. Course was immediately altered 40° to port to close the position of the disabled ship. The disposition of the battle squadron was *Warspite*, *Valiant*, *Formidable* and *Barham* in single line ahead. A light wind was blowing from the south-west and the sea was smooth with a low swell: there was no moon and a cloudy sky reduced visibility to about 2½ miles.

Nearly an hour passed before *Valiant*'s radar (the only one in the battle squadron) detected the 'stopped ship' on her port bow, eight to nine miles distant. Cunningham turned to the south-west at 2213 to close; this brought his squadron into quarter line. Radar reports continued to come in from *Valiant*, and in tense readiness the battle fleet held on its way. By 2220 the 'stopped ship' was reported by *Valiant* as only 4½ miles distant. Suddenly the situation changed dramatically. Every man on *Warspite*'s bridge was searching the dark horizon to port through their binoculars. Luckily Commander John Edelsten, Cunningham's chief of staff, decided to give the starboard horizon a sweep through his binoculars and immediately saw two large cruisers with a smaller one ahead of them, crossing the bows of *Warspite* from starboard to port, only 4,000 yards distant. Commander Manley Power, an ex-submariner whom Cunningham considered ' . . . an abnormal expert at recognizing the silhouettes of enemy warships at a glance', studied the dark, barely discernible shapes and pronounced them to be two *Zara*-class 8in gun cruisers, preceded by a smaller, unidentified class of cruiser. The three ships were in fact the heavy cruisers *Zara* and

Fiume, with the destroyer *Alfieri* ahead, which Admiral Iachino, unaware that Cunningham's battleships were pursuing him, had sent back to assist the crippled *Pola*: the 'stopped ship' on *Valiant*'s radar.

As Cunningham's ships altered course to starboard, which brought them back into single line ahead, *Formidable*, obviously of no value in a gun action, hauled out of the line.

'I shall never forget the next few minutes,' wrote Cunningham. 'In the dead silence, a silence

Warspite's Walrus being recovered. (Ron Martin)

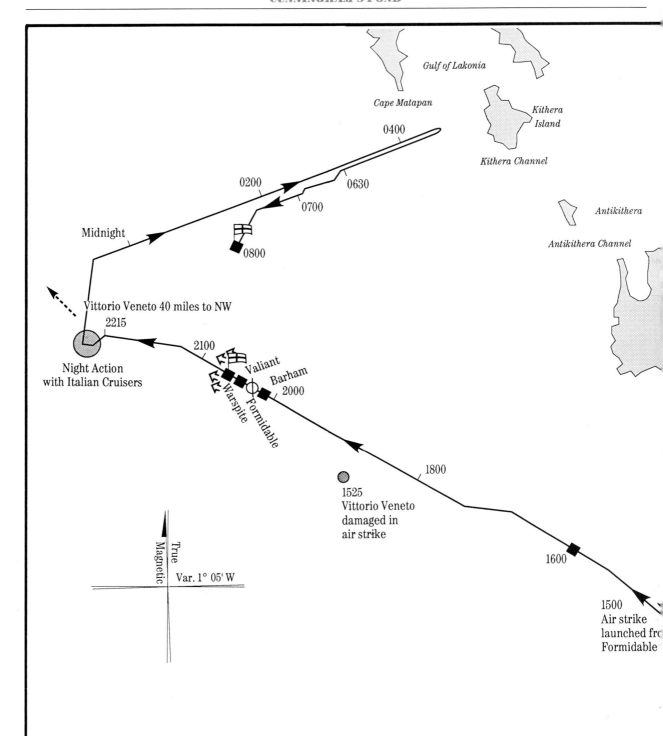

Gulf of Lakonia

Cape Matapan

Kithera Island

Kithera Channel

0400

0200

0630

0700

Antikithera

Antikithera Channel

Midnight

0800

Vittorio Veneto 40 miles to NW
2215

Night Action
with Italian Cruisers

2100

Valiant

Barham
2000

Warspite

Formidable

1800

1525
Vittorio Veneto
damaged in
air strike

1600

True

Magnetic

Var. 1° 05' W

1500
Air strike
launched fro
Formidable

Battle of Matapan, 28/29 March 1941

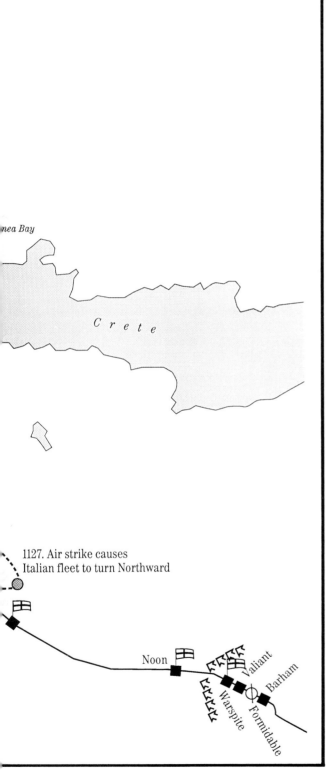

nea Bay

C r e t e

1127. Air strike causes
Italian fleet to turn Northward

Noon

Valiant

Barham

Warspite

Formidable

that could almost be felt, one heard only the voices of the gun control personnel putting the guns on to the new target. One heard the orders repeated in the director tower behind and above the bridge. Looking forward, one saw the turrets swing and steady when the 15in guns pointed at the enemy cruisers. Never in the whole of my life have I experienced a more thrilling moment than when I heard a calm voice from the director tower – "Director layer sees the target"; sure sign that the guns were ready and that his finger was itching on the trigger. The enemy was at a range of no more than 3,800 yards – point-blank!'[4]

The Fleet Gunnery Officer, Geoffrey Barnard, ordered the battleships to open fire. On *Warspite* at 2228 the 'ting – ting – ting' of the fire gongs preceded a great orange flash and a violent shudder as six of the 15in guns fired simultaneously ('Y' turret was not bearing). At the very same instant as the first salvo crashed out, searchlights from *Warspite* and the destroyer *Greyhound* illuminated the cruiser *Fiume*, third ship in line, just as five of *Warspite*'s huge shells smashed into her a few feet below the level of the upper deck, exploding with devastating effect. *Fiume*, which also received a full broadside from *Valiant*, burst into a sea of flame from just abaft the bridge to the after turret, which was blown clean over the side. Captain Fisher was heard to say in a voice of wondering surprise, "Good Lord we've hit her!" At a range of only 2,900 yards they could hardly have missed! Forty seconds after the first broadside, a second, eight-gun broadside from *Warspite* engulfed *Fiume* in flame and explosions. Listing heavily to starboard, burning fiercely along her entire length, her crew jumping overboard in panic, *Fiume* drifted out of line, and blew up and sank thirty minutes later.

Precisely one minute after opening fire on *Fiume*, *Warspite* swung her searchlights and guns on to *Zara* (second ship in line). Between 2229 and 2232 *Warspite* fired four full eight-gun broadsides at the luckless cruiser at a range of 3,000 yards. *Valiant* and *Barham* also joined in the cannonade, the latter having shifted her fire from the destroyer *Alfieri* (the leading ship) which had been set on fire and had made off westwards making smoke; she sank some time later. Between them *Warspite*, *Valiant* and *Barham* fired a total of sixty-two 15in shells at *Zara*, twenty of them hitting, reducing her to a blazing wreck. A big explosion forward hurled one of her turrets overboard, and masses of débris whirled

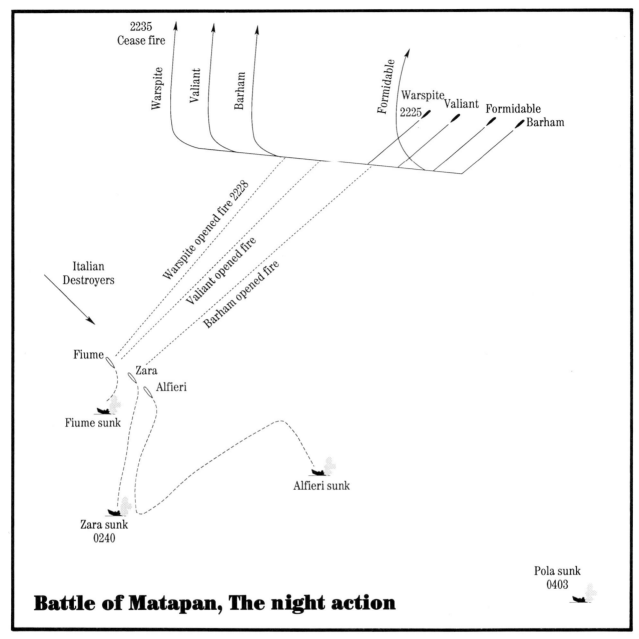

Battle of Matapan, The night action

through the air and splashed into the sea. Like *Fiume* before her, *Zara* drifted out of control to starboard. The Italian ships had been taken completely by surprise. Incredibly, their gun turrets, which were trained fore and aft when the action commenced, were not even manned because their crew had had no training in night firing! What is perhaps even more inexplicable is that the Italians did not see the huge silhouettes of three battleships and an aircraft carrier looming up only 3,000

yards distant, when their much smaller profiles were sighted by the British.

The moment *Warspite* ceased firing on *Zara*, three Italian destroyers, following in the wake of the unfortunate cruisers, were illuminated by *Warspite*'s sweeping searchlights. The port 6in battery was ordered to engage and at 2232 a salvo was fired at the lead destroyer at a range of 3,000 yards. No hits were scored; the salvo landing beyond the target. Making smoke, the three destroyers immediately turned away, firing torpedoes as they turned. To avoid this danger Cunningham ordered the three battleships to make a 90 degree turn to starboard. As *Warspite* turned her searchlights picked up another destroyer and two salvoes of 6in were let loose at her. All the shells missed, luckily, for the destroyer turned out to be HMS *Havock*, which had not switched on her fighting lights. Danger of a fratricidal battle also loomed on the opposite bearing when one of *Warspite*'s searchlights, sweeping the disengaged side in case further enemy ships were present, caught *Formidable* in its beam, five miles distant. The Control Officer of *Warspite*'s starboard 6in battery was restrained only seconds before ordering his guns to open fire on the carrier.

Commander Geoffrey Barnard, The Fleet Gunnery Officer, who was on *Warspite*'s bridge throughout the action, recorded the subsequent events in a memoir:

'ABC then, with supreme judgement, decided it was time for the battleships to disentangle from the confused in-fighting and cleared us off before sending the destroyers in to mop up the cruisers and anything else they could find. We had absolutely crippled the two big cruisers and a destroyer in about two minutes, and in addition there was the original 'stopped ship' and one or two mildly winged ones, so the destroyers had a marvellous night, finishing off the cruisers and shooting at everything they saw. [The blazing wreck of *Zara* was torpedoed and sunk by *Jervis* at 0240. The crippled *Pola*, the 'stopped ship', was sunk by torpedoes from *Jervis* and *Nubian* at 0403. *Havock* also accounted for a further destroyer, the *Carducci*]. . . . The cruisers never got off a round at us. Their destroyers fired quite gamely but wildly, and we could hear small stuff whistling overhead and occasionally see splashes near us, but we were never seriously in any danger except when they fired torpedoes at us from damn close range. Unfortunately nobody during the subsequent night of groping and confused fighting, found the damaged battleship [*Vittorio Veneto* was forty miles to the north-west of *Warspite* when the night action took place, and was well clear when the destroyers searched for the damaged cruisers]. . . . Next morning, at daylight, we reached the rendezvous point we had arranged with our scattered destroyers [SW of

Cape Matapan]: we were amazed and thankful when one by one they all turned up without a single scratch or casualty.'[5]

With the fleet reassembled, Cunningham set course for the scene of the previous night's encounters. A calm sea was covered with a film of oil, and strewn with boats, rafts, wreckage and floating corpses. Survivors in the boats and rafts waved white sheets and shirts. Destroyers were detached to save as many as possible (900 were picked up), but in the midst of the rescue work German Stukas made an attack, and the destroyers had to get under way, leaving hundreds of the Italians unrescued. Gallantly, ABC signalled their exact position to the Italian Admiralty. Telegraphist Gary Owen remembers that in reply to a signal from ABC regarding casualties and survivors, one of the destroyers signalled, "The Captain of the *Pola* has piles." To which ABC replied, "I'm not surprised!"

On the passage back to Alexandria a continuous fighter patrol was maintained over the Fleet by aircraft from *Formidable*. These dealt effectively with a Stuka dive-bombing attack which developed at 1530. The attack was directed mainly against *Formidable* and caused no damage beyond shaking her by two near misses. Without further incident the Fleet arrived in the approaches to Alexandria at 1730 on 30 March. As an enemy submarine had been reported in the vicinity, the destroyers cleared the approaches with a liberal sprinkling of depth-charges. These, of necessity, were set to explode at a very shallow depth, and Midshipman Binny recalls that *Warspite* shook violently each time the charges went off.

On the following morning a Thanksgiving Service was held on board *Warspite* for the victory off Cape Matapan, and a sacred icon of Saint Nicholas, the patron saint of sailors and travellers, was presented by the Patriarch of the Greek Orthodox church at Alexandria: this was placed in *Warspite*'s chapel. For the loss of one aircraft and three of its crew, Cunningham had not only sunk three heavy cruisers and two destroyers (with the loss of 2,400 men), but had ensured that the convoys to and from Greece were no longer threatened. After the shock of the battle the Italian Fleet remained supine and inactive for a whole year.

Source Notes

1. PRO ADM 186/797 The Bombardment Of Bardia.
2. The Midshipman's Log of D. Binny (IWM).
3. Cunningham, p. 303.
4. Cunningham, p. 332.
5. The Papers of Vice-Admiral Sir Geoffrey Barnard (IWM).

9.
DISASTER OFF CRETE

THE BOMBARDMENT OF TRIPOLI

Only four days after the battle of Cape Matapan, the tide of war turned against the British Army in North Africa. On 2 April Rommel's newly arrived 'Afrika Korps', together with the remnant of the Italian Army, launched a surprise attack at El Agheila, and by 16 April had driven the British forces all the way back to the Egyptian Frontier. In the short space of fourteen days, all the gains that General Wavell had won in the desert campaign of the previous winter were lost, and the defence of Egypt had become a perilous anxiety. As Tripoli was the only port on the North African coast capable of serving both the German and Italian forces as a main base for the reception of supplies, Churchill pressed heavily for a full-scale bombardment of the port, in the hope of putting the facilities out of action for a considerable period. Cunningham tried to veto the plan, believing it involved risks to the Fleet entirely incommensurate with the damage likely to be effected.

By comparison with Bardia, Tripoli was much better defended. The seaward defences consisted of fourteen batteries, mounting guns of 5in, 6in, 7.5in and 10in calibres. There were also numerous AA batteries, and outside the harbour a minefield. In addition there were two large airfields situated in the vicinity; one at Mellaga, six to seven miles east of Tripoli, and another at Castel Benito, fifteen miles to the south of the town. Immediate and continuous air attacks upon the bombarding force could therefore be expected. However, in preference to an alternative plan propounded by the Admiralty – to attempt to block the port by sinking *Barham* and an AA cruiser in the entrance – ABC reluctantly assented to the proposal.

In order to minimize the risk to the Fleet from air attack and the fire of the shore batteries, Cunningham decided to carry out the bombardment during the hours of darkness, relying on flares for illumination. Zero Hour was accordingly fixed for 0500, 21 April, on which day moonrise was at 0436, dawn at 0650 and sunrise at 0730. To assist the Fleet in making an accurate landfall in the darkness, the submarine *Truant* was to act as a lighthouse in a position four miles north of Ras Tajura (some ten miles east of Tripoli). In this position she was to show a white flashing light to seaward.

In order to deceive the enemy of his intentions, ABC decided that the Fleet should approach Tripoli from a position halfway between Malta and Alexandria, ostensibly to cover the passage of two convoys that were due to sail from Malta, and after dark on 20 April steam south at high speed so as to be in position to bombard Tripoli before dawn on the next morning. Accordingly, at 0800 on 18 April ABC, wearing his flag in *Warspite*, led the Fleet to sea. In company were *Barham*, *Valiant*, and the carrier *Formidable* with attendant cruisers and destroyers.

Reaching Suda Bay (Crete) at 1245 on the 19th, the Fleet sailed again at 1450, after the destroyers had refuelled, bound for Tripoli, which would be approached from a north-easterly bearing. The flashing light exhibited by the submarine *Truant* was sighted from *Warspite* at 0410 on the 21st, seven miles ahead. Tripoli was also illuminated by this time, with bomb explosions, fires, searchlights and anti-aircraft tracer – the result of an air raid by Wellington bombers from Malta. The weather was favourable, with a calm sea and no wind. *Warspite* rounded *Truant* at 0438, followed by *Valiant*, *Barham* and the light cruiser *Gloucester*; four destroyers swept ahead with paravanes in case of mines. *Formidable* with a destroyer screen stood out to sea. The anxious period of approach passed without any indication that the enemy had sighted the bombarding force.

At 0500 the harbour of Tripoli was fully illuminated by a dozen flares dropped by aircraft from *Formidable*, while *Warspite*'s Swordfish, which had been catapulted during the approach, reported 'Ready to Observe'. At 0502 *Warspite* opened fire with 'A' and 'B' turrets. Within a minute all the other ships were in action. *Warspite*'s allotted target was the 'Spanish Quay', a long breakwater enclosing the harbour to the west and north, which accommodated officers' quarters, barracks, shed and workshops.

In spite of the brilliance of the flare illumination, the observer in *Warspite*'s aircraft experienced difficulty in spotting the fall of shot, due to a vast cloud of dust and smoke, thrown up by the bombing raid, hanging over the town. Spotting from *Warspite*, firing at a range of 12,400 yards, was no better; all that could be seen was the occasional flash of bursting shells or the top of a splash of a 15in salvo when it landed in the harbour.

Complete surprise had been achieved, however, for, while the defences kept up a fine display of AA coloured tracer directed against the flares and spotting aircraft, the coastal batteries made no reply until the Fleet had completed its first run past Tripoli and was turning eastward to commence the second run. Although *Warspite* and the other ships were straddled by the fire from the shore batteries no damage was caused.

Cease-fire was ordered at 0545, and shortly afterwards the Fleet altered course to the north-eastward for the return passage to Alexandria. In total, 530 tons of high-explosive shell had been thrown into Tripoli: *Warspite*'s contribution being 135 15in and 106 6in shells. Despite this enormous weight of shells, the results were disappointng. Only 37 per cent of the 15in shells, and only 12½ per cent of the lesser calibres found a target. The remainder fell harmlessly into the waters of the harbour. One torpedo-boat was damaged; one merchant ship laden with fuel and bombs was sunk, and two other merchant ships were damaged. Unfortunately it was the town and its inhabitants that suffered far more damage than the shipping or the port facilities: one hundred dwellings were destroyed, and civilian casualties numbered one hundred dead and three hundred wounded. The objective of putting the facilities of the port out of action for a considerable time had certainly not been achieved: shipping movements from Italy to Tripoli were suspended for only 24 hours.

Surprisingly the expectation of heavy enemy air attacks on the Fleet did not materialize, and it wasn't until midday on 22 April, that three Stukas made an

Warspite in her wartime camouflage. (Ron Gilpin)

appearance. These were intercepted by aircraft from *Formidable*, which shot down two and drove off the third. The Fleet entered Alexandria harbour at 1100, 23 April, completely unscathed, to Cunningham's intense relief, who had feared the loss of at least one ship in a minefield, or heavy damage to them all through dive-bombing.

DISASTER OFF CRETE

Early in April the Germans invaded and quickly overran Yugoslavia and Greece. By 1 May 1941, the mauled and outnumbered British expeditionary force had been evacuated from the Greek mainland. Nineteen days later the Germans launched Operation 'Mercury', a great airborne assault against Crete, involving 13,000 para-troops and glider-borne troops, and 9,000 mountain troops brought in by Junker Ju-52 transports. To prevent the Germans sending seaborne reinforcements across the 50 miles of the Aegean separating mainland Greece from Crete, ABC immediately dispatched cruisers and destroyers to establish patrols to the north of the Island. To guard the light forces against the possibility of a sortie by the Italian Fleet, *Warspite*, *Valiant* and five cruisers took up a covering position 100 miles to the west of Crete. Before *Warspite* put to sea, Cunningham transferred his flag ashore, the better to co-ordinate the Fleet's work with the other services, and his flag was replaced on *Warspite*'s yard by that of Rear-Admiral H. B. Rawlings.

While cruising in the support position during 20 and 21 May, *Warspite* and her consorts were subjected to heavy bombing attacks by German aircraft. Once again

Warspite was unscathed, but her luck was running out. On the morning of 22 May, a group of cruisers and destroyers, which were running out of ammunition and suffering under intense bombing, began to withdraw westwards from the waters north of Crete. Learning of this group's predicament, Admiral Rawlings imme-diately set course for the Kithera Channel, between the islands of Kithera and Antikithera (NW of Crete), to lend close support.

At 1332, while passing eastwards through the Kithera Channel at 20 knots, *Warspite* was preparing to engage formations of enemy aircraft sighted on each beam, when three Messerschmitt Me 109 fighter-bombers suddenly appeared through smoke bursts right ahead. They were following one another closely in a shallow dive, and were not sighted until they were 2,000 yards from *Warspite* at a height of 800 feet. Captain Fisher immediately ordered the wheel to be put over hard a-port, and the starboard pom-poms and 4in guns to put up a barrage. It was too late. Before the change of course had begun to take effect, or the starboard AA guns could open fire, the three Messerschmitts had released their bombs from a range of 500 yards and a height of 500 feet. One bomb fell about 50 yards clear of the starboard side abreast the mainmast; another fell about 100 yards right ahead; the third, a 500lb armour-piercing bomb, hit *Warspite* on the starboard side, just before the foremost twin 4in gun mounting. The time elapsing between the Messerschmitts being sighted and the bomb hitting the ship was only ten seconds.

Striking the ship at an angle of 45°, the bomb penetrated the forecastle deck about six feet from the

Smoke from fires on *Warspite* after she had been hit by a bomb in the Kithera Channel off Crete, 22 May 1942. *Valiant* astern. (Ivor Silcock)

ship's side, plunged down through the 1in battery bulkhead, hit the baseplate of the aftermost starboard 6in gun, bounced up and burst about twenty feet from the ship's side about two feet above the upper deck.

The damage was extensive. The foremost starboard twin gun mounting was blown overboard, and the support of the after twin 4in guns was wrecked, rendering them unsafe for firing. The forecastle deck was blown upwards and ripped open to a length of ninety feet. The two after starboard 6in guns and their mountings were wrecked, and although the two forward guns were intact, they could not be fired due to damage to the surrounding structure. The upper deck was bulged downwards over an area 130 feet long and 30 feet wide, with a hole, 6 feet × 8 feet, under the point where the bomb burst. The explosion also blew out fifty feet of the ship's side between the forecastle and upper decks, and wrecked the fan downtake to number three boiler room. Smoke and fumes from the explosion and resulting fires were drawn through the damaged downtake by the fans, permeating the boiler room to the extent that it had to be abandoned. *Warspite*'s Executive Officer, Commander (now Admiral) Sir Charles Madden, has written a vivid account of the carnage the bomb caused.

'I was stationed in the Upper Conning Tower, listening through the voice pipe to what went on on the bridge. I heard the report: "Hit starboard side amidships," and left the U.C.T. to investigate. As I reached the back of the bridge I saw dense smoke coming from the starboard 4-inch battery. On reaching the upper deck level it was apparent that one 4-inch mounting had gone overboard completely, and that the other was at an angle. There was a huge hole in the deck between the two mountings from which smoke and flame were pouring out.

'I then went down to the port 6-inch battery to see if the fire parties were ready, and to try to get at the seat of the fire through the armoured door that connected the port and starboard 6-inch battery decks. I found the fire party lined up ready by this door, asked two ratings to enter with me, and told the fire parties to open the door and follow us in. We had great difficulty opening this door and had to use a sledge hammer. The handle was jammed by a dead man's head. Finally it gave, to display a gruesome scene. The starboard battery was full of flames and smoke, in among which the cries of burned and wounded men

could be heard. These were very unnerving and I remember thinking how accurate were the descriptions in C. S. Forester's books of the carnage on the gun decks in Nelson's day. The flames seemed pretty fierce and I was doubtful if we would make headway against them. However, my two volunteers came either side of me with their hoses and we walked into the battery. To my surprise the flames, which I suppose were dying down, seemed to subside before us, and soon we had the fire parties following us and were putting out the flames as we advanced.

'I was soon joined by more fire parties coming from the after end of the starboard battery, and felt confident that I could get the fires out, but was hampered by the continued cries of the burned men, which distracted the fire parties, who wanted to leave their hoses to assist their comrades. I therefore concentrated on administering morphia.

'About this time the smoke cleared in the hole in the deckhead, and I could converse with those on the deck above.

'I sent for all the officers with morphia, and soon had several on the job, which became the main task as soon as the flames were out. As it was dark and wounded men were thrown in all directions amidst piles of ironwork and rubbish this was not easy.

'The hole in the upper deck was now clear of smoke, and through it we could see the deep blue sky and the next wave of attacking aircraft coming at us. The 4-inch battery being out of action made it seem unpleasantly quiet, until the pom-poms started up, which a caused a lot of the broken ironwork to fall about. I can remember the pom-pom bursts filling up the area of sky we could see and the aircraft still coming on, and some of the fire parties dropping their hoses to shake their fists at them.

'I now had plenty of officers to take charge in the battery and we were moving the wounded out, so I went down to the mess decks under the battery. The port side was cleared for casualties, which were being laid out in rows. A surprising number of men had trickled along to look after their friends, and I had some trouble in reducing their number, as they were all being kind and helpful.

'I then went to the starboard mess decks, where a fresh and unexpected scene of carnage greeted me. The armoured deck overhead, that of the starboard 6-inch battery, had been pierced by the explosion, the force of which had decended into a mess deck where communication ratings off watch were resting. These, contrary to instructions, and because of the heat, were lightly clad, and there were heavy casualties from burns. The great amount of water we had pumped into the battery above to put out the fires had poured into the mess deck, which was in parts knee-deep in water, thus adding to the confusion of scattered mess tables, lockers and bodies.

'When all was under control I went to the bridge to report. The calm, blue afternoon seemed unreal after the dark and smelly carnage below.

'I then busied myself with removing the dead. I made as I thought sensible arrangements for laying them out in one of the after flats, but had not counted on the strong feelings of the men, who insisted that they should all be taken to the chapel – a tortuous journey through the armoured 'dips'. Sorting the dead out and identifying them occupied most of the dog watches, and they were sewn up in hammocks for burial with the last stitch traditionally put through the dead man's nose. The stout Corporal of Marines who served so cheerfully in the Wardroom bar, volunteered for and personally led this operation throughout the next two days till we returned to harbour.'[1]

In total, *Warspite* suffered 69 casualties: 38 (including one officer) were killed or died of wounds, and 31 men were wounded. The great majority of the casualties were sustained at the 6in and 4in guns. Thirteen dead were removed from the mess deck situated immediately under the bomb burst, while a few men had been injured at outlying positions above the explosions – lookouts and the crews of the pom-pom guns. Ironically it was among the crew of the starboard 6in gun battery that the majority of *Warspite*'s casualties were sustained at Jutland in May 1916. It is also ironic that the bomb hit was the first serious damage from enemy action that *Warspite* had suffered since Jutland, almost twenty-five years to the day.

Shortly after the attack on *Warspite*, Admiral Rawlings turned his squadron westwards to withdraw from the Kithera Channel. With her fires under control

and temporary repairs being effected to her damaged decks, *Warspite* was able to fight off and evade further attacks by high-level bombers, although practically all her starboard AA guns were out of action. Other ships in the squadron were not so lucky; one destroyer and two cruisers being sunk in bombing attacks, while *Valiant* was hit by two bombs but suffered no serious damage. At 1930 *Warspite*'s dead were committed to the deep. She arrived back in Alexandria during the early hours of 24 May (the day *Hood* was sunk by *Bismark*), and immediately landed her wounded. On the following day Cunningham rehoisted his flag in the ship and a memorial service was held for the shipmates who had lost their lives. Admiral Madden remembers that the following week was one of the worst of his life:

'With a working party from *Warspite* I spent the mornings digging out dead sailors and soldiers from one of the badly damaged cruisers, and the afternoons conducting their funerals. We started to do this in full ceremonial manner, but had to change the pall bearers into boiler suits as blood leaked out of the hastily made coffins.'[2]

After examining *Warspite*, dockyard officials declared the damage to be too extensive to be repaired with the limited facilities at Alexandria. Therefore, while temporary repairs were put in hand to make her seaworthy, arrangements were made for *Warspite* to undergo a refit at Bremerton Navy Yard near the American port of Seattle.

A month later when the temporary repairs were completed and *Warspite* was preparing for sea, she suffered more bomb damage. During a heavy air raid on Alexandria on the night of 23/24 June, a 1,000lb bomb fell close off her starboard side and detonated under water abreast 'A' turret. The plating of the upper and lower bulges were flooded for ninety feet. Some splinter damaged occurred, one motor boat was demolished and the occupants of the bridge were showered in water, mud and débris. Admiral Madden recalls that he was in the armoured Conning Tower when the bomb exploded:

'The armoured glass windows were blown in and we were all flung across the place, landing up against the other side of the armoured tower. I suffered some damage to my neck which has left it restricted in movement, but this was the only slight injury I received in the war.'[3]

AMERICAN INTERLUDE

The damage, however, did not seriously affect the seaworthy qualities of the ship, and on 25 June 1941 *Warspite* set sail for Seattle. Her route took her via the Suez Canal and the Red Sea, Colombo (Ceylon), Singapore, Manila (Philippines) and Honolulu, where she arrived on 2 August. There *Warspite*'s crew, long used to the austerities of war, enjoyed comforts and hospitality of a nature which they must have almost forgotten existed. Enormous numbers of visitors came on board, and great interest was taken in inspecting *Warspite*'s damage. On 4 August she sailed for the Canadian west coast port of Esquimault, on Vancouver Island, very near the Canada–United States border. Anchoring there on the 10th, a draft of 284 officers and men were landed for transfer back to Britain. That evening she sailed under American escort for Seattle and, looking rusty and weather-beaten, berthed in the Puget Sound Navy Yard, Bremerton on 11 August. Half her remaining officers and men were transferred home, some 600 remaining aboard to help with the refit. Hundreds of those who did remain were 'adopted' by American families, and enjoyed all the comforts of home in their off-duty periods. Those who were not so lucky were accommodated in a converted ferry berthed in the Navy Yard.

ALTERATIONS TO *WARSPITE* DURING HER REFIT AT BREMERTON, USA, 11 AUGUST– 28 DECEMBER 1941

(Prior to this refit there had been only one wartime alteration to the ship. This was the fitting of one 3.7in howitzer in 1939.)

1. Bridge superstructure modified:
   (a). Signal platform extended aft.
   (b). Admiral's bridge widened and the sides of the foremost section enclosed.
   (c). Pom-pom director sponsons on each side of the compass platform enlarged to accommodate further air defence positions.
2. Type 271 surface search radar installed in a lantern on the foremast starfish platform.
3. Fore topmast re-positioned abaft the mast.
4. Type 281 air search radar fitted on the fore and main topmasts, with the transmitting office sited abaft No. 2 bridge platform on the starboard side.
5. Two Type 284 aerials fitted on the high-angle control system directors, with offices fitted aft in the Admiral's bridge.
7. A Type FM2 medium-frequency direction-finding

Warspite en route to Bremerton, USA, from Alexandria, to effect repairs to the bomb damage suffered off Crete. (Ivor Silcock)

Part of *Warspite*'s ship's company parading through the streets of Bremerton, USA, during the ship's refit in the navy yard. (Stan Lawrance)

aerial installed on the bridge front.

8. Steel screens fitted outboard of the 4in high-angle twin mountings.

9. Davits for 32ft life-cutter removed.

10. Surface look-out positions fitted abreast funnel.

11. Outboard compartments beneath the pom-pom sponsons heightened.

12. The Vickers 0.5in machine-guns removed and replaced by fifteen 20mm Mk IV single Oerlikons in Mk III mountings, fitted in sponsons about the ship.

13. The 3.7in howitzer removed.

While the refit was underway, Captain Fisher toured America and Canada giving lectures on Britain's war effort. Commander Madden who, at 35, was the youngest serving Commander in the navy at that time, was left in command of *Warspite* during the Captain's absence, and at the end of October the Vancouver Board of Trade invited him to give a talk entitled 'War Experiences of *Warspite*'. Tickets, which cost $1, quickly sold out and 1,600 people crowded into the ballroom of the Hotel Vancouver to hear Commander Madden's 'talk', which was wildly reported in the American Press on the following day.

Warspite's refit lasted four months. Apart from the repairs to her bomb damage, the bridge superstructure was modified, surface search, air search and surface gunnery radar sets were fitted; and her anti-aircraft armament was improved by the addition of fifteen 20mm single Oerlikons. A major difficulty of the refit was the necessity of replacing five of *Warspite*'s 15in guns, which were badly worn. This was a complicated affair, for the spare guns had been dispersed in Britain for greater safety, and the special 'gun-seats' used for transporting these enormous 100-ton weapons by rail had to be located. Having brought the guns and the gun-sets together they had then to be moved to a seaport; and to spread the risk the guns were sent across the Atlantic in three different ships. Unshipped at Norfolk, Virginia on the east coast, the Americans provided special railway trucks to transport the guns across the entire breadth of the United States to Bremerton on the west coast. *Warspite* was finally re-commissioned in Puget Sound Navy Yard by Captain Fisher on 28 December 1941. In the meantime the whole face of the war had been transformed by the Japanese attack on Pearl Harbor.

Source Notes
1. The Privately Printed Memoirs of Admiral Sir Charles Madden, Bt, GCB, DL.
(hereinafter cited as Admiral Madden).
2. ibid.
3. ibid.

10.
THE 'OLD LADY'

EASTERN WATERS

Warspite sailed from Bremerton on 7 January 1942. Many new officers and senior ratings had joined the ship during the preceding weeks, but there was still a good leavening of those who had stood her decks during the previous commission. After working-up efficiency in Canadian waters off Vancouver Island, she set off on 22 January escorted by two Canadian destroyers for the long passage to Ceylon, where she was to reinforce the Eastern Fleet. Sailing south-westwards across the vast expanse of the Pacific, she arrived in Sydney, Australia on 20 February, and thence around the southern Australian coastline to Fremantle and then north-west across the Indian Ocean, under the escort of British destroyers from the Eastern Fleet, to Ceylon. Luckily the Japanese were ignorant of her movements and she

Warspite working-up efficiency in Canadian waters after her refit at Bremerton Navy Yard, January 1942. (US Naval Archives)

made the journey unmolested. Exactly two months after leaving Canadian Waters, on 22 March, *Warspite* dropped anchor in Trincomalee harbour. Five days later Captain Fisher was relieved by Captain F. E. P. Hutton, and on that same day, in a tropical downpour, Admiral Sir James Somerville, C-in-C. Eastern Fleet, hoisted his flag in *Warspite*.

Somerville was faced with an impossible situation. Apart from *Warspite*, he had four slow, unmodernized and therefore very vulnerable battleships of the 'R' class, two large and one small carrier and a few cruisers and destroyers. With such a force Somerville knew he would be courting disaster if he became embroiled in a daylight action with the large Japanese fast carrier strike force which intelligence indicated was intending to attack Ceylon. Luckily when the Japanese attack took place on 5 April (Colombo and Trincomalee were bombed by carrier-based aircraft), the majority of the Fleet was in a secret anchorage at Addu Atoll, some 600 miles to the south-west of Ceylon. Only the small carrier

and two cruisers which were in the waters near Ceylon were caught and sunk before the Japanese withdrew. There can be little doubt that if the large Japanese carriers (the same force that attacked Pearl Harbor) had got within striking range of Somerville's fleet, all five battleships would have been sent to the bottom.

Later that April *Warspite* went to Bombay to embark General Wavell, C-in-C. India, and carry him to Ceylon for a conference. Admiral Madden recalls this occasion in his memoirs:

'We visited Bombay where the crews had leave and I had a difficult time controlling the

Eastern Fleet 1942–3. Captain F. E. P Hutton (left) commanded *Warspite* from 22 March 1942 to 1 March 1943; Admiral J. F. Somerville (centre) hoisted his flag in *Warspite* as C-in-C, Eastern Fleet on 27 March 1942; and Commander Sir Charles Madden, *Warspite*'s Executive Officer 1941–2. (Stan Lawrance)

picket boats, trying to land them all at the "Gateway to India Steps", which were small and in shallow water. We embarked General Wavell … He was a quiet man and a great contrast to the effervescent James Somerville, who asked me to look after the General for a morning. He was not easy to entertain, but he visited the mess decks and spoke rather shyly to a number of men. I rather tentatively asked him if he would like to speak to some of the officers about the war on land, of which we knew nothing, and he said he would speak to the whole ship's company if I could arrange it. It was dead calm and we rigged up the quarterdeck with a huge map of the Eastern War Zone and a platform. General Wavell gave the officers and men a clear description of our defeats and the present difficulties and his plans for the future as one would expect to a group of Senior Staff Officers. He was absolutely frank and riveted his audience, who sat in absorbed silence. It was a

masterly performance and deeply impressed us all'[1]

During June 1942, the American naval victory off Midway Island effectively eliminated the threat of the Japanese Fleet moving west of Singapore in strength; with the result that the remaining nine months of *Warspite*'s service in the Eastern Fleet passed without great incident.

In March 1943, exactly one year after *Warspite* arrived in Trincomalee, she was ordered to Home Waters. Docking at Durban en route on March 31, Captain H. A. Packer embarked and relieved Captain Hutton. Packer was no new boy to *Warspite*, having served in her as the first Sub-Lieutenant of her gunroom

Captain Hutton (right) and Commander Sir Charles Madden, aboard *Warspite* in 1942. (Stan Lawrance)

in 1915–17, and as her gunnery officer in 1926. In a letter to his wife Joy, Captain Packer expressed his feelings about his new command:

> 'I am delighted with my new ship – or rather old ship. I have fine officers as far as I can see and a happy ship's company . . . I also have in my ship's company Able Dog Pluto. Born during the siege of Tobruk he came to this ship via a destroyer in which he was in many engagements . . . Pluto is very impressive . . . He is always the first on the scene when the Cable Party is piped to muster before anchoring. Straight away when the Cable Party Bugle sounds he dashes up forward, through the guard rails into the very eyes of the ship and stands there, strong and vigilant, until he is satisfied that the anchor has been cleared away and is all ready for letting go. Then he trots back and joins up with the common sailors until the anchor goes and the cable roars out. Then he trots aft sedately to the quarterdeck to supervise the marines lowering the after-gangway.'[2]

Sailing from Durban at 1300 on 16 April 1943, *Warspite* joined up with a homeward-bound troop convoy off the Cape which she escorted to Home Waters. During the voyage *Warspite*'s steering gear jammed causing her to turn in circles. Captain Packer had been able to observe at first hand the whimsical ways of *Warspite*'s steering gear, when she turned circles under the Germans guns at Jutland. It was as if she were reminding Packer of her gremlin – still present nearly thirty years later! On 10 May she berthed at Prince's Dock, Clydeside, where repairs were undertaken to her capricious steering gear: an attempt to set things right, which was to prove as unsuccessful as all previous attempts.

OPERATION 'HUSKY'

After carrying out bombardment exercises off Scapa during the first two weeks of June, *Warspite* set sail for the Mediterranean to join the great fleet being assembled for Operation 'Husky' – the invasion of Sicily. Embarking Rear-Admiral A. W. la T. Bissett at Gibraltar on 23 June (who hoisted his flag on *Warspite*'s yard as second in command, 'Force H') she arrived in Alexandria on 5 July; the base she had formerly known so well, and from which she had last sailed to America, a severely damaged ship, on 26 June 1941. Zero Hour for the landing of the Allied troops on Sicily was 0245 on 10 July 1943. To lend support to the invasion fleet in case of a sortie by the Italian Fleet, which still had six battleships in commission, *Warspite*, in company with *Valiant* and *Formidable*, put to sea from Alexandria at 1100 on 7 July. At dawn on the 9th they joined up with the other half of 'Force H', based on Oran: the battleships *Nelson* and *Rodney*, the carrier *Indomitable* and a large number of destroyers and cruisers. After dark they

Ammunitioning ship with the huge 15in shells, Kilindini, 1942. (H. Hawkins)

set course so as to arrive off the assault area at daylight on the following morning. Action was sounded off in *Warspite* at 0430, but apart from two air alarms, which proved to be false, nothing happened. While the Allied landings on Sicily were successfully effected, *Warspite* calmly cruised back and forth with the remainder of 'Force H', 60 miles off Cape Passero, on the south-east tip of Sicily. Much to everybody's disappointment the Italian Fleet did not sortie, and Commander Duckworth, serving in *Warspite* at the time, could only record in the following day's entry in his diary: 'Another monotonous day spent patrolling up and down. Sighted Mount Etna at 0515 faintly sixty miles away. We might as well be on a Mediterranean pleasure cruise!'[3]

Apart from putting into Malta for a few hours to refuel on 12 June, *Warspite* continued her uneventful patrol off Cape Passero until the morning of the 16th. In the early hours of that day the carrier *Indomitable* was hit and damaged by a torpedo-bomber, and *Warspite* was detailed off to escort her to Malta. While she was berthed in Grand Harbour, Captain Packer took the

opportunity to visit Admiral Cunningham and vent his frustration that *Warspite* had not been in action during the invasion. 'Well,' said the C-in-C, 'I can't get hold of the Italian Fleet, tie them down and let you have a go at them.' To which Packer answered, 'No, but I'm told Sicily is the biggest island in Europe, and I'm sure we could hit it if told to go and bombard.' Leg-pulling Cunningham said, 'I doubt it. *Warspite* was always the worst gunnery ship in the Mediterranean in peacetime.' To which Packer retorted, 'And in War?' 'She never missed,' said the Admiral. 'She's one of those all right on the night ships.' Within twenty-four hours Packer had his wish. At 0800 on 17 July, *Warspite* and *Valiant* left Grand Harbour for the anchorage of Marsaxlokk on the

Eastern Fleet, 1942. Warspite taking it green over her bows. View taken from the flight deck of the carrier Illustrious. (Stan Lawrance)

Captain H. A. ('Bertie')
Packer onboard *Warspite*.
He commanded the ship
from 31 March to 12
December 1943. (Stan
Lawrance)

south side of Malta. On entering the anchorage *Valiant's* propellers fouled the anti-submarine nets, and she became so entangled that she was held fast. This was unfortunate, for at noon both battleships were ordered to sail at once to bombard the Sicilian town of Catania. The bombardment was to precede an assault by British troops, and timing was of the essence. At *Warspite*'s top speed there was barely enough time to cover the distance to Catania. *Valiant*, therefore, had to be left behind to disentangle herself from the nets.

Age was taking its toll of *Warspite*'s engines; during the first hours of the dash for Catania, her maximum speed averaged only 22½ knots. Captain Packer calculated that at this rate they would be half-an-hour late reaching Catania. It was only by forcing the engines eight revs over the maximum, that an extra knot of speed was obtained and the schedule became possible. Then, contrary as ever, the gremlin in the steering gear made it jamb, and *Warspite* turned a complete circle narrowly missing one of her escorting destroyers. Ten

precious minutes were lost getting the auxiliary steering connected, and it wasn't until 1843 that *Warspite* finally passed through the Open Fire Position. Commander Duckworth, who was on *Warspite*'s bridge, recorded the event in his diary.

'1843 opened fire with five salvoes spread about every minute. Difficult to spot our hits – so much white smoke drifting southwards over the town. Our target is the north of the town, leaving the station and harbour untouched. Guns [the gunnery officer] had the fall of shot all planned out in squares marked out on the map of the town plan. A destroyer on our starboard beam sighted a

Warspite's port side 4in and 6in guns firing during the bombardment of Catania, 17 July 1943. (Ron Martin)

submarine, fired a gun and turned towards us at high speed and dropped eight depth-charges. Some ineffective fire from shore batteries dropped amongst the destroyers to which they replied. Suddenly two Fw 190s roared down our starboard side at sea level machine-gunning like fury. We loosed off all our AA guns at them and scared them off. Our 'Y' [special] intercepts of the enemy radio transmissions heard one Hun pilot say to the other, "Let's go home now"! We ceased fire at 1900 and turned away to the east, the destroyers making a smoke-screen astern of us. Then we turned south.'[4]

Air alarms continued all night, and the AA guns were constantly in action, but by 0700 on the 18th *Warspite* was safely back in Marsaxlokk harbour. To Captain Packer, Admiral Cunningham signalled, 'Operation well executed. When the old lady lifts her skirts she can run.' Henceforth, as a result of this signal *Warspite* became known as the 'Old Lady'; although the

veterans who once stood her decks, and now form the HMS Warspite Association, prefer the title 'Grand Old Lady'.

Sicily was overrun by Allied troops in thirty-eight days. In preparation for the assault on mainland Italy, *Warspite* and *Valiant* steamed into the narrow Straits of Messina on the morning of 2 September, to bombard gun emplacements south of Reggio, on the toe of the Italian boot. *Warspite's* target was a 6in gun battery, and for thirty minutes she fired 15in gun salvoes from a range of only three miles. Her aircraft was catapulted for spotting purposes before the bombardment commenced, and the observer, a South African called Webb, got carried away when the shells began bursting near the target. Instead of the formal spotting reports he blast and splinters from seventeen near misses put all the enemy 6in guns out of action. The bombardment was carried out without reply from the shore batteries, or from air attack. But the 'Old Lady' did not have it so easy on her next operation.

On 8 September Allied troops landed at Salerno in an attempt to capture Naples. *Warspite* in company with the other three battleships and the two carriers of 'Force H' stood out to sea in support. That night they were heavily attacked by German aircraft. Captain Packer takes up the story:

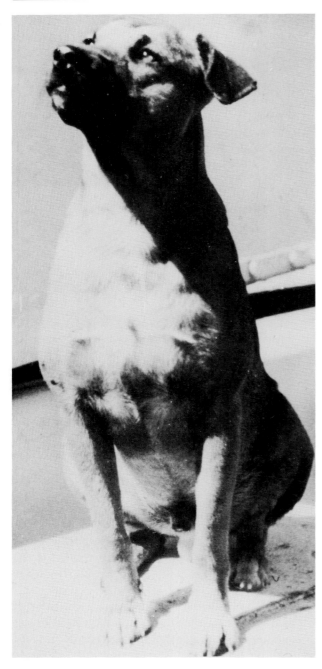

Able Dog Pluto. *Warspite's* mascot, 1942–3. (Ron Martin)

Warspite in Grand Harbour, Malta, 1943. (Ron Martin)

began shouting, 'O.K., O.K., give them all you've got. You're plastering them. Repeat, repeat. Give them the works!' This enthusiasm caused much amusement on *Warspite's* bridge. Although no direct hits were scored,

'At 2130 it started. We were relentlessly attacked by German aircraft with bombs and torpedoes – intensively until midnight and then sporadically. The moonlight is a gift for determined aircraft. They attack up moon. They can see us and we can't see them . . . I had one moment as bad as any this war. I heard, above the sound of our pom-poms, Oerlikons, 4-inch and 6-inch guns, an aircraft roaring in. It skimmed down the safe edge of our barrage about 40° on the port bow . . . I saw this Ju 88 drop his torpedo and I saw it splash, and down the voice pipe to the Quartermaster I roared "Port 35!" I didn't think we had a hope of it missing us and it seemed about a thousand years before I saw the electric repeat from the rudder-head showing that the rudder was 35° to port. The torpedo – they travel forty knots or so – had been dropped about 600 yards away and we were steaming eighteen knots . . . I can honestly say that I was holding on to things waiting for the bump and so was everyone else on the bridge. I steadied up with my course parallel to the track of the

Warspite after 1941 refit at Seattle

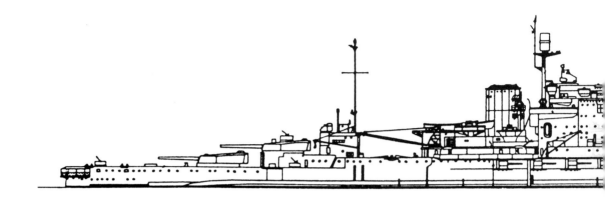

Noël Coward arriving on
board *Warspite* to be
greeted by Captain Packer,
Malta 1943. (Ron Martin)

Warspite in Grand
Harbour, Malta, 1943. (Ron
Martin)

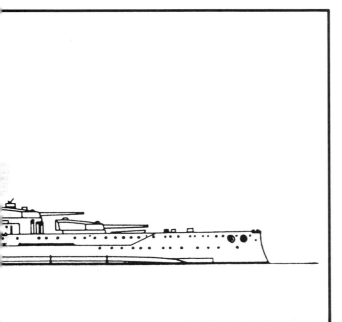

torpedo and it literally missed the stern by feet. The parallel track was so close that I had to climb up on the side of the bridge and look over the edge to see it. Just then Admiral Bisset roared up the voice pipe, "Good God! What are you doing? Can't you see you are broadside on to the moon?" "Look over the port side!" I sang out. "You will see a torpedo track parallel to us. Can you see it?" "Yes I can," he said. "Well done!" So that was O.K.'[5]

On the following day while still off Salerno, *Warspite* received a signal to proceed in company with *Valiant* and an escort of destroyers, to a position off the Algerian port of Bône (now Annaba), where they were to receive the surrender of part of the Italian Fleet on the morning of the 10th. News of the Italian surrender had been received on the previous day. Throughout the remainder of the 9th, and through the night *Warspite* and her consorts proceeded south at twenty-one knots.

At 0835 on the following morning, the dim shapes of the Italian ships were sighted from *Warspite* on her port

bow, 23,000 yards distant, steering north-west at 20 knots. Commander Duckworth lamented that the horizon was so hazy; the first overcast day experienced in three months! The majority of *Warspite*'s crew were at action stations; the gun cages were loaded, with guns trained fore and aft. The remainder of the ship's company, in tropical rig, were 'fell in' on the upper deck, while Able Dog Pluto raced up and down the forecastle barking at the Italian ships. For Commander Duckworth and many other 'old timers', the scene rekindled memories of the surrender of the Kaiser's High Seas Fleet, twenty-five years before.

Leading the Italian line were the two 15in gun battleships *Vittorio Veneto* and *Italia*, followed by five cruisers and nine destroyers. By 1030 *Warspite* and *Valiant* had taken up position ahead of the Italian ships, and were leading them eastwards towards Malta.

Off Bizerta ABC came out in the destroyer *Hambledon* to watch his old enemies go by. As he passed by *Warspite* he signalled, 'Glad to see my old Flagship in her proud and rightful position at the head of

View taken from *Warspite* of the Italian Fleet surrendering, September 1943. An Italian heavy cruiser is leading a battleship of the *Vittorio Veneto* class. (Stan Lawrance)

the line.' To which Captain Packer replied, 'The Old Lady will look after them all right.' Grand Harbour was reached at 0900 on 11 September, and ABC immediately made his famous signal to the Admiralty, 'The Italian Fleet now lies at anchor under the guns of the fortress of Malta.'

At midnight on the 12th, *Warspite* put to sea again to receive the surrender of two more Italian ships, which had sailed from Venice and Taranto. They were sighted from *Warspite* at 0745 off Cape Passaro (Sicily). One of them was *Giulio Cesare*, which *Warspite* had hit with a 15in shell during the action off Calabria in 1940.

A battleship of the *Vittorio Veneto* class viewed from *Warspite*'s forecastle. (Stan Lawrance)

View, taken from *Warspite*'s stern, of *Valiant* and the surrendered Italian Fleet in line ahead en route to Malta. (Stan Lawrance)

Admiral Cunningham addressing the ship's company aboard *Warspite*, after the surrender of the Italian Fleet, Malta 1943. (Stan Lawrance)

DISASTER OFF SALERNO

Early in the evening of 14 September 1943, *Warspite*, in company with *Valiant* and the carrier *Illustrious*, sailed from Malta bound for Britain, where the 'Old Lady' was to undergo a refit. They had not gone far when, at 2000, an urgent signal from Malta, ordered *Warspite* and *Valiant* to proceed at full speed through the Messina Straits to Salerno Bay. The American troops ashore at Salerno had met with stiff German opposition and battleship guns were needed to silence the German heavy artillery which was shelling the beaches from the hills close inland.

Arriving amid the mass of shipping off Salerno at 1045 on the 15th, *Warspite*'s gunnery officer was immediately taken over to the US flagship, to liaise with the Americans as to the particulars of the targets to be engaged. Before fire was opened at 1752, *Warspite*'s Captain of Marines was landed ashore with a wireless set, to observe and report the fall of shot. Moving into a position only half a mile from the beaches, *Warspite*'s 15in guns engaged the German gun positions in the hills and troop and traffic concentrations, with an accuracy that the Captain of Marines reported as 'very satisfactory'. Nineteen of the thirty 15in rounds fired fell exactly on target. According to Commander Duckworth, it was a cloudless, scorching hot day, and the ship's company were dripping with perspiration in their anti-flash and action clothing. Firing ceased at 1900 and *Warspite* stood out to seaward. Sporadic attacks by Fw 190 fighter-bombers occurred during the bombardment, and all through the evening and night *Warspite*'s anti-aircraft guns were in action as she steamed up and down outside the bay.

At dawn on the following morning *Warspite* moved inshore, and came to in the position she had occupied on the previous afternoon. Just after 1300 her great guns again belched forth flame and huge clouds of cordite smoke, and her 1-ton shells screamed over the American troops to explode with great effect among enemy traffic concentrations and on ammunition dumps. Despite the fact that the wireless signals from the Captain of Marines, reporting the fall of shot, was jammed by the Germans, fifteen of the thirty-two rounds she fired fell dead on target, with a further eight falling within 100 yards. From the American flagship Admiral Hewitt signalled to *Warspite*, 'Am grateful for your efficient support which has aided so much the forces ashore.'

Firing ceased at 1400, and at 1410 *Warspite* began steaming at ten knots to a more northerly bombardment position. The ship's company were fallen out from action stations for lunch. Petty Officer (now Lieutenant) Ron Martin recalls:

'In my mess we resumed our game of cards (Solo) and I was dealt thirteen Hearts! (practically a mathematical impossibility) and as I opened my mouth to shout "Royal Abundance Declared!" the alarm bells rang and in my hurry I threw the cards all over the mess. I returned to my action station as rangetaker in the port 4in gun director. At 1425, twelve Fw 190 fighter-bombers attacked the ship, diving out of the sun. These were heavily engaged by the AA guns and driven off, but this attack was only a diversion to mask the presence of German bombers at 20,000 feet. I was standing up in my Director and looking up I saw three black objects approaching downwards at great speed. I looked at them in an almost detached manner – curious is the word! The first one seemed to me to go straight down the funnel!'[6]

The three black objects, as Lieutenant Martin described them, were in fact FX1400 radio-guided armour-piercing bombs, whose fall could be corrected by a radio beam from the aircraft launching them (each bomb weighed 3,000lb, the weight of the explosive charge being 600lb). The first bomb hit the boat deck just abaft the funnel and plunged on down through the port hangar, wardroom galley, stokers' after mess deck, kit locker flat, and No. 4 boiler room before bursting in a double bottom reserve feed tank. The explosion holed the outer bottom over a length of twenty feet and for a width of 7–14 feet; the inner bottom being blown upwards over this area. The shock was very violent, and at first it was thought that *Warspite* had broken her back, and that the mast, which rocked and whipped, would crash to the deck. Casualties were nine killed and fourteen wounded.

The second bomb detonated about six feet off the starboard side abreast No. 5 boiler room at about the level of the lower edge of the bulge. The explosion corrugated the inner and outer bottom plating and holed and distorted the bulge plating. The third bomb hit the sea and exploded off the starboard side aft but did no damage.

As a result of the direct hit and the near miss, Nos. 2, 3, 4 and 6 boiler rooms flooded almost immediately, and No.5 flooded shortly afterwards, but the ship was able to steam slowly on her starboard engines with main

The cone of the radio-controlled bomb which hit *Warspite* off Salerno. The cone was found in No. 4 boiler room. (H. Hawkins)

steering until 1500, when No.1 boiler was contaminated with sea water and all steam failed. Also flooded were the double bottom air spaces, oil fuel tanks, lower bulges and the cable passages adjacent to the machinery spaces. Slow flooding in the engine rooms, No.1 boiler room, two dynamo rooms, shaft passages, and a number of other compartments abreast the machinery spaces was brought under control.

Initially, Captain Packer, unaware of the extent of the damage, attempted to keep under way with the object of reaching the northerly bombardment position. By the time he was made aware that *Warspite* had shipped some 5,000 tons of sea water, the engines had given up the ghost, and she would not steer. Helplessly the 'Old Lady' began drifting around in circles towards an unswept minefield. A minesweeper flashed frantic

November 1943. *Warspite* under the tow of four tugs on her 1,035-mile passage from Malta to Gibraltar, for repairs to be effected to the bomb damage suffered off Salerno. (H. Hawkins)

signals of the danger, but there was nothing Packer could do. Due to the flooding her draught had increased by three feet and she was listing 4° to starboard.

Warspite's position was desperate. There was a likelihood of further air attacks at any moment; her radar was out of action due to the loss of aerials and shock damage, and U-boats were reported to be in the vicinity. In addition, her 15in guns were inoperable due to the loss of hydraulic power. To counterbalance these disabilities, the AA armament was intact, wireless communications had been maintained, two diesel generators were still running and steering was re-established by changing over to mechanical. Good weather prevailed, a flooding boundary had been established, and hatches on the main deck had been shored. Later some of the lower bulge compartments on the port side were counter-flooded to bring the main deck, starboard side, above the waterline. Assistance came in the form of the two US salvage tugs *Hopi* and *Moreno*, which had the crippled battleship in tow (in tandem) by 1700. Stoker James Hartford was on deck when the tugs came alongside and he remembers that, ' . . . one ran into us pretty heavily, and somebody shouted, "don't put any more holes in her, we have enough already".[7] Under tow, *Warspite* began to withdraw from Salerno Bay at four knots. The cruisers *Delhi*, *Euryalus* and *Scylla* had joined up as escorts by 1930 to provide AA cover. Luckily no further air attacks were made that evening or throughout the bright moonlit night.

By 0200, nearly twelve hours after the bomb hit, *Warspite* was still only fifteen miles from Salerno. Below decks conditions were extremely unpleasant. With no fans running to ventilate the ship, the atmosphere became stiflingly hot and fetid. All the lights had failed and in the dim glow from battery lamps, hundreds of men toiled in semi-darkness to control the spread of flooding with pumps and bailing buckets. To make matters worse there was no drinking water, only a strictly limited quantity of lemonade; and nothing but biscuit and corned beef to eat.

'With the dawn [17 September] the situation had worsened,' Captain Packer relates, 'and there was much fatigue for no one had had much stand-off during the past few days, and since the hit everyone was on their feet, either at the guns, hauling in wires, pumping or shoring up. Men were beginning to sit down and rest and drop off to sleep as they sat. But they were all marvellously cheerful, willing and fatalistic . . . I see them naked on the deck washing each other from buckets of salt water dipped over the side. Bailing out compartments with buckets in this heat is hard work. About 200 men are at it all the time . . . '[8]

The tugs *Nimble* and *Oriana* joined the tow at 1015, and although *Warspite*'s list to starboard had increased to 4½°, and her draught had increased by another two feet, the speed of the tow increased to six knots. Early that evening the salvage ship *Salvedor* and the US tug *Naragannset* took up position on either beam, to help the 'Old Lady' navigate the difficult passage through the narrow Messina Straits. It proved to be a nightmare. She became completely unmanageable in the treacherous rip-tides and whirlpools of the Straits. From midnight until 0500 on the 18th, she was carried along by the tide

sideways, with all tow lines parted except one. Off Reggio the tide turned and began to carry *Warspite* back up the Straits. It was only by positioning a tug port and starboard aft to straighten her up, that the lead tugs could get some way on the ship. The rest of the passage passed without incident, and finally, with her dead committed to the deep, her weary sailors lined up on deck, and her band playing, the defiant 'Old Lady' entered Grand Harbour at 0800 on Sunday, 19 September 1943.

HOMEWARD BOUND

On 12 October, while temporary repairs were under way, Captain Packer left the ship to join the staff of the C-in-C Mediterranean in Algiers. With no immediate replacement available, *Warspite*'s executive Officer, Commander the Hon. D. Edwards, assumed temporary command. Dry docking in Gibraltar was necessary to repair the damaged hull, so at 0700 on Monday, 1 November 1943, under the tow of four ocean rescue tugs and an escort of four destroyers, the 'Old Lady' set off on the 1,035-mile journey, with more than 3,000 tons of sea water still in her flooded compartments. For the first twenty-four hours she was able to assist the tow by steaming on one shaft at seven knots. But when the few operational boilers packed in, the speed of the tow dropped to five knots. She eventually reached Gibraltar at 0800 on 8 November, and four days later went into dry dock. When the flooded compartments were pumped dry later that day, the bodies of three casualties from the bombing were found: one in No. 3 boiler room and two in No. 4.

Warspite remained at Gibraltar for four months. During this period there occurred what veterans of the ship refer to as the 'fish incident'. Lieutenant Ron Martin explains what happened:

'*Warspite* was *always* a happy ship. The ship's company were cheerful, efficient and well-behaved. It was unusual to say the least for any protests or misbehaviour to occur. Now it was usual for the ship's company to have a cold supper on Sundays only, to give the long-suffering cooks a break after Sunday dinner. On this particular occasion the Cooks of Messes went to collect supper from the galley, and returned with large roasting tins full of herrings in tomato sauce – an unpalatable, unpopular dish by any standards. On this occasion it was all rotten and smelt to high heaven! To a man all this food was returned to the galley and left outside piled up in the tins. We were issued with cheese and pickles in lieu. However, two or three especially rebellious crew members took several tins to the Paymaster Commander's cabin (he was responsible for the purchase of ship's victuals) whilst he was having supper in the wardroom, and smothered his cabin, bunk, uniform lockers, everything, with this muck, without being spotted! Shore leave was stopped whilst investigations began, and I'm afraid I have no recollection of the outcome except that herrings in tomato sauce was never served up again!'[9]

When the 'Old Lady' sailed from Gibraltar for Home Waters at 0600 on Thursday, 9 March 1944, her repairs were far from complete. Only two of her 15in gun mountings had been made serviceable and No. 4 boiler room remained non-operational: apart from placing a caisson over the hole in the double bottom, nothing had been done to repair this totally wrecked boiler room, under which the glider bomb had exploded.

In the Straits of Gibraltar *Warspite* joined a homeward-bound convoy, carrying 67,676 troops. 'A wonderful sight,' according to Commander Duckworth. 'Twenty-four monster liners of every company. Fascinating to watch, like a Spithead Review under way.' On clearing the Straits the 'Old Lady' left the Mediterranean for the very last time. The Commodore of the troop convoy, unaware of the true condition of *Warspite*, was obviously delighted to have the apparent protection of a battleship. In fact it was more a case of the convoy escorting *Warspite*!

After parting company with the convoy off the Clyde, the 'Old Lady' sailed around the north of Scotland to Rosyth where she dropped anchor at 2330 on 16 March. Two days later she was dry-docked for further repairs, and on the same day Captain M. H. A. Kelsey assumed command.

D-DAY

Warspite had been recalled to Home Waters because she was required to be part of the fleet of ships which would bombard the Normandy beach-head during the Allied invasion of Europe. In the short time available, Rosyth dockyard could not complete all the extensive repairs required, with the result that when *Warspite* put to sea on 27 April, one of the 15in gun mountings ('X' turret) remained non-operational and would be so for the rest of her career. Number 4 boiler room was also unserviceable; despite this, and the large caisson stuck over the hole in her bottom, the 'Old Lady' managed a maximum speed of 21 knots. For the remainder of April and the early part of May she carried out bombardment practices in Scottish waters. On 12 May she berthed in the Clyde off Greenock amidst a mass of shipping that was to take part in the D-Day invasion.

Warspite sailed from the Clyde in company with the 2nd Cruiser Squadron during the evening of 4 June 1944. Lieutenant Ron Martin recalls:

'On 5 June we were off the Eddystone lighthouse, where we embarked several Press correspondents, a Russian Admiral and General and a fat Chinese naval officer! That same evening we arrived south of the Isle of Wight to an amazing sight. Over 6,000 vessels of all shapes and sizes were steaming up and down in well-ordered confusion! We could see the poor soldiers in their landing craft being seasick, poor devils. As dusk fell we lined up behind forty minesweepers and crept slowly towards the French coast at action stations. The Chaplin read prayers over the tannoy.'[10]

Warspite, with the battleship *Ramillies*, the 15in gun monitor *Roberts*, five cruisers and fifteen destroyers, were allocated to cover 'Sword Beach', the most easterly section of the invasion beach-head, from a position eleven miles west of Le Havre. The 'director layer' in the after gun director, E. Wilson, recalls that during the last minutes of the approach:

'The hydraulic pipes in the Director sprang a leak as it was turning. As the position was cramped, there was not much room for myself and the ordnance artificer who came to repair the pipe, so I sat on top of the director and had a grandstand view of the gliders going in overhead and the general assembly of ships off the beaches. Suddenly I heard a 'plop' in the sea quite near, and I assumed someone had thrown something over the side. Seconds later there was a horrible whine and a shell landed in the sea alongside. I was down and under the cover of the Director [10in armour plating], regardless of space, in seconds!'[11]

The shells landing close to *Warspite* were fired by a German battery at Bénerville-sur-Mer. *Warspite* successfully 'discouraged' them with three salvoes fired

'Blind' at 0530. At 0545 two salvoes were fired at a battery at Villerville without aircraft spotting, and a few minutes later, enemy torpedo-boats and patrol craft were observed to be approaching from Le Havre. At 0609 they were engaged and at 0612 one of the torpedo-boats was hit by a 15in high-explosive shell abreast the after end of her engine room. The target turned sharply to starboard, heeled and sank rapidly by the stern with her bows sticking out of the water. Her consorts retired to Le Havre.

At 0630 Villerville was engaged and one of the batteries was knocked out with three direct hits. At 0738 fire was opened on Gonneville-sur-Mer, but visibility was poor and the spotting aircraft had its tail shot away. At 0755 Villerville was re-engaged; this battery replied with anti-personnel shells which cut some of *Warspite*'s exposed electric leads. The ship shifted her position at 0821. When she resumed the bombardment of Villerville at 0901 visibility was down to 200 yards in the target area.

Gliders passing above *Warspite* and *Ramillies*, as the two battleships approach their bombardment position on D-Day, 6 June 1944. (Ron Martin)

At 0952 fire was shifted to Bénerville, which was again engaged at 1219 and 1309, while between 1440 and 1503 the ship was called upon to deal with enemy transport and scored four direct hits on vehicles. Lieutenant Ron Martin recalls that:

'During this period it was heartbreaking to see dead bodies of Allied troops drifting past the ship. The only light relief was that the fat Chinese naval officer, who had been allocated to my 4-inch gun Director, ate all the Director crews' action rations himself! While on the bridge Captain Kelsey took one bite of his Cornish pastie and said to the Paymaster Commander, "This is wholesome." before throwing it overboard!'[12]

Warspite's port 4in gun crew, D-Day, 1944. Note the empty shell-cases. (Ron Martin)

At 1520 the 'Old Lady' turned her guns on German Headquarters and a 4in gun battery which was knocked out. Her principal target, however, was Villerville, at which, in bombardments between 1112 and 1200, 1551 and 1621, and 1710 and 1814, she fired seventy-three rounds, knocking out guns as the enemy brought them up to take the place of those already destroyed. Nine direct hits on guns were scored and fifty salvoes fell within 100 yards of their targets.

By the end of D-Day 133,000 men, more than 6,000 vehicles and 4,000 tons of stores and ammunition had been landed over the beaches in the British sector, and the leading troops were already six to eight miles inland. *Warspite* withdrew to seaward during the hours of darkness, anchoring in eight fathoms about four miles off shore.

Next day the 'Old Lady' engaged various targets of opportunity such as transports at a cross-roads, guns, an anti-aircraft battery in which four out of five guns were knocked out, and an area strong-point which was destroyed with thirteen out of twenty rounds fired Blind (i.e., without air or forward observer spotting). In the afternoon Bénerville was set on fire with eight salvoes.

By this time *Warspite* had fired a total of 314 15in shells (181 high-explosive and 133 armour-piercing). To replenish with ammunition and make good damage caused by the blast of her own guns, she sailed for Portsmouth. Arriving at Spithead at 0330 on 18 June, she moved up harbour that afternoon, and the ship's company worked all that evening and night taking on ammunition.

While re-crossing the Channel on the 9th, she was ordered to the western sector of the Normandy beaches, as the American bombarding ships were running out of ammunition. The target was enemy guns, which were engaged between 1627 and 1850, under direction of USS

Warspite bombarding the Normandy beach-head, D-Day, 1944. (Ron Martin)

▶

Hoisting a battle ensign in *Warspite* on the morning of D-Day. (Stan Lawrance)

Warspite bombarding the Normandy beach-head, D-Day. (Stan Lawrance)

Warspite's 'A' and 'B' turrets
prepare to open fire on
D-Day. (Stan Lawrance)

Quincy. These guns were mounted on a narrow neck of the foreshore, with a marshy lagoon behind them, and were thus extremely difficult targets. The fall of shot was practically invisible from *Warspite*, but ninety-six rounds were fired with results which won a complimentary signal from the American Commander.

On 11 June *Warspite* switched back to the eastern sector, taking up a bombarding position off 'Gold Beach'. Her target was a concentration of German tanks in a wood at Hottot-les-Bagues, which she engaged between 1520 and 1530. Liaison between the ship and the spotter aircraft was so good and accurate that Captain Kelsey gave an order unique in Royal Navy

gunnery: 'Fifty rounds 15-inch rapid fire.'! Due to natural and increasing human error of the big guns following pointers quickly, it had the effect of the shells chasing the German tanks out of the woods into the open. Another troop concentration was engaged between 1555 and 1606. On both occasions the General commanding 50th Division sent congratulations on *Warspite*'s good shooting.

The D-Day landings seen from *Warspite*. (Stan Lawrance)

A German 9in gun emplacement; one of *Warspite*'s targets on D-Day. (Stan Lawrance)

Warspite firing her main armament on D-Day. (Stan Lawrance)

Warspite off Normandy, 7 June 1944. View taken from *Ramillies*. (Stan Lawrance)

That night she returned to Portsmouth to refuel and embark still more ammunition. As *Warspite*'s guns were badly worn, however, it was decided to send her to Rosyth where the nearest replacements were located.

MINED!

Warspite, accompanied by the destroyers *Southdown* and *Holmes*, sailed from Portsmouth at 2200 on 12 June, bound for Rosyth, east about. She was the first capital ship to pass through the Straits of Dover since the German battlecruisers *Scharnhorst* and *Gneisenau* broke home from Brest in February 1942. Heavy gun batteries on the French coast opposite Dover opened

fire as she passed, but the RAF dropped 'window' to disrupt the German radar and the 'Old Lady' ran the gauntlet unscathed. But once again her luck was running out.

At 0748 on 13 June when *Warspite* was about 28 miles east of Harwich, she ran over an acoustic or pressure-operated mine, containing a charge of 1,500lb of aluminized hexanite. The mine detonated off the port side abreast 'Y' turret. Eye-witnesses reported an area of violently disturbed water close to the ship's side, which was thrown up generally to upper deck level, and that there was a thin column in the centre rising some distance above this level. They estimated that the centre

of the explosion was about twenty feet from the port side. When the mine detonated, *Warspite* was steaming at sixteen knots. The ship was very severely shaken by the explosion which jammed her rudder to starboard and after making a tight turn she came to a standstill 140° off her course. Extensive flooding of the after portion of the lower bulge compartments caused the ship to list 3½° to port within five minutes. The list later increased to a maximum of 4½°. There was also leakage into a few double-bottom and hold compartments. In all she shipped 690 tons of sea water.

The damage to the hull was extensive. The port bulge plating was corrugated over a length of 150 feet abreast the engine and after magazine compartments: flooding occurred through a number of ruptures and strained seams. The outer bottom in the area below the damage to the port bulge was corrugated, and the bulge structure between 'X' and 'Y' turrets was forced inboard to a maximum of two feet. Minor buckling also occurred over 90 feet of the starboard bulge plating and there was also slight damage to the inner bottom.

Both main and auxiliary machinery were extensively damaged by shock. The port outer shaft seized up solid and several plummer-blocks on the port inner shaft were fractured. The mounting of the port and starboard inner turbines were also fractured, and the

Warspite being fitted with a new outfit of 15in guns, Rosyth, July 1944.
(H. Hawkins)

gearing and thrust block of the port inner turbine were put out of action.

Immediately after the explosion, all the radar sets were completely out of operation. The majority of failures were due to smashed valves, meters or broken leads, in addition to the loss of power. The Type 281 transmitter was severely damaged and its aerial mast was bent.

The main machinery was shut down for half-an-hour for examination. During this period the list to port was corrected by counter-flooding and the transference of oil fuel from the port to starboard tanks. When the machinery was restarted neither the port outer nor the port inner shafts could be turned. At 0835, however, *Warspite* was able to proceed, using her starboard shafts only. The maximum speed attained was 10 knots and she arrived at Rosyth, drawing forty-two feet aft, at about 2130 on 14 June. The battleships *Anson* and *Howe* and other warships lying below Forth Bridge, all 'cleared lower deck' to cheer the battered 'Old Lady' as she slowly passed by.

Warspite was dry docked for two months for partial repairs to be carried out, sufficient to allow her to be used operationally as a bombardment ship. A new outfit of 15in guns was also fitted. Normally the distorted propeller shafts would have been drawn out and straightened in machine-shops. But as this was a lengthy process repairs were attempted *in situ*. The result was that the port outer shaft remained seized up, while the two inner shafts were operational but remained far from perfect. Only the undamaged starboard outer shaft was running true. During trials carried out in the second week of August, the 'Old Lady' could only manage a maximum speed of 15.5 knots with her three shafts.

THE BOMBARDMENT OF BREST

On 24 August 1944 *Warspite* went back to war with one 15in turret, one shaft and one boiler room out of action, plus a very battered hull and numerous other defects. During August 1944, the Americans were investing a powerful force of 40,000 German troops which was cut off and squeezed up in the tip of the Brest peninsula. The lynch-pin of their defences was a girdle of old French forts dating from the time of Louis XVI (1774–93) and casemates armed with heavy guns. In the confined space of the peninsula the Americans could not take these fortifications, which commanded all land approaches, except at a heavy cost in casualties. *Warspite*,

therefore, was called upon to silence them with her 15in guns. At 0815 on 25 August, the 'Old Lady', with five escorting destroyers (designated 'Force 112'), sailed from Plymouth bound for Brest. She reached her bombarding position a few miles off the northern shore of the peninsula at 1500 the same day. The targets were about fifteen miles to the south, hidden from sight by hills. As *Warspite* would be firing Blind, Spitfires were detailed to act as spotters. Fire was opened at 1507. Carl Olsson, a reporter for the *Illustrated*, who was on the ship's compass platform, vividly describes the opening of the bombardment:

'The Brest coastline showed up strangely placid and serene as we came up to the firing point. Through a rangefire telescope I watched a farmer with two horses carting corn sheaves in an upland field. A mile or two away near a lighthouse there was a solitary angler in a boat, his back to us intent on his lines and a pleasant afternoon's fishing. It was as unwarlike a scene as you can imagine, and so it was a sudden shock when the action bells went near my ear, and the loudspeaker ordered us all to put on our anti-flash hoods, gauntlets and lifebelts. The compass platform where I stood was now packed with the ship's executive officers, muffled to the eyes in anti-flash gear. In his forward corner sat the captain in his chair, watching the coastline through glasses and giving brief orders as we slowed to our position in the tide drift. In the wings of the platform the aircraft lookouts were ceaselessly watching the sky, and at the stern end sat an Army gunner captain, the bombardment liaison officer, in front of his charts and earphones. He was in direct touch with the far-off Spitfires which would spot for us, and with the Army control ashore. Telephones buzzed on the platform, orders were given and the great 15-inch turrets swung slowly to starboard. The gun muzzles probed the sky. I made my way to the portside, putting a steel housing between myself and the expected blast. Salvo firing from the 15-inch guns was a new experience for me and when it came, a few seconds after a double ring on the firing gong, the appalling blast in spite of the steel partition behind my back, sent me reeling across the deck. When I had picked myself up after the first blast, I had another look through the rangefinder telescope. The fisherman was madly windmilling his oars towards the shore. His boat was practically airborne. Relentlessly the double "ting-ting" of the fire gong went on. At varying moments later, "Wham!" as salvo after salvo went on its way.'[13]

The control station ashore gave five targets to be engaged; fifty rounds to be fired on each in thirty minutes. Firing to be completed in 2½ hours, before the assault by the attacking troops commenced.

TARGET 1:

Keringar 11in gun battery in turrets (called *Graf Spee* by the Germans). Target was found with four ranging salvoes. Spotting aircraft reported near misses on all gun turrets. Fifty-seven rounds expended.

TARGET 2:

Les Rospects 6in battery in casements. Range 29,000 yards. Eight salvoes were fired before firing for effect. All salvoes after the fifth were in the target area. Twenty-two salvoes were fired – 47 rounds expended.

TARGET 3:

Toulbroch Fort, including two batteries running 1,000 yards to the west. Range 32,200 yards. Target was found with two salvoes. Eleven salvoes were fired – 32 rounds expended.

TARGET 4:

Minou Fort. Range 31,800 yards. Target was found in three salvoes. Several salvoes were not seen owing to smoke and dust over target area. Eighteen salvoes were fired – 51 rounds expended.

TARGET 5:

Montbarey Fort. Range 32,000 yards. Target was found in four salvoes – 26 rounds expended.

German gun emplacements in the old French forts surrounding Brest, which were bombarded by *Warspite*: 1, Toulbroc'h; 2, Les Rospects; 3, Keringar. (Charles Le Goasguen)

▼1

▲ 2   ▼ 3

It was while *Warspite* was engaging Montbarey Fort, that the control station ashore made the signal at 1745, 'Afraid your time is up, cease fire.' Simultaneously with the receipt of this signal, came the first reply by the enemy. Huge fountains of sea-water rose near *Warspite* from 11in shells falling short, fired by the Keringar battery. Ten salvoes were fired at *Warspite*, three of which fell so close on the starboard bow and beam, that splinters from the shells hit the funnel, motor-cutter and starboard HA Director. With her task completed *Warspite* turned away northwards at fifteen knots, while the destroyer *Fame* laid a smoke-screen.

In total *Warspite* had fired 213 high-explosive and armour-piercing shells. Results were disappointing. Although one of the forts and a few of the batteries were silenced, others survived practically intact, and were able to put up a stiff resistance to the attacking troops.

THE BOMBARDMENT OF LE HAVRE

Early on the morning of 10 September 1944, *Warspite*, in company with the destroyer *Ulysses* and HM tug *Growler*, sailed from Portsmouth bound for a bombarding position thirteen miles west of Cap Le Havre, which she reached at 0945. The object of the bombardment was to assist the British First Corps's assault on Le Havre by silencing enemy gun batteries. Spotting was by aircraft.

Four out of five allotted targets, and two others indicated by aircraft, were engaged at the extreme range of 32,000 yards. In all *Warspite* expended 304 15in shells.

Captain M. H. A. Kelsey, who commanded *Warspite* from 18 March until 29 August 1944 and from 11 September until 30 December 1944. (Stan Lawrance)

Able Cat Pinnochio,
Warspite's mascot,
1943–4. (Stan Lawrance)

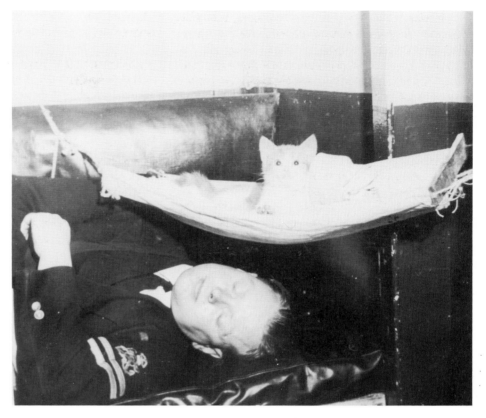

The first of these targets, engaged at 1005, consisted of three 170mm (6.7in) guns in casements. Despite two direct hits and a third in the mouth of one of the emplacements, two of these guns were still firing at *Warspite* when the ship withdrew; 183 rounds were expended at this target.

The second target was a battery of four guns. Fire commenced at 1134. Aircraft reported that most of the fifty rounds expended landed in the target area. A fierce fire, thought to be an ammunition dump, resulted.

Fire on the third target opened at 1236, but fire was checked after only three salvoes, when the spotting aircraft reported that no guns could be seen in the target area.

Two targets of opportunity, indicated by the aircraft, were also engaged, commencing at 1253. One direct hit and several near misses, out of 36 rounds, were scored on a battery of six guns, and two direct hits, out of ten rounds, silenced a battery of four guns.

The fourth target, a battery of four guns, was engaged on two occasions at 1331 and 1554; 22 rounds were expended but no observable results were reported.

OPERATION 'INFATUATE'

Nearly eight weeks after the bombardment of Le Havre, the 'Old Lady' set off from Portsmouth for what was to be her last wartime operation. Calling at Deal on 30 October, she set out on the following morning, in company with the monitors *Erebus* and *Roberts*, for the mouth of the River Scheldt. Her function was to bombard the German defences during Operation 'Infatuate' – the assault on the Dutch island of Walcheren.

At 0800 on 1 November 1944 *Warspite* stopped in her bombarding position ten miles west of the West Kapelle lighthouse. At first, due to bad weather, no air spotting was available, but fire was opened soon after 0815 in direct shooting at the considerably dispersed guns of the enemy batteries. Later, spotting aircraft arrived and extremely satisfactory results were obtained; out of 21 salvoes fired by *Warspite*, fifteen were hits and the targets were reported to have been wrecked. At 1613 the ship scored hits with eight salvoes in succession on the 'Domburg' battery of 8.7in guns.

During the course of the day the 'Old Lady' fired 353 15in shells. When fire was checked at 1723, her huge guns fell silent forever. Never again would she engage the enemy. At 1730 she withdrew so as to have the advantage of the high tide for crossing the South Walls Bank, and returned to Deal.

Later *Warspite* returned to Portsmouth where, on 1 February 1945, the Admiralty ordered her to be paid off into reserve. She was thirty years old, her armament and machinery were badly worn, and there was so much partially repaired damage, that to make her fit for further service would have necessitated a long and costly refit.

DEFIANT TO THE END

During the second week of February 1945, the 'Old Lady' was moored at the Reserve Fleet buoy off the Mother Bank, Spithead. There she remained, with a skeleton crew, until August 1946, when, as a result of the decision to scrap the ship, she was towed into Portsmouth harbour to be stripped of all useful fittings, including her eight 15in guns.

When it became public knowlege that *Warspite* was destined for the scrapyard, there was a call for what

was the most famous of all British battleships to be saved and preserved as a museum ship. Unfortunately the protests went unheeded.

The process of preparing her for the ship-breakers lasted seven months. Finally, on 12 March 1947, the gutted remains of the 'Old Lady' were towed out of harbour to Spithead. There Metal Industries Ltd., who had purchased the hull for scrap, took her over. In April she left under tow of the tugs *Bustler* and *Mytinda III*, bound for Faslane in the Gareloch, Clyde. On board were only eight (civilian) crew members. On the way down the Channel she ran into a fierce gale. At 1930 on Monday, 20 April, as *Warspite* pitched and rolled fifteen miles off Land's End in 70-mile-an-hour winds, one of

Warspite's No. 2 boiler room. This photograph was taken while the ship was under way to bombard Brest. (H. Hawkins)

Breech of one of *Warspite*'s 15in guns. (H. Hawkins)

Reduced to a hulk, her great guns removed from the turrets, *Warspite*, under the tow of tugs, begins her last voyage from Spithead bound for the breaker's yard, April 1947. (Stan Lawrance)

her turrets worked loose and the 5in steel hawser connecting her to *Bustler* snapped. To make matters worse *Warspite* began shipping water as her forecastle rose and plunged into the heaving seas. Still linked to *Mytinda III*, the 'Old Lady' drifted miles off course, while the crew of *Bustler* struggled to get a new line attached. They succeeded on the following afternoon. With both tugs pitching so steeply that at times their screws came out of the water, they managed to tow *Warspite* into Mount's Bay off Penzance, where, on Tuesday night, the battleship dropped anchor three miles off shore. Such was the fury of the gale that, despite being in the lee of the land, at 1630 on 23 April, *Warspite* broke anchor and was carried pitching and rolling eastwards across Mount's Bay where she ran aground on the Mountamopus Ledge. At high tide she floated clear, only to be carried a further 500 yards to the eastward on to the rocks of Prussia Cove. There, with her bows stove in and her forward compartments flooded, she stuck fast, down by the bows and listing to port.

At 1730 the Penlee lifeboat put out into the heaving seas to rescue the eight men still on board the 'Old Lady'. Coxswain Edwin Madron took the lifeboat to the windward of her, turned, and with the gale behind, approached the battleship's bows. *Warspite*'s forecastle was awash and the seas were breaking around 'B' turret. The waves were thirty feet high. Her starboard side was close to the shore. Off her port side, and at her stern, the coxswain could see rocks appearing and disappearing in the breaking seas. But between the battleship and the rocks was a channel about forty yards wide. Down this channel coxswain Madron took the lifeboat, with the rocks on his starboard hand and right ahead. In normal circumstances, approaching from windward, he could have anchored, veered down on his cable, fired a line and hauled the men into the lifeboat by breeches-buoy, but in the narrow channel he dared not attempt it, for fear of yawing on to the rocks. His only alternative was to try and get alongside. Madron chose a spot at the far end of the quarterdeck, turned in the narrow channel, and brought the lifeboat near the battleship, head to the wind. In a momentary lull, he threw two veering lines on board *Warspite*. Then began the perilous task of holding the lifeboat close enough for the men to jump into her. The rise and fall of the seas was so great that at times the lifeboat's crew were looking down on the battleship's deck, and next moment the boat was in grave danger of being smashed against the bulge near the battleship's water-line.

Warspite aground in Prussia Cove. (E. Wilson)

Her bows awash, *Warspite* lies grounded on the rocks of Prussia Cove; 23 April 1947. (Stan Lawrance)

Watching each sea, the coxswain went full speed ahead to meet it as it broke round 'B' turret, and then, as it passed him went full-speed astern again. For thirty-five minutes he was manoeuvring in this way, and as the lifeboat swung close enough to the battleship, he would call on the men to jump one by one. Seven of them jumped as soon as they were called, but the eighth took a long time before he dared risk it. Throughout those thirty-five dangerous minutes two mechanics were kneeling under the lifeboat's canopy in front of their controls. They could see nothing and one error on their part in carrying out the coxswain's stream of orders would have meant disaster for the lifeboat. In this way all eight men were rescued and landed at Newlyn harbour that evening.

The damage to *Warspite*'s hull was so extensive that it was impossible to refloat her. Contrary as ever, the 'Old Lady' made sure she had the last word! She did not escape the scrapmen, however. The wreck was subsequently purchased by the Wolverhampton Metal Co. Ltd., and she was scrapped in her position on the rocks of Prussia Cove, a process that took until 1956 to complete.

For her service, which spanned from Jutland in 1916 to Walcheren in 1944, *Warspite* lays claim to have given the greatest value for money of any battleship ever put afloat. I will let Lieutenant Ron Martin, Hon. Secretary of the H.M.S. Warspite Association, write her requiem:

> 'I joined *Warspite* in 1942 in Mombasa, transferring from the *Royal Sovereign* in a large crew swop. I left the worst ship I ever served in to the best! It was like a breath of fresh air. Many people cannot understand the affection this magnificent ship generated in all who had the privilege to serve in her. By some strange quirk of fate *Warspite* seemed to attract the finest crews – both officers and men. She was an efficient and happy ship – and that says it all!'

Source Notes

1. Admiral Madden.
2. Joy Packer. *Deep As The Sea*, pp. 254–8. Hereinafter cited as Packer.
3. The Diary of Captain A. D. Duckworth (IWM). Hereinafter cited as Duckworth.
4. ibid.
5. Packer.
6. Lieutenant R. Martin (HMS Warspite Association).
7. James Hartford (HMS Warspite Association).
8. Packer.
9. Lieutenant R. Martin.
10. ibid.
11. E. Wilson. (HMS Warspite Association).
12. Lieutenant R. Martin.
13. *Illustrated*, September 1944.

The remains of the 'Old Lady' being broken up in Prussia Cove, April 1949, two years after she grounded. (MPL)

All that remained of the hull by October 1952. The remains had been beached on Marazion Sands. (MPL)

Parade by veterans of the 'Old Lady', who now form the HMS Warspite Association, at Montbarey Fort, Brest, 1988. The fort was one of *Warspite*'s targets during the bombardment of Brest. (Ron Martin)

Visit by the HMS Warspite Association to Fort Keringar, Brest, 1988. The guns of Keringar were the only ones to return fire at *Warspite* during the bombardment. (Ron Martin)

The dedication of the standard of the HMS Warspite Association by the Chaplain of the Fleet, May 1988. (Ron Martin)

SOURCES

Author's correspondence and interviews with the patron and members of the HMS *Warspite* Association: The Patron Admiral Sir Charles Madden, Bt, GCB, DL; Lieutenant-Commander F.C. Rice, RN; Lieutenant R. C. Martin, RN; Lieutenant D. W. Toms, RN; Tom Brown; R. Burrows; P. S. Cooper; R. E. Gilpin; H. Hawkins; J. P. Hartford; V. Holdsworth; L. A. Jesset; J. H. Kingdon; S. F. Lawrance; J. Nelson; G. J. Owen; E. Rose; I. Silcock; E. S. Wilson; Mrs. A. P. Morrow and Mrs. M. Schuttleworth.

For information and photographs of the fortifications at Brest, I am indebted to Capitaine de Frégate Jacques Gury and Colonel Charles Le Goasguen.

Unpublished Admiralty manuscript sources in the Public Record Office, Kew:
1. Naval Staff History of the Second World War. Battle Summaries:
   Adm 234/319. Naval Operations of the Battle for Crete.
   Adm 234/323. The Action off Calabria.
   Adm 186/795. The Battle off Cape Matapan.
   Adm 186/797. The Bombardment of Bardia and Tripoli.
   Adm 186/798. Naval Operations of the Campaign in Norway.
2. Admiralty War History, Cases and Papers:
   Adm 199/445. Naval Operations in the Mediterranean, 1940–2.
   Adm 199/476. The Second Battle of Narvik.
   Adm 199/1396. Invasion of Normandy: British Assault Area War Diary.
   Adm 199/1397. Invasion of Normandy: Allied Naval Commander War Diary.
3. Director of Naval Construction Damage Reports:
   Adm 267/54. Bomb Damage to *Warspite* (Salerno).
   Adm 267/63. Mine Damage to *Warspite* (1944).
   Adm 267/65. Bomb Damage to *Warspite* (Crete).

Unpublished archive material in the Department of Documents, Imperial War Museum:
Papers of Commander J. Bostock, DSC, RN.
Papers of Dr. G. H. Bickmore.
Diary of Commander A. H. Ashworth, RN.
Papers of John Chessman.
Diary of Commander H. C. Burton, RN.
Papers of Commander Lycett Gardner, RN.
Diary of Surgeon Captain G. E. D. Ellis, RN.
Papers of Admiral E. H. Philpotts.
Papers of Commander N. S. Griffiths, RN.
Papers of Commander P. E. Vaux, RN.
Diary of Captain A. D. Duckworth, RN.
Midshipman's log of D. Binney.
Papers of Vice-Admiral Sir Geoffrey Barnard.

Published Sources:
Cunningham, Viscount. *A Sailor's Odyssey*, Hutchinson, 1951.
Macintyre, Captain D. *Narvik*, Evans Bros., 1959.
Marder, A. J. *From The Dreadnought To Scapa Flow*, vol. 3, Oxford, 1978.
Packer, J. *Deep As The Sea*, Eyre Methuen Ltd., 1976.
Raven, A., and Roberts, J. *Queen Elizabeth Class Battleships*, Bivouac Books Ltd., 1975.
Roskill, Captain S. W. *H.M.S. Warspite*, Collins, 1957.

APPENDIXES

WARTIME ALTERATIONS TO *WARSPITE* POST-BREMERTON REFIT

1942

1. A further four 20mm Mk IV single Oerlikons fitted (a total of 19 being carried).
2. Type 271 surface search radar replaced by a Type 273.
3. Original Wasteney-Smith sheet anchors replaced by Byers anchors.

1943

1. A further sixteen 20mm Mk IV single Oerlikons fitted (a total of 35 being carried).
2. Aircraft catapults and associate equipment removed.

Aircraft hangars converted to other uses including employment as cinemas. Catapult deck used for boat stowage.

1944

1. Four 20mm single Oerlikons removed. Replaced by four 20mm Mk IV twin Oerlikons in Mk IV mountings (31 single and 4 twin Oerlikons being carried).
2. All 6in guns removed and casemates plated over.
3. Type 284 surface gunnery radar replaced by Type 274.
4. Type 281 air search radar replaced by Type 281b.

BATTLE HONOURS AND CAMPAIGNS OF HM SHIPS WHICH HAVE BORNE THE NAME *WARSPITE*

BATTLE HONOURS

21 June 1596	Cadiz
25 July 1666	Orfordness
28 May 1672	Sole Bay
28 May and 4 June 1673	Schooneveld
11 August 1673	Texel
19–24 May 1692	Barfleur
13 August 1704	Velez Malaga
10 March 1705	Marbella
17–18 August 1759	Lagos
20 November 1759	Quiberon Bay
31 May–1 June 1916	Jutland
10 and 13 April 1940	Narvik
9 July 1940	Calabria
28–9 March 1941	Cape Matapan
20 May–1 June 1941	Crete
September 1940–June 1942	Libya
8 November 1942–20 February 1943	North Africa
10 July–17 August 1943	Sicily
9 September–6 October 1943	Salerno
6 June–3 July 1944	Normandy
1 November 1944	Walcheren

CAMPAIGNS

Atlantic	1939–45
English Channel	1939–45
North Sea	1939–45
Biscay	1940–45
Mediterranean	1940–45
Malta Convoys	1941–42

CAPTAINS OF HMS *WARSPITE* 1915–45

Name	Assumed command	Relieved
E. M. Philpotts	8 March 1915	18 December 1916
C. M. de Bartolome	18 December 1916	3 June 1918
H. Lynes, CB, CMG	3 June 1918	17 January 1919
E. K. Loring	17 January 1919	5 May 1920
F. Clifton-Brown, CB, CMG	5 May 1920	4 April 1922
R. N. Bax, CB, ADC	4 May 1922	4 April 1923
R. M. Burmester, CB, CMG	4 April 1923	2 September 1924 (paid off for refit)
G. K. Chetwode, CB, CBE	6 April 1926	4 August 1927
T. N. James, MVO	5 August 1927	7 November 1927
H. S. Monroe, DSO	7 November 1927	1 December 1927
J. F. Somerville, DSO	1 December 1927	1 September 1928
J. W. Carrington, DSO	1 September 1928	9 January 1929
A. H. Walker, OBE	9 January 1929	8 July 1930
C. A. Scott	8 July 1930	6 September 1930
O. H. Dawson	6 September 1930	25 April 1931
St. A. B. Wake	25 April 1931	2 August 1932
L. D. I. MacKinnon	27 August 1932	15 December 1933 (paid off for refit)
F. H. W. Goolden	24 February 1937	1 May 1937 (for trials)
V. A. C. Crutchley, VC, DSC	1 May 1937	27 April 1940
D. B. Fisher, CBE	27 April 1940	22 March 1942
F. E. P. Hutton	22 March 1942	1 March 1943
H. A. Packer	31 March 1943	12 October 1943
Hon. D. Edwardes	12 October 1943	18 March 1944
M. H. A. Kelsey	18 March 1944	29 August 1944
C. P. Frend	29 August 1944	11 September 1944
M. H. A. Kelsey	11 September 1944	30 December 1944
M. H. Evelegh	30 December 1944	9 February 1945
G. F. Blaxland	9 February 1945	15 March 1945
P. H. Calderon	15 March 1945	26 July 1945 (paid off)

INDEX

BASEBALL™
THE · AMERICAN · EPIC

SHADOW BALL
THE HISTORY OF THE NEGRO LEAGUES

BY GEOFFREY C. WARD
AND KEN BURNS, WITH JIM O'CONNOR

ILLUSTRATED WITH PHOTOGRAPHS

ALFRED A. KNOPF 🐎 NEW YORK

Photo credits:
Archive Photos: 71; Associated Press: 63, 74, 76; Bettmann Archive: 62;
Brooklyn Public Library: 54, 61 *(top)*; Chicago Historical Society: 17; Phil
Dixon: 27 *(top)*; Mary R. Eckler: 44; William Gladstone: 52; Dennis Goldstein:
24 *(center right)*, 25, 34, 45; Hal Lebowitz: 38; Los Angeles Dodgers,
Inc./Maurice Terrell: 49; Jerry Malloy and Negro Leagues Baseball Museum,
Inc.: 7; National Baseball Library & Archive, Cooperstown, New York: title
page, 5, 8, 10 *(bottom)*, 12, 13, 14, 15, 18, 19, 21, 22, 24 *(center left, bottom)*,
26–27 *(bottom)*, 28, 29, 30, 31, 32 *(left)*, 33, 35, 36, 37, 39, 40-41, 47, 48, 51,
53, 56, 58, 61 *(bottom)*, 68, 69, 70, 72, 73, 75, 78–79; Buck O'Neil: 32 *(right)*;
Ohio Wesleyan University: 43; Joseph M. Overfield: 9; The Sporting News: 16
(bottom), 23, 57, 65; Sports Illustrated/Mark Kauffman: 42; Sports
Illustrated/Neil Leifer: 67; John Thorn: 59; Transcendental Graphics/Mark
Rucker: 4, 10 *(top)*, 11, 20; UPI/Bettmann: 55, 60; Western Reserve Historical
Society: 16 *(top)*, 46.

Library of Congress Cataloging-in-Publication Data
Burns, Ken.
Shadow Ball : a history of the Negro leagues / Ken Burns,
Geoffrey C. Ward, with Jim O'Connor.
p. cm. — (Baseball, the American epic)
Includes index.
ISBN: 0-679-86749-X (trade) — ISBN: 0-679-96749-4 (lib. bdg.)
1. Negro leagues—History—Juvenile literature. 2. Baseball—United
States—History—Juvenile literature. [1. Negro leagues—History.
2. Baseball—History.] I. Ward, Geoffrey C. II. O'Connor, Jim. III. Title.
IV. Series.
GV863.A1B87 1994
796.357'0973—dc20
94-5552

Manufactured in the United States of America
2 4 6 8 0 9 7 5 3 1

CONTENTS

A GENTLEMAN'S AGREEMENT.

The crowd stirs with anticipation as the Indianapolis Clowns, an all-black team, take the field for their warm-ups. The second baseman's glove snaps back when he snags a quick peg from first. He hurls the ball to the third baseman, whose diving catch brings the fans to their feet. Then a batter steps to the plate. The pitcher sets, gets his signal, winds up, and throws. The batter swings. He hits it! The shortstop leaps to his right and makes a tremendous backhand stab.

He jumps up, whirls, and throws to first just ahead of the sprinting runner. The low throw kicks dirt up by the first baseman's outstretched glove. The runner is out! The crowd roars.

But wait! There's no ball in the first baseman's glove. The batter didn't really hit it. The Clowns were warming up in pantomime—hurling an imaginary ball so fast, making plays so convincingly, that fans could not believe it wasn't real.

They called it shadow ball—and it came to stand not only for the way the black teams warmed up, but the way they were forced to play in the shadows of the all-white majors. Many black ballplayers were as good—if not better—than the big leaguers. All that kept them out was the color of their skin.

Since the mid-1800s, baseball has been played by young and old, rich and poor, men and women, in big cities and tiny villages across the country. It is the all-American game.

But for years baseball team owners and managers, players and even fans, did everything they could to keep African Americans from playing on professional teams. To some whites, the idea of being struck out by a black pitcher or throwing a home run pitch to a black batter was unthinkable.

In 1867, just two years after the end of the Civil War, which freed African Americans from slavery and promised them equal opportunities, organized baseball made its first attempts to ban blacks. The National Association of Base Ball Players—which later became the National League—refused to allow an all-black team from Philadelphia to join the league.

Nevertheless, during the next twenty-five years, more than fifty blacks managed to play on white teams. The first was Bud Fowler, born near Cooperstown, New York, in 1858. Fowler was a true all-around player—he was a good catcher, first baseman, and pitcher but was best at second. In 1872 he joined a white professional club in New Castle, Pennsylvania.

Bud Fowler is credited with inventing the first shin guards. White players were spiking him so often that he began taping pieces of wood to his legs to protect himself. And although he batted over .300 every season, no team would keep him very long. As soon as a competent white player came along, Fowler lost his job.

One season he played for five different teams. By the end of his career, Fowler had played for fourteen teams in nine different leagues. Eventually, worn down by years of bouncing from team to team, Fowler returned to Cooperstown and became a barber.

"MY SKIN IS AGAINST ME."

—BUD FOWLER

MOSES FLEETWOOD
WALKER, CATCHER FOR
THE TOLEDO BLUE
STOCKINGS

The first black to make it to the majors was Moses Fleetwood Walker, on Ohio clergyman's son. Walker joined the Toledo Blue Stockings of the American Association as a catcher in 1884 and immediately ran into a wall of racism.

As the catcher, it was Walker's job to tell the pitcher, using hand signals, what kind of pitch to throw next. But one Blue Stockings pitcher ignored Walker's signals because he refused to take orders from a black man.

That pitcher was not alone. There was opposition to black players everywhere. The Buffalo Bisons of the International League, a minor league, signed Frank Grant to play second base. Grant was an outstanding athlete, but like Bud Fowler before him, he was the constant target of white opponents' spikes.

One player, Ned Williamson, vividly recalled Grant's harassment: "The players of the opposing team made it a point to spike this brunette Buffalo. They would tarry at second when they might easily make third just to toy with the sensitive shins of the second baseman. The poor man played only two games out of five, the rest of the time he was on crutches."

Meanwhile, the Newark Little Giants signed fastballer George Washington Stovey, who became one of the dominant pitchers of the International League.

Stovey soon caught the eye of John Montgomery Ward, captain of the New York Giants. In 1887 word got out that Ward wanted Stovey to pitch for the Giants. Cap Anson, manager of the Chicago White Stockings, announced that neither he nor any of his players would ever play a team on which blacks were welcome.

Anson's threat worked. The Giants did not sign Stovey.

"YOU CANNOT HIT 'EM WITH A CELLAR DOOR."

—A REPORTER DESCRIBING GEORGE WASHINGTON STOVEY'S PITCHES

Other baseball officials were just as vocal with their racism. One International League umpire declared that he would always call the close plays against a team that included black players.

The message was clear. That year the owners of all the major league ball clubs entered into a "gentleman's agreement"—an unwritten policy to sign no more black players. The minors formally declared that blacks were no longer welcome.

The color line was being drawn all over the country, and by 1899 blacks were completely out of organized baseball. But they would soon demonstrate—to the delight of fans everywhere—that nothing could keep them from playing the game they loved.

JOHN MONTGOMERY WARD

THE CHICAGO WHITE STOCKINGS OF 1888. CAP ANSON *(STANDING, SECOND FROM RIGHT)* THREATENED NOT TO LET THEM PLAY AGAINST ANY TEAM THAT HAD A BLACK PLAYER.

THE NAME OF THIS PLAYER, PHOTOGRAPHED IN 1888, HAS LONG BEEN LOST.

"THE BEST MAN IS HE WHO PLAYS BEST."

—THE NEWARK CALL IN AN ARTICLE CRITICIZING THE "GENTLEMAN'S AGREEMENT"

BARNSTORMING. By 1900 America was baseball mad, and the sport had grown into a full-fledged industry. But because of the gentleman's agreement, African Americans—roughly one-tenth of the nation's citizens—were denied jobs in that industry. Black athletes realized that if they were ever going to play professional ball, they would have to form their own teams.

The first professional black team was the Cuban Giants, originally a group of waiters from the Argyle Hotel in Babylon,

Cuban Giants,

COLORED CHAMPIONS.

1887. AND. 1888.

OMES

TRUSTY

THOMAS

WILLIAMS

HARRISON

BOYD.

THE CUBAN GIANTS,
ORIGINALLY A GROUP OF
WAITERS FROM NEW YORK

OPPOSITE:
THE CUBAN X GIANTS

Long Island. They called themselves "Cuban" to hide the fact that they were African Americans, and "Giants" (like several other black teams) after the popular all-white New York Giants. It was said that they spoke gibberish to each other in the field so that fans would think they were Spanish.

Soon black fans had dozens of teams to cheer for: the Cuban X Giants, New York's Lincoln Giants, Meridian Southern Giants, Indianapolis ABCs, French Lick Plutos, and the Page Fence Giants.

The all-black teams of the early 1900s spent much of their time on the road. No black team could draw the same crowds as the white professional teams, so in order to make enough money to cover expenses, black teams had to be willing to play all the time.

THE PAGE FENCE GIANTS WERE SPONSORED BY A WIRE MANUFACTURER. WHEN THEY ARRIVED IN A NEW TOWN, THEY WOULD RACE THROUGH THE STREETS ON BICYCLES TO DRUM UP INTEREST IN THEIR GAMES.

"ORGANIZE YOUR TEAM."

— ADVICE TO YOUNG BLACK MEN FROM W. E. B. DuBOIS, CO-FOUNDER OF THE NATIONAL ASSOCIATION FOR THE ADVANCEMENT OF COLORED PEOPLE

They crisscrossed America in buses, traveling wherever there was a team—black or white—that would play them. When the white major league clubs went on the road, black teams rented their stadiums and scheduled doubleheaders. During the winter months they often headed south to Mexico or Cuba and played teams of white all-stars from the major leagues.

Almost every game was an away game, and the road trips stretched for weeks and sometimes months. The players called their nomadic life barnstorming.

It was a tough and wearying way to live. A team might play two or three games in a single day—sometimes in two or three different towns. Then the players would drive most of the night to get to the next day's first game.

It wasn't easy for the teams to find hotel rooms or restaurants—especially in the South, where many states had passed laws legalizing segregation, or the separation of the races. Blacks and whites went to separate schools, ate in separate restaurants, drank from separate water fountains. Black ball teams often had to stay in hotels or boarding houses in the black section of town, or split up and sleep in people's homes. If the weather was warm, they slept on the ground next to the ball field.

SHORTSTOP POP LLOYD PLAYED BASEBALL UNTIL HE WAS 58.

Barnstorming brought some of the best players to small towns everywhere. In the days before radio and television, these games were often the only games many fans—black and white—ever saw. Factories and schools closed early when a black team came to town. No one wanted to miss the game.

Two players dominated black baseball in its early years. John Henry "Pop" Lloyd was called "the black Honus Wagner" because he was considered equal to the great Pirate shortstop. Wagner said he was honored to be compared to Pop Lloyd.

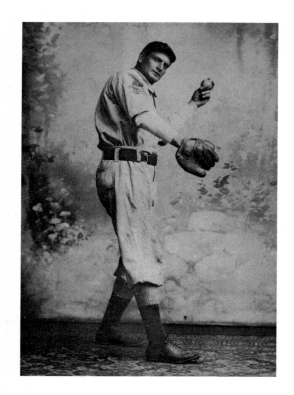

"You could put Wagner and Lloyd in a bag together," said Connie Mack, owner of the all-white Philadelphia Athletics, "and whichever one you pulled out, you wouldn't go wrong."

In the winter of 1911 Lloyd took part in a classic confrontation with another baseball superstar. The other player was Ty Cobb, the white Detroit Tiger center fielder and American League batting champ. Lloyd was playing in Cuba for the Havana Reds, one of Cuba's top teams, when the Tigers came through on a tour.

Cobb, who had hit .385 the previous season, hit a sizzling .370 in Havana. But Lloyd was better—in twenty-two trips to the plate he got eleven hits, for an even .500.

Cobb was also a superb base stealer and bragged that he would show the Cubans how they stole bases in the American League. But Lloyd and Havana catcher Bruce Petway stopped Cobb every time he tried to steal second. When the five-game exhibition series ended, Cobb vowed never to play against blacks again.

The other black star of the era was Andrew "Rube" Foster. Foster had signed with the semi-professional Fort Worth Yellow Jackets when he was only 17 years old. The massively built young Texan moved up quickly to the Leland Giants and then on to the Cuban X Giants, who were based in Philadelphia. In 1902 the Cubans played an exhibition game against the Philadelphia Athletics. Foster pitched and beat the great Rube Waddell. His teammates nicknamed him Rube in honor of his victory.

The next year John McGraw of the New York Giants came calling. McGraw had been one of the toughest and dirtiest players of his time. He was just as tough as a manager and was always looking for a player who could help his team win. McGraw didn't care what color the player was. In 1901 he had tried to sneak the Page Fence Giants' Charlie Grant onto the Baltimore Orioles by claiming that Grant was a Cherokee named Chief Tokahoma. But Grant had been recognized and never got to play.

"WASTE A LITTLE
TIME ON HIM."

—RUBE FOSTER'S ADVICE TO PITCHERS
FACING A BATTER WHO SEEMS EASIER TO HIT

After that experience, McGraw knew there was no chance of slipping Foster into the big leagues. Instead, he paid Rube to teach Christy Mathewson, the Giants' star pitcher, his "fadeaway," or screwball pitch.

Foster later took most of the Cuban X Giants back to the Leland Giants. In those days it was common for players to jump from team to team, depending on how much money each owner offered. And although the owners believed that players should honor their contracts, there was little they could do when a player left.

Foster was an unbeatable pitcher. In 1904 he won fifty-one games and lost only five, using a combination of physical skill and psychology to dominate opposing batters.

"The real test comes when you are pitching with men on base," Foster said. "Do not worry. Try to appear jolly and unconcerned. Where the batter appears anxious to hit, waste a little time on him. Waste a few balls and try his nerves; the majority of times you will win out by drawing him into hitting a wide one."

In 1911 Foster and John Schorling, a white tavern owner, founded the all-black Chicago American Giants. In addition to being a player and part owner, Rube was also the team's manager. He was about to begin a career that would change black baseball forever.

GIANTS PITCHER
CHRISTY
MATHEWSON
LEARNED HOW
TO THROW A
SCREWBALL
FROM RUBE
FOSTER.

CHAPTER 3

TWO INNINGS AHEAD OF EVERYONE ELSE. In 1919 the bloodiest race riots since the Civil War swept the United States. The worst took place in Chicago. It started when a black boy was stoned to death because his rubber raft floated too close to a white beach. By the time it ended, thirty-eight people were dead and over five hundred injured. For many of the blacks who had moved north to escape the harsh anti-black laws of the South, the riots confirmed their worst fears—racism was everywhere.

AN UNIDENTIFIED
KANSAS CITY
MONARCHS PLAYER

OPPOSITE: THE ST. PAUL
GOPHERS, 1909

But as a result of the riots, African Americans began to assert themselves. Marcus Garvey, the black nationalist, urged blacks to look to themselves for help. "No more fears," he wrote. "No more begging and pleading." Blacks began to set up their own businesses. Few would become more successful than Rube Foster.

In the year of the riot, Foster began organizing the Negro National League. He believed that a black-owned and -operated league would keep black baseball from being controlled by whites and would give black players the opportunity to make as much money as white players. And, he said, he wanted to "do something concrete for the loyalty of the race."

There were eight teams in the league: the Kansas City Monarchs, Indianapolis ABCs, Dayton Marcos, Chicago Giants, Detroit Stars,

RUBE FOSTER
(IN JACKET AND TIE)
WITH HIS CHICAGO
AMERICAN GIANTS, 1919

"WE ARE THE SHIP, ALL ELSE THE SEA."

— RUBE FOSTER ON THE NEGRO NATIONAL LEAGUE

St. Louis Giants, Cuban Giants, and Foster's own Chicago American Giants.

The owner of the Kansas City Monarchs was a white man named J. L. Wilkinson. Foster believed that all the clubs should be owned by blacks, but he agreed to let the Monarchs into the league because of Wilkinson's long, impressive history in black baseball. He had founded the barnstorming All Nations team, whose members were black, Indian, Asian, and Hispanic.

Under Rube Foster's leadership, the American Giants seldom lost a game. One year he led them to a 123–6 record. The Giants were so successful that they sometimes drew bigger crowds than the Cubs or the White Sox, Chicago's two white major league clubs.

Foster, one fellow Negro leaguer recalled years later, was always "two innings ahead of everyone else." As a manager, he insisted that his teams play "smart baseball"—a fast, aggressive game built around bunts, steals, hit-and-runs, and crafty pitching.

By comparison, white baseball was a slower, quieter game. After Yankee slugger Babe Ruth belted fifty-four home runs in 1920 and brought thousands of new fans to his team, major league managers built their strategy around hitting the long ball.

No player stayed on Foster's American Giants unless he could bunt a ball into a circle drawn along one of the foul lines. Any Giant who was tagged out standing up had to pay a five-dollar fine. "You're supposed to slide," Foster told them.

The result was a fast-paced, exciting game, and the Negro National League was a huge success. In the 1923 season alone, over 400,000 fans attended league games. Foster's creation became one of the largest black-owned businesses in the country.

YANKEE SLUGGER BABE
RUTH WITH BLACK FANS

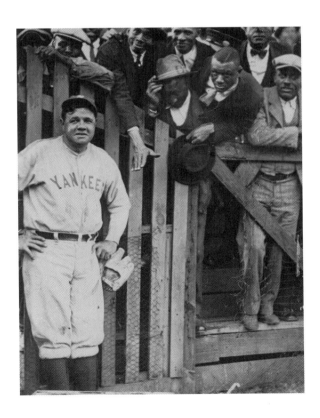

BULLET JOE ROGAN
(BELOW LEFT) OF THE
KANSAS CITY MONARCHS.
HIS "PALM BALL" BAFFLED
EVERY BATTER.

OSCAR CHARLESTON
(BELOW RIGHT), "THE
BLACK TY COBB"

Three players dominated the league: Pitcher Smokey Joe Williams, who stood 6' 5", threw so hard that his team had to change catchers after four or five innings because their hands would swell up from the pounding.

Bullet Joe Rogan could throw heat like Smokey Joe, but he had another weapon in his arsenal. He invented the "palm ball"—a change-up that "walked up" to hitters who were waiting for his fastball. It totally baffled them.

Oscar Charleston was a fierce, hard-hitting center fielder who could outrun any ball. When a young baseball writer once suggested that Charleston was "the black Ty Cobb," an old-time reporter corrected him. "Cobb," the reporter said, "is a white Oscar Charleston."

The Negro National League's success attracted the attention of a group of white businessmen who saw the profits to be made in black baseball. In 1922 they formed the Eastern Colored League, which included the Philadelphia Hilldales, Brooklyn Royal Giants, Lincoln Giants, Baltimore Black Sox, Atlantic City Bacharachs, and New York Cuban All-Stars.

THE BALTIMORE BLACK SOX

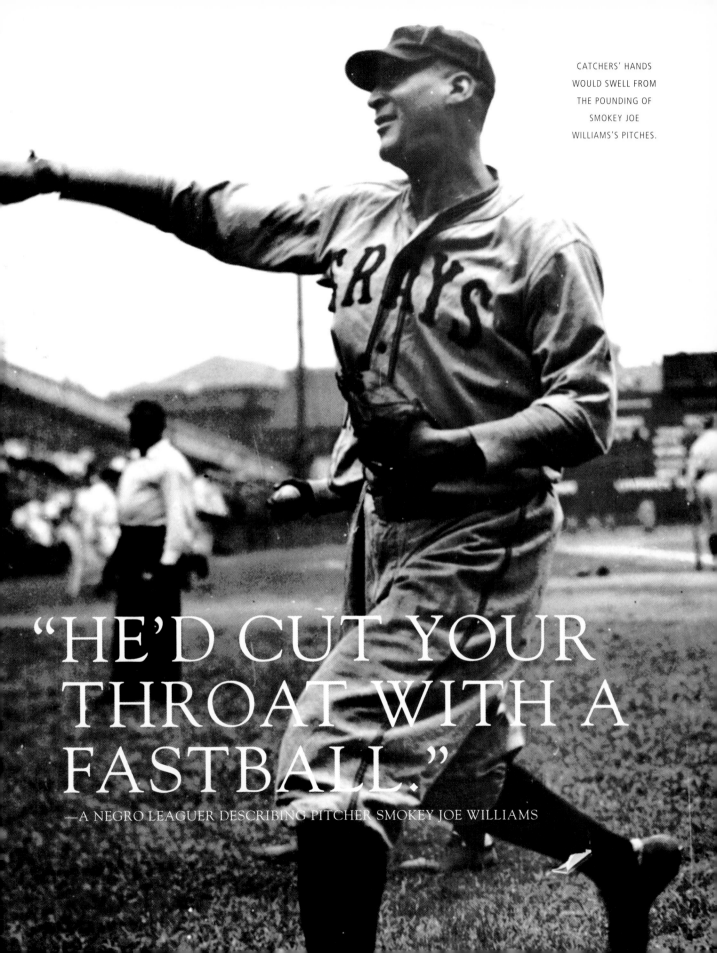

CATCHERS' HANDS WOULD SWELL FROM THE POUNDING OF SMOKEY JOE WILLIAMS'S PITCHES.

"HE'D CUT YOUR THROAT WITH A FASTBALL."

—A NEGRO LEAGUER DESCRIBING PITCHER SMOKEY JOE WILLIAMS

The Eastern League immediately began raiding the Negro
National League for its best players. This enraged Foster, and he refused
to schedule a World Series that had been planned with the Eastern
champion for 1923.

"FOLKS COMING OUT LIKE BEES HIDDEN AWAY ALL WINTER."

—THE CHICAGO *DEFENDER* DESCRIBING OPENING
DAY OF THE 1923 NEGRO LEAGUE SEASON

In 1924 Foster's business sense prevailed, and the first Negro World Series was held between the Kansas City Monarchs and the Philadelphia Hilldales. The Monarchs won in a tough ten-game series.

The emotional and financial strain of running the league—and watching his best players being lured away to the rival Eastern League—started to wear Foster down. In 1926 he suffered a nervous breakdown. One day he was found chasing imaginary fly balls in the street near his house. Finally he was sent to a mental hospital, where he died in 1930.

On the day Foster was buried, one reporter wrote that his coffin was closed "at the usual hour a ball game ends." Three thousand fans braved a cold, icy rain to attend the funeral of the man they called "the father of black baseball."

AT FOSTER'S GRAVESITE, MOURNERS LEFT FLORAL TRIBUTES IN THE SHAPE OF A BASEBALL AND A BASEBALL DIAMOND.

CHAPTER 4

THE GUY PEOPLE WANTED TO SEE.
In 1929 the stock market crashed and the
American economy collapsed. It was the
beginning of the Great Depression.
Wealthy people were wiped out overnight,
and thousands of homeless families
roamed the streets and countrysides.
Fifteen million men and women—one out
of every four Americans—would soon be
out of work.

    The Depression hit baseball too.
Attendance fell dramatically, because few
people could afford to buy food, let alone a

PRECEDING PAGES—
RIGHT: THE CHICAGO
AMERICAN
GIANTS, 1927.
LEFT: J.L. WILKINSON
AND
THE KANSAS CITY
MONARCHS IN
FRONT OF THEIR
TEAM BUS, NICK-
NAMED DR. YAK, IN
THE 1930s.

fifty-cent ticket to the ballpark. The Eastern League had disbanded in 1928, and despite the efforts of the Monarchs' J. L. Wilkinson, the National League failed in 1931. Most of the teams survived by barnstorming, but now the road trips were longer and the players were paid only a fraction of what they had made before—when they were paid at all.

Fortunately, there were people who had the desire—and the means—to revive the league. One of them was Gus Greenlee, a black gambler from Pittsburgh, Pennsylvania, who was known as Big Red. Greenlee ran Pittsburgh's "numbers" racket—an illegal game in which a bettor picked a three-digit number and bet as little as a nickel. The 100-to-1 payoff meant that a person could win five dollars on a nickel bet. Runners, or messengers, went around black neighborhoods every day collecting bets and delivering payoffs. It was a popular and profitable enterprise that made Greenlee a rich man.

Greenlee also owned a nightclub called the Crawford Grill. It featured famous black musicians like Count Basie, Lena Horne, and Duke Ellington.

When Greenlee bought a local semi-pro team called the Pittsburgh Colored Giants, he renamed them the Crawford Colored

THE PITTSBURGH
CRAWFORDS IN
1932

Giants. Eventually the name was shortened to the Crawfords.

Pittsburgh's other black team, the Homestead Grays, was owned by Cum Posey, the son of a wealthy banker and real-estate developer. Posey had built the Grays into an all-star team. They had not been part of either black league, but they had played—and beaten—most of the teams. In 1931 they won 136 games and lost ten.

Posey often traveled with the Grays, booking the ballparks and looking after his players' every need. He even made sure they got their favorite sandwiches after the game.

But Posey's rival, Gus Greenlee, was determined to build the best team in black baseball. His method was simple—he bought up the finest players on the Homestead Grays.

One of them was Oscar Charleston. Although Charleston was nearing the end of his career, Greenlee hired him to manage the team as well as play first base.

Another player, center fielder James "Cool Papa" Bell, was such a fast runner that he could make it from first to third on a bunt. In one game he hit three inside-the-park home runs. A teammate who often roomed with Bell on the road swore that Bell could flip off a light switch and be in bed before the room was dark.

COOL PAPA BELL,
MASTER OF THE
INSIDE-THE-PARK
HOME RUN

THE HOMESTEAD
GRAYS, 1931.
CUM POSEY IS
AT THE FAR LEFT,
IN KNICKERS.

Third baseman William "Judy" Johnson, nicknamed Mr. Sunshine because he was cheerful and optimistic, always seemed to know what the other team was going to do. He could figure out the opposing manager's hand signals just by watching him for a few innings. Then, by whistling a coded message, he'd pass the signals on to his teammates.

Catcher Josh Gibson, who already had a reputation for hitting 500-foot home runs, caught Greenlee's eye in 1931 when he slammed seventy-five homers for the Homestead Grays. By the next season he was playing for the Crawfords. Legend has it that the only home run ever hit out of Yankee Stadium was a Gibson blast during a Negro league game.

Buck O'Neil of the Kansas City Monarchs, who spent six decades in baseball as a first baseman, manager, coach, and scout, played with or against nearly every important black athlete in the game. He never forgot Josh Gibson.

JUDY JOHNSON
(BELOW LEFT) HAD A
KNACK FOR READING
THE OTHER TEAM'S
SIGNALS.

BUCK O'NEIL *(BELOW RIGHT)* PLAYED WITH OR AGAINST NEARLY EVERY IMPORTANT BLACK ATHLETE IN THE GAME.

LEONARD

WEST
PHILA
STARS

TAYLOR

BROWN
PHILA
STAR

1937

BUCK LEONARD OF
THE HOMESTEAD
GRAYS EASES INTO
FIRST IN A 1937
GAME AGAINST THE
PHILADELPHIA STARS.

"He and Ruth had power alike," O'Neil recalled, "but Ruth struck out maybe 115 times a year. Josh Gibson struck out maybe fifty times a year. The best hitter I've ever seen. Would have been outstanding [in the majors]. Would have rewritten the record book as far as home runs are concerned."

The Crawfords quickly became the strongest team in black baseball. "We played everywhere. In every ballpark," one Crawford player recalled. "And we won. Won like we invented the game."

Greenlee spared no expense for his team. When his players were refused permission to use the locker rooms at the Pittsburgh Pirates' Forbes Field, Greenlee decided to build his own stadium.

Completed in 1932, Greenlee Field cost $60,000 and seated 7,500. It was the first stadium ever built for a black team. Greenlee also bought the Crawfords a luxurious new Mack bus to travel in. On some

trips, he would squeeze his 6' 2" frame into the driver's seat and chauffeur his club himself for a day or two.

As the Depression grew worse, owners struggled to keep their teams going. The only people with money in the black community were gamblers like Gus Greenlee. Before long, most of the black teams were owned by "numbers kings."

THE PITTSBURGH CRAWFORDS POSE BEFORE THEIR CUSTOM-BUILT TOUR BUS IN FRONT OF THE ENTRANCE TO GREENLEE FIELD.

"THEY WOULD HAVE BEEN STEEL TYCOONS, AUTO MOGULS, HAD THEY BEEN WHITE."

—NOVELIST RICHARD WRIGHT ON
THE BLACK NUMBERS KINGS OF THE 1930s

ALEX POMPEZ

EFFA MANLEY,
MANAGER OF THE
NEWARK EAGLES

Tom Wilson had the Baltimore Elite Giants; Alex Pompez, the Cuban Stars; Ed Bolden, the Philadelphia Stars. In New York the Black Yankees were supposedly owned by dancer Bill "Bojangles" Robinson, but Ed "Soldier Boy" Semler had really purchased the team. And in Newark, the Eagles were owned by Abe Manley, the numbers king of Trenton, and managed by his wife, Effa.

In 1931 Greenlee signed one of the greatest pitchers of all time—Leroy "Satchel" Paige. Paige had earned his nickname at age seven when he worked as a porter in a Mobile, Alabama, train station, carrying passengers' suitcases, or satchels. The pay was ten cents a bag. To make more money, Paige carried several bags at one time on a pole across his shoulders. Someone said he looked like "a walking satchel tree." Soon everyone was calling him Satchel.

Paige's main weapon was a blazing fastball. He had many names for it—Long Tom and Little Tom, the bee ball (so fast it hummed as it flew), jump ball, trouble ball, midnight rider, and four-day creeper. No matter what he called it, it was impossible to hit.

"He was tall," Cool Papa Bell said, "between 6' 3" and 6' 4", but he only weighed about 180, so it seemed like he was all arms and legs. He could put that big fastball right at your knees all day long. It seemed to come right out of his foot."

Above all, Satchel Paige was a great showman and crowd pleaser. He liked to arrive late so that he could make a grand entrance—sometimes with a police escort. Then he would take his time walking to the mound.

"I like walking slow," Paige said. "Moving that way got them to laugh. Laughing is a pretty sound. But I never joked when I was pitching."

On barnstorming trips, Paige often promised to strike out the first nine men he faced in a game—and he usually did. Sometimes he would call his outfielders in and finish an inning with just the infielders. The

The Great
Satchell Paige

"I JUST PUT THE BALL
WHERE I KNOW HE
CAN'T HIT IT."

—SATCHEL PAIGE

'SATCHEL' PAIGE'S own story

Pitchin' Man

As told to HAL LEBOVITZ   TWENTY FIVE CENTS

ONE OF TWO
AUTOBIOGRAPHIES
PAIGE PUBLISHED

fans loved it. As Buck O'Neil said, Paige was "the guy that people wanted to see."

Like Ruth, Satchel had learned to play ball in reform school. When he was 12, he had stolen some toys from a store. A hard-hearted judge sent him to the Industrial School for Negro Children.

"My time there made me a man," Paige would always say. "I played ball, sang in the choir, and got a pretty fair education."

When he left reform school five years later, the Mobile Tigers gave him a tryout. After throwing ten unhittable strikes past the manager, Satchel signed his first contract—for one dollar a game.

Paige would sign many more contracts. If there was one thing he did better than pitching, it was jumping from team to team. He called himself "the travelin' man," and during his career he played for over 250 teams.

In January 1933 Greenlee put together a new Negro National League. There were six teams—the Crawfords, the Chicago American Giants, Columbus Blue Birds, Detroit Stars, Indianapolis ABCs (who were soon replaced by the Baltimore Black Sox), and Nashville Elite Giants.

When major league baseball had its first All-Star game in July 1933, in an attempt to bring fans into the ballpark and save their ailing businesses, Greenlee and the other black team owners thought that was a fine idea. Two months later they held the first all-black East-West All-Star game, in Chicago's Comiskey Park. Fans came from around the country to cheer on the teams they had helped pick with their votes in the Chicago *Defender* and the Pittsburgh *Courier*, two black weekly newspapers.

Unlike the black World Series, which never caught on because
black fans didn't have the time or money to attend a series of games,
the annual East-West All-Star game was an immediate success. The
huge crowds sometimes numbered 50,000. It was "the glory part of our
baseball," one player recalled.

THE CHICAGO
AMERICAN GIANTS,
1931

Buck O'Neil remembered how much the fans loved the game, and how far they would travel to see it:

"People would come, like we used to say, 'two to a mule.' We would have excursions running from New Orleans to Chicago. And they would pick people up in Mississippi, Memphis, Tennessee. Right

on to Chicago. And everybody came to that ball game. You would look up, and there's Joe Louis and Marva Louis [the black boxing champ and his wife] sitting in a box seat down front. All of the great entertainers in Chicago at that time. They would come and we had something to show. Yeah. We had something to show."

BUCK LEONARD
STANDS FAR LEFT, IN A
GRAYS UNIFORM.
JOSH GIBSON,
ALSO IN A GRAYS
UNIFORM, STANDS
THIRD FROM RIGHT.

CHAPTER 5

THE GREAT EXPERIMENT. Branch Rickey was an Ohio farm boy whose family's Methodist faith was at the center of their lives. He grew up pious and hardworking— and crazy about baseball, learning to play in the backyard with a ball sewn by his mother. To help pay his way through college, Rickey got a job coaching the baseball team, for whom he was also the catcher. Their star player was first baseman Charles "Tommy" Thomas, the only black man on the team. The racism that Thomas experienced made a lasting impression on Rickey.

PRECEDING PAGES—
LEFT: JACKIE ROBINSON.
RIGHT: BRANCH
RICKEY'S COLLEGE
TEAM. TOMMY THOMAS
STANDS AT THE CENTER.

BRANCH RICKEY,
BASEBALL'S GREAT
REVOLUTIONARY

On a road trip one season, a hotel refused Thomas a room. Rickey was outraged and finally persuaded the hotel manager to let Thomas room with him.

Later, when Rickey went to their room, he found a tense and brooding Thomas standing in the corner. Rickey tried to reassure him, but Thomas, angry and humiliated, was too upset.

"Tears spilled down his face," Rickey recalled years later, "and splashed on the floor. Then he rubbed one great hand over the other with all the power of his body, muttering 'Black skin...black skin. If I could only make 'em white.'"

After college Rickey played briefly with several professional teams, then became a lawyer. But he quickly returned to baseball as a scout, and by 1913 he was managing the St. Louis Browns.

In those days baseball players trained as little as possible. They would usually arrive at spring training overweight and out of shape. They believed they could "play themselves into shape" in a few short weeks—while still drinking and smoking after practice.

Branch Rickey had different ideas. He believed in a "scientific" method of baseball. In 1916 he crossed town to join the St. Louis Cardinals, where he made his players run wind sprints and practice sliding into sandpits. He would not allow them to drink, play poker, or swear during training. He started every day with a blackboard lecture on baseball tactics. His players didn't know what to make of him, but his efforts paid off, and the Cardinals began to win.

When Rickey saw how hard it was to acquire first-rate players from other teams, he developed a system of minor league clubs that he called "farm teams." These teams would "grow" new talent for the Cardinals. The idea worked brilliantly, and within a few years the farm teams were producing a steady supply of good young players ready to move up to the majors.

In 1943, after nearly thirty years with St. Louis, Rickey moved east and became president and general manager of the Brooklyn Dodgers. The Dodgers, who had never won a World Series, had most of the players they needed to win the pennant and maybe even the championship. Rickey intended to take them all the way—and he had a revolutionary plan for doing it.

Rickey believed the time was right to integrate baseball—to end segregation and sign black players to major league clubs. Black athletes were already competing against whites in other sports. Jesse Owens had won four gold medals in the 1936 Berlin Olympics. A year later Joe Louis won the world heavyweight boxing championship from Jim Braddock. World War II was raging overseas, and black and white soldiers were fighting and dying side by side.

JERRY BENJAMIN AT BAT FOR THE HOMESTEAD GRAYS, 1942

And there was money to be made. Black fans flocked to Negro league games, and the teams were flourishing. Rickey knew the same fans would come to major league games if black players were on the teams.

But integrating baseball would not be easy. Baseball commissioner Kenesaw Mountain Landis, who had been brought into baseball after the 1919 White Sox scandal to "clean up the game," was a lifelong opponent of integration. He had done everything he could to keep the old "gentleman's agreement" in effect. "The colored ballplayers have their own league," he said. "Let them stay in their own league."

In 1944 Landis died and was replaced by A. B. "Happy" Chandler, a former governor of Kentucky and a United States senator. Chandler proved to be a very different commissioner. When questioned about allowing blacks in major league baseball, he said, "I'm for the Four Freedoms. If a black boy can make it on Okinawa and Guadalcanal [two World War II battlefields], he can make it in baseball."

BASEBALL COMMISSIONER
KENESAW MOUNTAIN LANDIS,
A LIFELONG OPPONENT OF
INTEGRATION

"IF WE ARE ABLE TO STOP BULLETS, WHY NOT BALLS?"

—AFRICAN AMERICAN PICKET SIGN SEEN AT YANKEE STADIUM

Still, Rickey knew he would have to move carefully and choose just the right man to break the color barrier. He found that man in a talented young athlete named Jack Roosevelt Robinson.

Like Rickey, Jackie Robinson came from a poor family. He was born in Cairo, Georgia, in 1919, the grandson of a slave and one of five children of a sharecropper who deserted them when Jackie was a baby. Jackie's mother moved the family to Pasadena, California, where they were the only blacks in an all-white neighborhood. The white children threw rocks at the Robinson kids—until Jackie and his older brothers started throwing them back.

Robinson was a superb athlete and went to Pasadena Junior College and the University of California at Los Angeles (UCLA) on scholarships. He starred in football, basketball, track, and baseball. He was a strong, proud man who stood up for his rights.

During World War II, while Robinson was stationed in Texas, the army desegregated, ordering that whites and blacks must be treated equally on all its bases. But one day a bus driver told Robinson to sit in

AT UCLA, JACKIE ROBINSON WAS A STAR ATHLETE IN FOOTBALL, BASKETBALL, TRACK, AND BASEBALL.

the back of a military bus at Fort Hood. Robinson, who was one of the army's first black officers, refused even when he was told he would be arrested. He was given a court-martial—a military trial—and found not guilty. A few months later he received an honorable discharge and signed as a shortstop with the Kansas City Monarchs for $400 a month.

The Monarchs were one of the strongest teams in the Negro leagues. Owner J. L. Wilkinson had a good eye for talent and filled his roster with stars like Bullet Joe Rogan, Buck O'Neil, and Satchel Paige.

Wilkinson is also credited as the "father of night baseball." Although a few night games had been played as far back as 1880, the lights were never bright enough or very dependable. In 1930 Wilkinson designed a lighting system that was carried from field to field on the back of a truck. The lights were raised on fifty-foot telescoping poles and powered by a huge generator mounted on the Monarchs' touring bus. Attendance skyrocketed at night games, with the crowds sometimes reaching 12,000.

"I WAS IN TWO WARS."

—JACKIE ROBINSON (*LEFT*), REFERRING TO
FIGHTING WORLD WAR II OVERSEAS
AND PREJUDICE AT HOME

In 1945, when Jackie Robinson signed with the Monarchs, he took an immediate dislike to playing in the Negro leagues. Baseball was not his favorite sport, and he hated the informality of the league—Satchel Paige seemed to come and go on his own private schedule, and in Baltimore one day the official scorekeeper left in the middle of the game. Robinson also hated the endless bus rides and the segregated hotels and restaurants.

Jackie was quiet and kept to himself. To some of his teammates, it seemed that he thought he was better than they were. But they were impressed by his determination to be treated with respect.

"We'd been going for thirty years to this filling station in Oklahoma where we would buy gas," Buck O'Neil recalled. "We had two fifty-gallon tanks on that [bus]. We'd buy the gas, but we couldn't use the rest room. Jackie wanted to use the rest room.

"The man said, 'Boy, you can't go to that rest room.'

"Jackie said, 'Take the hose out of the tank.' This guy ain't gonna sell one hundred gallons of gas in a whole month. 'If we can't go to the rest room, we won't get any gas here. We'll get it someplace else.'

"The man said, 'Well, you boys can go to the rest room, but don't stay too long.'

"So, actually, he started something there. Now, every place we would go we wanted to know first could we use the rest room. If we couldn't use the rest room—no gas."

Despite his unhappiness with barnstorming, Robinson had a great year with the Monarchs and finished the season with a .387 average.

Branch Rickey had heard about Robinson and thought he might be the man he was looking for. He sent one of his scouts to talk to Robinson.

Meanwhile, Rickey created a diversion to fool the other teams. He announced that the Dodgers were forming a black baseball club—the Brooklyn Brown Dodgers—as part of a new all-black league. Now Rickey could interview black players without arousing any suspicions.

COMING! COMING! COMING!
KANSAS CITY MONARCHS NIGHT BASEBALL

We have successfully lighted every kind of a ball park in the country, including both Major Leagues, AND CAN REPEAT IN ALL OF THEM.

The Greatest Drawing Card Outside the Major Leagues

Actual Photograph of One of the Many Towers Supporting Our Flood Lights

WORLDS~ COLORED CHAMPIONS

Headquarters 420 East Ninth St., Kansas City, Mo.

Actual Photograph of Trucks Used to Transport the Monarch Lighting Plant and Towers

Rickey and Robinson met in Rickey's Brooklyn office on August 29, 1945. Rickey quickly got to the point. He knew that Robinson had the physical skill to play for the Dodgers. But, he said, the first black player would face more abuse from other players and fans than any athlete in the history of the game. Rickey spent the rest of the meeting demonstrating that abuse. He cursed and yelled, threatened and screamed, threw punches that barely missed Robinson's face.

Then he told Robinson, "You can't retaliate."

"Mr. Rickey, do you want a ballplayer who's afraid to fight back?" Robinson asked.

Rickey responded: "I want a ballplayer with guts enough *not* to fight back. You will symbolize a crucial cause. One incident, just one incident, can set it back twenty years."

Rickey asked Robinson to promise that he wouldn't retaliate, no matter what happened, for three years. After thinking it over, Jackie agreed. Rickey had found his man.

Two months later the Brooklyn Dodgers announced that they had signed Jackie Robinson and were sending him to play for the Montreal Royals, their International League farm club in Canada.

As Rickey had predicted, the other major league clubs did not support his move. They voted fifteen to one against letting Robinson into the league. But Happy Chandler overruled them and approved the deal.

From the very first game, Robinson was under tremendous pressure. He knew there were people who wanted to see him strike out every time and drop every ball so that he would fail and be sent back to the Negro leagues.

He ignored the taunts that Branch Rickey had warned him about. He did not complain when he had to stay in different, and inferior, hotels from his white teammates, or eat in "Negro" restaurants. But his silence took its toll. By the end of the season, Robinson was racked by stomach pain. His wife, Rachel, thought he might have a nervous breakdown.

Robinson held on, however, and had a great season. With Jackie leading the way, now playing second base, the Royals won the league championship and then the minor league Little World Series.

Even after such an outstanding year, Robinson would still have to prove himself when he moved up to Brooklyn. Some of the Dodgers were Southerners who didn't like the idea of playing with a black man. Three of them drew up a petition saying they didn't want Jackie on the team. When they presented the petition to Dodger manager Leo Durocher, he tore it up.

Spring training came and went without incident. The Dodgers moved Jackie to first base because they had veteran player Eddie Stanky at second.

Finally, on Opening Day, April 15, 1947, Jackie Robinson made history by becoming the first black man in modern times to play major league baseball. More than half of the 26,623 fans at Brooklyn's Ebbets Field that day were black. Robinson failed to get a hit in the game, but the crowd was thrilled. The Dodgers won, 5–3.

It was a tough season for Robinson. When Philadelphia arrived for a three-game series, he nearly cracked. Led by their manager, Ben Chapman, the Phillies pulled out all the stops. "Nigger," they yelled, "go back to the cotton fields!" "We don't want you here, nigger!" "Hey, snowflake!"

Only his promise to Branch Rickey kept Robinson from exploding. By the third game of the series, the rest of the Dodgers were fed up. Stanky, one of the players who had circulated the petition to keep

SINGER LENA HORNE VISITS THE MONTREAL ROYALS, WITH WHOM JACKIE ROBINSON PLAYED BEFORE MOVING UP TO THE DODGERS.

Robinson off the team, challenged the Philadelphia bench: "Listen!" he shouted. "Why don't you yell at somebody who can answer back?"

Later that season, when the Dodgers played Cincinnati and some fans started in on Robinson, Pee Wee Reese put his arm around his teammate's shoulder. Reese was a Southerner and a big favorite with the Cincinnati fans. His gesture quieted them immediately. Robinson was becoming a member of the team.

By the end of the season, Jackie Robinson had a .297 average, including twenty-nine stolen bases and twelve home runs. He was named Rookie of the Year by *The Sporting News*.

Robinson's aggressive, Negro league style of play had an immediate impact on the game.

"At the time [major league] baseball was a base-to-base thing," said Buck O'Neil. "You hit the ball, you wait on first base until somebody hit it again. But in our baseball you got on base if you walked, you stole second, you'd try to steal, they'd bunt you over to third and you actually score runs without a hit. This was our baseball."

Robinson and the other black players who followed him into the majors eventually made it everyone's baseball. Branch Rickey's "great experiment," as sportswriters came to call it, would succeed far better than anyone had imagined.

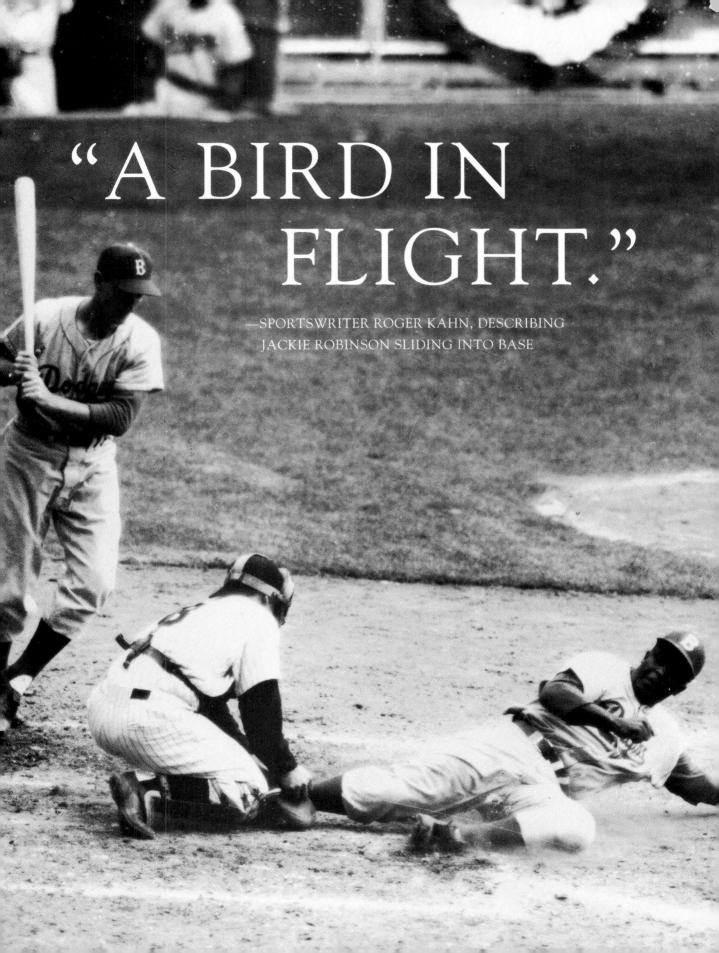

"A BIRD IN FLIGHT."

—SPORTSWRITER ROGER KAHN, DESCRIBING
JACKIE ROBINSON SLIDING INTO BASE

THE OLDEST ROOKIE IN THE GAME.

On July 9, 1948, a tall, not-so-young rookie walked slowly from the Cleveland Indians' bullpen to the pitching mound. "I didn't go fast," he remembered. "No reason wearing myself out just walking." That day Satchel Paige, who was either 38, 42, 44, or 48 years old (Satch liked to make himself younger or older depending on how well he was pitching), became the oldest rookie ever to play in organized baseball.

Paige had wanted to be the first black player in the majors. This was his chance to

prove how wrong the white world had been all these years. A lot of people thought that signing Satchel was just another publicity stunt by Bill Veeck, the flashy young owner of the Indians. The editor of *The Sporting News* wrote, "Were Satchel white, he would not have drawn a second thought from Veeck."

"If Satch were white," Veeck responded, "he would have been in the majors twenty-five years earlier and the question would not be before the house."

The Indians were behind 4–1 when Paige took the mound. After twenty-two years, his fastball wasn't the mighty weapon it had once been. The first batter he faced rapped a base hit to left field. Paige's teammates looked at one another—what was going on? Had Satchel lost his stuff?

Paige quickly put their fears to rest. He pitched two brilliant innings, dazzling the St. Louis Browns with the same pitches that had won him nearly 2,000 games in his Negro league career.

"I used my single windup," he said, "my triple windup, my hesitation windup, and my now windup…my step-and-pitch-it, my sidearm throw, and my bat dodger."

"I USED TO OVERPOWER 'EM; NOW I OUTCUTE 'EM.

—SATCHEL PAIGE

When he was the starting pitcher in a game against the Washington Senators, 72,000 fans jammed Cleveland Stadium, setting a new night-attendance record. Paige notched his first major league win, 4–3.

Paige finished the season with a 6–1 record. The Indians clinched the pennant and went on to win the World Series.

It turned out to be the high point of Paige's major league career, for age had indeed caught up with him and he never pitched as well again. He stayed with Cleveland for a while and then moved over to the St. Louis Browns. In 1954 he went back to barnstorming. One of his few regrets, he told a sportswriter, was that he'd never had a chance to strike out Babe Ruth in the major leagues.

In 1946 Branch Rickey had recruited another talented black player—catcher Roy Campanella, who had already spent nine years in the Negro leagues playing for the Baltimore Elite Giants.

Campanella, who was 25 when he joined the Dodgers, had grown up in an integrated neighborhood in Philadelphia. Until he was recruited by Baltimore at age 15, he did not know that blacks couldn't play in the majors.

When Campanella first met Branch Rickey, he assumed that Rickey wanted him to play for the Brown Dodgers. Like everyone else, Campanella had been fooled by Rickey's story about starting an all-black team. But Rickey wanted Campanella to be the first black catcher in the majors.

Campanella spent a year at the Dodgers' Nashua, New Hampshire, farm team and much of the following year with Montreal. In 1949 he took over behind home plate for the Dodgers.

ROY CAMPANELLA

"Mr. Rickey told me, 'You are going to have to be a diplomat to talk to the ten or eleven different pitchers on this team, to make them use your judgment in calling and giving all the signals. The catcher runs the team in the major leagues.'"

Campanella ran the Dodgers for nearly ten years and was named the National League Most Valuable Player three times.

Just as Campanella moved up to the major leagues, Jackie Robinson's three years of silence ended. He had turned the other cheek just as he'd promised Branch Rickey. Now things would be different. "They better be prepared to be rough this year," he said, "because I'm going to be rough on them."

Robinson became more aggressive on the field and more assertive when away from it. In St. Louis he demanded—and got—a room in the same hotel as the rest of the team. He encouraged black fans to demand "what you got coming." Some sportswriters who had once applauded him began to criticize him, saying he should be a player and not a crusader.

Robinson fired back: "As long as I appeared to ignore insult and injury, I was a martyred hero to a lot of people. But the minute I began to sound off—I became a swell-headed wise-guy, an 'uppity nigger.'"

But Robinson's anger didn't affect his playing. He had his best season ever, leading the league in batting average and stolen bases and finishing second in RBIs. So many fans came out to see him play when the Dodgers were on the road that the team accounted for one third of the entire National League's attendance. When the season ended, Robinson was voted Most Valuable Player.

AS HIS WIFE, RACHEL, WATCHES NERVOUSLY, JACKIE ROBINSON CRASHES HIS WAY INTO HOME PLATE.

WILLIE MAYS DIVES INTO
HOME IN A GAME
AGAINST PHILADELPHIA,
A YEAR AFTER JOINING
THE MAJORS.

OPPOSITE: MAYS
MAKES ONE HIS
FAMOUS SEEMINGLY
IMPOSSIBLE CATCHES,
THEN HURLS IT TO
SECOND FOR THE
DOUBLE PLAY,
SEPTEMBER 29, 1954.

In 1951 Leo Durocher, who was now manager of the New York Giants, needed a center fielder for his club. He heard about an outfielder playing for the Birmingham Black Barons named Willie Mays. Mays had everything—speed, a great glove, and a powerful bat. The Giants purchased Mays's contract from the Barons and sent him to their farm club. He hit a hot .357 in Trenton, New Jersey, and then an unbelievable .477 in Minneapolis, Minnesota.

Mays, the oldest of twelve children, was born in Westfield, Alabama, in 1931. His father had been a star in a local industrial league. He had started Willie playing baseball before he could walk, rolling a ball to him across the living room floor. By the time Mays was 16 he was playing for the Barons, but home games only—his teachers said no to road games because they were afraid Willie wouldn't do his homework.

"WHEN I WAS 17, I REALIZED I WAS IN A FORM OF SHOW BUSINESS."

—WILLIE MAYS

When Durocher told Mays, who was only 19, that he wanted to bring him up to the Giants in 1951, Mays panicked. He didn't think he was ready for the majors. Durocher tried to reassure him—he didn't have to hit .477 for the Giants; .250 would be fine. Mays agreed to give it a try.

At first his fears seemed justified. He went 1 for 26 at the plate. One day Durocher found him crying in the dugout after a game.

"Mr. Leo," said Mays, "I just can't hit up here."

"As long as I'm manager of the Giants," Durocher answered, "you're my center fielder."

Mays got two hits the next day and snapped out of his slump. His hard hitting and astonishing fielding skills electrified the Giants, and they went on to win the pennant in 1951. When it was over, Durocher said, "If he could cook, I'd marry him."

Willie was outgoing but not good at remembering names. Whenever he saw a familiar face, he would greet the person with "Say hey." Soon he was called the Say Hey Kid. He was a great showman, too. He always wore a cap that was too large so that it would fly off his head as he chased long fly balls in center field.

Willie Mays spent twenty-two years in the majors and had one of the most outstanding careers in professional baseball history. He led the league in home runs four times, hitting fifty-two in 1965, and finished his career with 660.

Another home run hitter came into the majors from the Negro leagues at the same time as Mays. Hank Aaron had started playing ball with the semi-pro Black Bears in his hometown of Mobile, Alabama, while he was still in high school. His next stop was with the Indianapolis Clowns, where he hit .467 and led the Negro American League as a rookie.

Like many young blacks at the time, Aaron had been inspired by Jackie Robinson's success in the majors.

"I felt that if Jackie could play in the big leagues and make it, Henry Aaron could do the same thing," he said. "I knew it was going to be a hard road, but I felt like if Jackie could do it, then he had given every black kid in America that little ray of hope that they could do it."

Aaron signed with the Milwaukee Braves in 1952 and was sent to their Jacksonville farm club in the South Atlantic, or Sally, League. He did well in Jacksonville and was named Most Valuable Player for the 1953 season, but he hated the racism he encountered in the all-Southern league.

HANK AARON

"I was one of the first blacks playing in the Sally League," Aaron remembered. "I was literally going through hell down there. Name-calling, racial slurs, resentment for playing against whites."

Jacksonville's manager, Ben Geraghty, visited Aaron in his room nearly every night to talk to him and help keep him going.

Aaron moved up to the Braves in 1954 as their center fielder, and by 1956 he had won his first batting championship with a league-leading .328 average. The next season he led the Braves in their conquest of the Yankees in the World Series.

The Braves moved to Atlanta in 1966, and season after season Aaron added to his home run total. He hit so many that fans began to call him the Hammer. Nearly twenty years after joining the majors, he passed the 700 mark.

Suddenly fans and sportswriters woke up to an incredible possibility: Babe Ruth's record of 714 career homers just might be broken.

A lot of people didn't want to see Ruth's record overtaken—especially by a black man—and Aaron began to receive hate mail. Many of the letters threatened to harm Aaron or kidnap his children if he didn't stop.

Hank kept silent about the hate mail, but word soon got out and letters of support began to flood in. "I don't care what color you are," a 12-year-old wrote. "What do these fans want you to do? Just quit hitting?"

Aaron began the 1974 season two homers short of breaking Ruth's record. The pressure was tremendous. Over 300 reporters were traveling with the Braves, waiting for history to be made.

On April 5, 1974, Aaron tied Ruth's record. Three days later, with his proud parents sitting in the stands, he hit a pitch over the left field fence to break Babe Ruth's record.

He remembered how he felt as he rounded the bases:

"I was in my own little world. It was like running in a bubble, and I could see all these people jumping up and down and waving their arms in slow motion. Every base seemed crowded, like there were all these people I had to get through to make it to home plate.

I just couldn't wait to get there. I was told I had a big smile on my face as I came around third. I purposely never smiled as I ran the bases after a home run, but I suppose I couldn't help it that time."

The game was halted for a ceremony at home plate. Hank hugged his parents and family. How did he feel? a reporter asked.

"Thank God it's over," Aaron said.

By the end of his career, Hank Aaron had hit 755 home runs— a record that still stands today.

HANK AARON IS ENGULFED BY FANS, INCLUDING HIS MOTHER *(CLOSEST TO THE CAMERA)*, AFTER BREAKING BABE RUTH'S HOME RUN RECORD ON APRIL 8, 1974.

"THE ONLY MAN I IDOLIZE MORE THAN MYSELF."

—MUHAMMAD ALI, FORMER BOXING CHAMPION, SPEAKING ABOUT HANK AARON

CHAPTER 7

THE DEATH KNELL FOR OUR BASEBALL.

Team by team, black athletes followed Jackie Robinson into the majors. Don Newcombe joined the Dodgers right after Roy Campanella, in 1946. The Newark Eagles' Larry Doby, who led the Negro leagues with a .414 average, was signed by the Cleveland Indians in 1947. That same year, Hank Thompson and Willard Brown of the Kansas City Monarchs joined the St. Louis Browns. Most of the big league clubs didn't pay the Negro league teams by buying

LARRY DOBY, WHO
FOLLOWED JACKIE
ROBINSON INTO
THE MAJORS

OPPOSITE: THE
NEWARK EAGLES,
1946

up the players' contracts, as they did when they hired a player away from a major or minor league team. Even Branch Rickey, who signed up sixteen players for the Brooklyn organization, had an excuse for this theft of talent.

Many of the Negro league owners were numbers runners, Rickey told reporters. That made the league a "racket" that wasn't entitled to compensation.

Effa Manley, manager of the Newark Eagles, fired back. "He took players from the Negro leagues and didn't even pay for them. I'd call that a racket."

But no one wanted to slow down the integration of the major leagues. "It was the death knell for our baseball," said Buck O'Neil. "But who cared? Who cared?"

The Negro leagues struggled on for a few more years. But as the better players left for the majors, the teams became mere shadows of themselves. Black fans began following major league teams with black players.

Jackie Robinson's Brooklyn Dodgers were wildly popular. When they played in Cincinnati, Ohio, black fans took a train nicknamed the Jackie Robinson Special, which ran from Norfolk, Virginia—600 miles away— so they could see their hero play.

Most Negro leaguers would never be asked to join the majors. They were too old or not good enough to take a white regular's spot. At the same time their jobs were in danger because attendance at Negro league games was plunging and the leagues were collapsing. Every team was losing money.

At the end of the 1949 season the New York Black Yankees and the Newark Eagles closed their doors forever. It was the end of the Negro National League.

Some of the other teams survived for a few years by barnstorming, but by 1953 there were fewer blacks playing ball for a living—in any league—than at any time in the century. The Negro American League, now composed of only four teams, survived until 1960.

In 1957, Walter O'Malley, who now owned the Brooklyn Dodgers, announced that he was moving the team to Los Angeles, California. Roy Campanella, the Dodgers' star catcher, did not accompany the team. In January 1958 he was permanently paralyzed when his car skidded on ice and crashed into a telephone pole.

Jackie Robinson chose to retire rather than move west. He had been a symbol of integration for thousands of African Americans. Now he became more active in his crusade for racial equality, refusing to attend old-timers' games because there were no blacks in baseball management.

In 1962 Robinson was elected to the Baseball Hall of Fame—the first African American to receive that honor.

Three years later, the United States Congress passed the Civil Rights Act of 1965. The act forbade segregation in public places. Black players could now stay in the same hotels and eat in the same restaurants as their white teammates in every state in the union.

That same year Branch Rickey died. Jackie Robinson attended the funeral with several ex-teammates, including Bobby Bragan, who had tried to keep Robinson off the team. Now Bragan came to honor Rickey because, as he said, Rickey had made him a better man.

The following June, Ted Williams was inducted into the Hall of Fame. Like many white players of his era, Williams had faced some of the great Negro league stars in exhibition games. Now, in his acceptance speech, the Red Sox slugger talked about the exclusion of Negro league players from the Hall of Fame:

"I hope someday Satchel Paige and Josh Gibson can be added here as a symbol of the great Negro league players. They are not here only because they didn't get a chance."

AT HIS HALL OF FAME INDUCTION IN 1966, TED WILLIAMS *(ABOVE)* CALLED FOR THE INCLUSION OF NEGRO LEAGUE PLAYERS IN THE HALL.

OPPOSITE: JACKIE ROBINSON LEAVES THE DODGERS' DRESSING ROOM FOR THE LAST TIME.

Five years later, in 1971, Paige became the first Negro league player to enter the Hall of Fame. He was followed in 1972 by Josh Gibson and Buck Leonard, the Homestead Grays' first baseman. Eventually seven other Negro leaguers were selected by a special committee: Rube Foster, Cool Papa Bell, Judy Johnson, Newark Eagles' third baseman Ray Dandridge, Pop Lloyd, Oscar Charleston, and Cuban pitcher Martin Dihigo. Today there is a section of the Hall of Fame devoted to the Negro leagues and the history of black baseball.

SOME OF THE NEGRO LEAGUE STARS WHO MADE IT INTO THE HALL OF FAME: CLOCKWISE FROM TOP LEFT: BUCK LEONARD (INDUCTED 1972);
COOL PAPA BELL (1974) WITH HIS WIFE, CLARABELLE; JUDY JOHNSON (1975), AND JOHN L. USRY, ACCEPTING FOR POP LLOYD IN 1977

"JACKIE STOLE HOME AND HE'S SAFE."

—REVEREND JESSE JACKSON AT JACKIE ROBINSON'S FUNERAL

Jackie Robinson's last public appearance was at the opening game of the 1972 World Series in Cincinnati. He was 53 years old and suffering from diabetes and heart disease, but he was still crusading for more opportunities for blacks in baseball. Before he threw out the first ball, Robinson had this to say:

"I am extremely proud and pleased to be here this afternoon but must admit, I'm going to be tremendously more pleased and more proud when I look at that third base coaching line one day and see a black face managing baseball."

Jackie Robinson died less than two weeks later.

Since that time, few blacks have had the opportunity to manage a big league team. And even though the winning manager of the 1992 and 1993 World Series was a black man—Cito Gaston of the Toronto Blue Jays—the first four decades of integrated play have produced only a handful of black managers. Bill White, the black broadcaster and former first baseman, was president of the National League from 1989 to 1993. But there are still no black owners.

Baseball is not perfect—it reflects both the strengths and weaknesses of American society. When Jackie Robinson stepped onto Ebbets Field from the shadows of the Negro leagues, many hoped it would bring an end to racism in America. It was a good beginning, but it also marked a loss for African Americans.

The Negro leagues were a source of pride for black people throughout the country. They had employed hundreds of blacks and poured thousands of dollars back into the black community. They had enabled some of the finest athletes in America to earn a living playing a game they loved.

"Because of baseball," said Cool Papa Bell, "I smelled the rose of life. I wanted to meet interesting people, to travel and to have nice clothes. Baseball allowed me to do all those things, and most important, it allowed me to become a member of a brotherhood of friendship which will last forever."

The Negro leagues withered away during the 1950s, finally dissolving completely in 1964. The last original Negro league team, the Indianapolis Clowns, played their final game in 1968.

Negro league records are sketchy because reporters did not write many stories about black athletes until Jackie Robinson broke into the majors in 1947.

Recently, however, people have been filling the gaps in those records—donating photographs to libraries and combing through box scores in old newspapers—in order to create an accurate picture of the leagues. Their efforts will guarantee that the accomplishments of these remarkable athletes—and their place in American history—survive beyond the memory of the players who still live and the people who were lucky enough to see them play.

AN EXHIBIT IN THE HALL OF FAME IN COOPERSTOWN, NEW YORK, DEVOTED TO THE NEGRO LEAGUES AND THE HISTORY OF BLACK BASEBALL

"THERE WAS ALWAYS SUN SHINING SOMEPLACE."

—JUDY JOHNSON, RECALLING LIFE ON THE ROAD IN THE NEGRO LEAGUES

INDEX

Page numbers in **boldface** refer to illustrations.